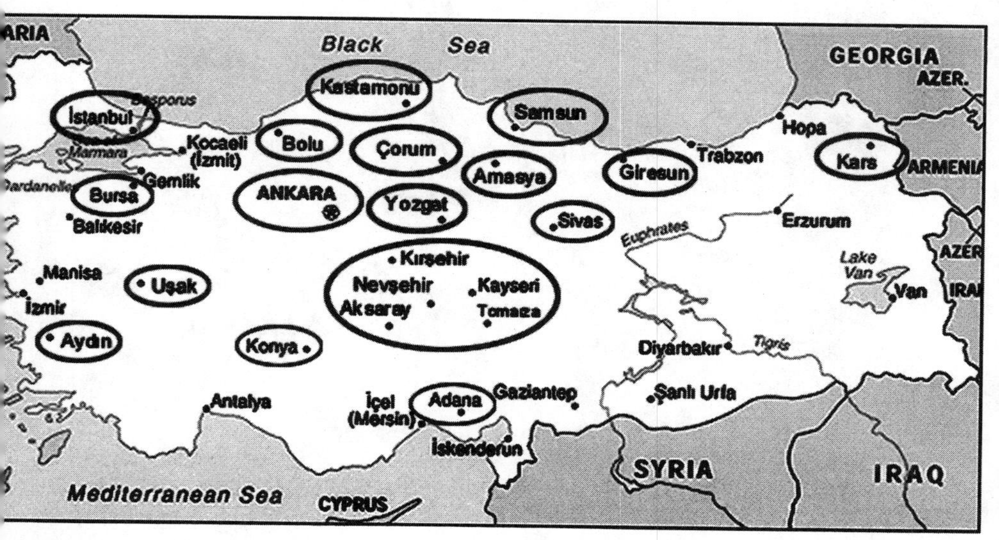

of Turkey. Circled regions are native towns and villages of participants in this study.

Map of Netherlands.

Communication and Identity in the Diaspora

Communication and Identity in the Diaspora

Turkish Migrants in Amsterdam and Their Use of Media

Christine Ogan

LEXINGTON BOOKS
Lanham • Boulder • New York • Oxford

LEXINGTON BOOKS

Published in the United States of America
by Lexington Books
4720 Boston Way, Lanham, Maryland 20706

12 Hid's Copse Road
Cumnor Hill, Oxford OX2 9JJ, England

British Library Cataloguing in Publication Information Available

Library of Congress Cataloging-in-Publication Data

Ogan, Christing L.
Communication and identity in the Diaspora : Turkish migrants in Amsterdam and their use of media / Christine Ogan.
p. cm.
Includes bibliographical references and index.
ISBN 0-7391-0269-9 (cloth : alk. paper)
1. Mass media and minorities—Netherlands—Amsterdam. 2. Turks—Netherlands—Amsterdam—Communication. 3. Turks—Netherlands—Amsterdam—Ethnic identity. 4. Immigrants—Netherlands—Amsterdam. I. Title.

P944.5.M552 N446 2001
305.89'4350492352—dc21

2001029435

Printed in the United States of America

™ The paper used in this publication meets the minimum requirements of American National Standard for Information Sciences—Permanence of Paper for Printed Library Materials, ANSI/NISO Z39.48–1992.

Contents

Acknowledgments

As I was conducting the research and writing this book, I realized that I had been preparing to do this work for most of my life. My involvement with the Turkish people and their culture began when I met my husband in the mid-1960s in Ithaca, New York. Not only did I fall in love with him, but I came to embrace Turks and Turkey with a passion. Over the years, I have conducted considerable research in Turkey. In the process of doing that, I learned a lot about the political, social, economic, and communication structure of the country. But I also enjoyed myself enormously. Since most of the research involved talking to people, I have had many wonderful experiences as a guest in Turkish homes over the years. I wish to thank all of those people who participated in this study and those with whom I have previously talked who helped me to frame the inquiry.

When I became curious about the impact of satellite television on Turkish communities in Europe, I came to know Turkish people in a new setting. Thanks to Marisca Milikowski, research fellow at the Amsterdam School of Communications Research at the University of Amsterdam, with whom I first worked, I was able to locate the first group of Turkish people in Amsterdam for the study. Those people introduced me to others, and on it went. Prof. Milikowski and I had many long talks about migrants and many other topics when she graciously invited me to her home. We coauthored two articles written prior to this book. She also introduced me to Sema Razak, a former student at the Amsterdam School of Communications Research, who helped me locate participants, participated in many of the interviews, and discussed the research with me in informal meetings. I am grateful to both of them for their insights and work on this project.

In the Netherlands I also came to know and enjoy interacting with Dutch people. I found them to be as gracious and as helpful as the Turks. They assisted me by providing much useful information about the history of migration to the Netherlands and orienting me to the city of Amsterdam. But as you will see in this book, the two groups have a long way to go to understand one another and to appreciate the rich cultures of each other's societies. My hope is that this book will help in that process.

Veldkamp, a market research organization in Amsterdam, generously provided data for secondary analysis. Through the research Veldkamp conducted, I was able to obtain baseline demographics and media use statistics.

Several faculty members associated with the Institute for Migration and Ethnic Studies were extremely helpful. They shared their own research with me and allowed me to engage them in interviews, both on-line and in person. In particular, my thanks go to professors Rinus Penninx, Jan Rath, and Jean Tillie.

My dear friends Harold and Clary de Bock welcomed me into their home on several occasions and endured many conversations about the Netherlands, migrants, and the migration process. Carin Mulié-Velgersdijk, manager of two research institutes associated with the University of Amsterdam, also opened her home to me. Without the wonderful place to stay that she provided, I would not have been able to complete the fieldwork. I will always be grateful for her help and for the many conversations we had about the research.

When I returned to Bloomington and began to write, I realized that I had several documents that needed translation. Stella Hooker, a native of the Netherlands and Bloomington resident, did an excellent and speedy job when I needed it. Her husband John, who has written one book and translated another about the Netherlands and Dutch culture, was also extremely helpful.

My great thanks also go to my home institution. The School of Journalism at Indiana University supported me with one summer research grant, and several of my colleagues have provided good criticism of my work—specifically Radhika Parameswaran and Betsi Grabe. Lisa Holstein, my doctoral advisee, was the expert copy editor for the manuscript. And Kara Alexander, the school's photography lab administrator, did a wonderful job of helping me digitize and edit the photos. Truthfully, she did more of the work on getting them into proper format than I did—but I learned much in the process. Thanks also go to my good friend Janice Harste, who helped with the final formatting of the text.

Finally, my appreciation goes to my family. Pekin, my husband, faithfully read and commented on everything I wrote. He also provided constant encouragement. My daughters Banu and Elif served as real-life examples of second-generation migrants in the United States. Though they have only one foreign-born parent, they grew up with a sense of belonging to both the United States and Turkey. Both of them also provided encouragement when I was most discouraged about the project. Foofwa d'Imobilite, Banu's fiancé, continues to experience issues related to migration. As the son of a Brazilian mother and a Swiss father, Foofwa grew up in Switzerland, but settled in New York as an adult. He tells me he often feels like his identity lies somewhere in the middle of the Atlantic Ocean. He has been incredibly supportive of this effort. I hope he enjoys the final product. And I hope all the people who were involved with the research on some level are pleased with the outcome.

Chapter 1

Introduction

> Life for me here is still not easy. Even when I have lived here for thirty years—it is still a foreign place. Everything is foreign—the lifestyle, the methodology—customs. I get tired in school meetings. You have to process the Dutch, translate to Turkish, and then prepare a response. And you don't get the proverbs and idioms. I have just never been able to process Dutch firsthand. It means that the language has just not set with me.
>
> If my feet are here, my head is in Turkey. But my best days have been spent in Turkey. I am filled up there. I get no intellectual satisfaction here—or people who are on the same intellectual wavelength to communicate with. And it is hard to find true friends here.
>
> Ayfer, a teacher of Turkish in the Amsterdam schools

Though she is a professional who owns her home in a new district in Amsterdam where she lives with her two teenaged daughters, Ayfer says she is only really happy when she returns to Turkey for her summer holiday. She is not alone. She is one of thousands of Turkish migrants in the Netherlands who feel that way. And likely she is one of millions of migrants worldwide who long for their homeland though the chances for a permanent return are slim to none.

I call these people a diasporic community, though technically that is not true. A diaspora is "the collective forced dispersion of a religious and/or ethnic group"[1] that is usually precipitated by a political or other disaster. The Turks who live in Amsterdam went there by choice. The first migrants came at the invitation of the Dutch government to fill a labor need in the 1960s. And since the migrants' home country still exists and is a place to which the migrants frequently return for visits, they are not a dispersed population.

These days diasporic communities are thought of more broadly, however. They continue to retain their identity through a collective memory in the new home.[2] More important than why a diasporic community came together say Chaliand and Rageau is "the will to survive as a minority by transmitting a heritage."[3] The Turkish migrants in Amsterdam certainly have this will for the moment. Their memories are refreshed continuously from exposure to television from Turkey, from their regular trips back to Turkey, and from their interaction in communities that contain Turkish shops and cultural centers.

This book is about those Turkish migrants. It is based on interviews with more than a hundred people in Amsterdam conducted over a period of two-and-a-half years, from 1997 to 1999. The purpose of the study was to discover what role the influx of Turkish media into the European media environment played in the lives of the Turkish community. The in-depth interviews about many phases of the migrants' lives in Amsterdam, their use of media, their religious beliefs and practices, and their hopes and dreams for the future were conducted with all types of people. Those people included individuals who had been elected to public office; young educated professionals; youth who were attending school as well as those who had dropped out of school; factory workers and their spouses; unemployed men and women of all ages; retired workers; illiterate housewives; and journalists working in the Dutch and Turkish media. Every attempt to obtain a comprehensive understanding of the community was made. Subjects for the study were located through a variety of means.

In Europe for many years the availability of media from Turkey was limited to print. And since many of the migrants had little formal schooling, they were even more cut off from their homeland. In the early 1990s the Dutch cable began to carry the Turkish Radio and Television's international public channel. And a short while later private television carried by satellite became available at a reasonable cost. Many of the respondents claimed it changed their whole lives to be able to receive news and public affairs information, entertainment, and even religious programs in their native language. Others said the arrival of television in the Turkish language had minimal impact on their lives. This book tells the story of those changes, large and small. It also tells the stories of how these people manage to survive in a land with radical differences from their country of birth—differences in climate, religious orientation, language, and culture. Some of the migrants adapted rather well to their new environment. Others still feel like foreigners, even after twenty or thirty years. To understand the reasons for differences between those who adapted well to the changed cultural environment and those who did not also was a goal of this study.

About the Study

In many ways I have been conducting this study for more than thirty years. I have had my own experience of living as a migrant when I married and lived in Turkey. Later, when my husband, a Turkish native, and I moved to the United States, he became the migrant. My two daughters, at various points in their lives, have felt somewhat torn between two cultures, much the way many of the participants in this study do. The actual study began in February 1977 when I spent a week in Amsterdam, exploring the possibility of researching the Turkish migrants' use of television and other media from Turkey. Over the next two-and-a-half years, I returned to Amsterdam three times, staying several weeks on each visit, interviewing people and collecting the documents that were used to produce this book.

More than 100 participants for this study were interviewed for about two hours each in their homes or offices. I can't provide an exact number of interviews, because many people I talked with were interviewed informally. Others were interviewed in groups in their homes. Great effort was taken to locate people who represented different socioeconomic levels, religious and political points of view, and attitudes toward the Dutch society. Participants were located through a variety of methods, ranging from cold approaches on the street, or in shops or at outdoor festivals, to contacts through friends and colleagues. A snowball approach (asking one respondent to suggest other people who might be appropriate to interview) was also used to locate people who represented particular political or religious positions that might have implications for their media use. At the end of the interviewing in the summer of 1999, I felt that I had a reasonable grasp on the diversity represented among the Amsterdam Turkish community, as I began to hear points of view and life stories that sounded very similar to others I had been told. Names of people in this study have been changed to protect their privacy. However, when professionals in the media or government are cited, their actual names are used. Though most of the interviews were with Turks, and conducted in Turkish, some Dutch people were also interviewed. Those conversations were in English.

What to Call the Participants

It is difficult to know what to call the people of my study without using stereotypical or inaccurate terminology. The Dutch, as well as other Europeans, refer to them as Turkish migrants. But most of them no longer fit that description. The first waves of migration took place throughout the decade of the 1960s. So I wonder when a migrant can shed that adjective. It is now thirty-five to forty years after the first Turkish workers arrived in the Netherlands. Many of their children were never migrants. They were born in the Netherlands and grew up there. They may have always had Dutch citizenship. Doesn't that make them Dutch? And to refer to the group as "ethnic Turks" may be accurate, but does not suit many of the younger people who wish to be called European-Turks or Dutch-Turks. So however politically incorrect it may be, it is hard for me to make clear reference to those who contributed to this study without using one of the inappropriate terms. I apologize for that, but will say that many of the people with whom I talked called themselves Turks—and perhaps that is what I should do, too.

I also accept what Gerd Baumann says in his book, *The Multicultural Riddle,* about the essentializing of such terms as ethnicity and culture. Calling the nation-state, ethnicity, and religion the three poles of multiculturalism, Baumann argues that ethnicity "invokes biological ancestry and then claims that present-day identities follow from this ancestry."[4] However, this notion involves at least four fallacies, Baumann says, including the following:

1. Descent, that is the tracing of persons from ancestors, is an act of present-day memory looking back, as opposed to an authentic act of genealogical bookkeeping. . . .
2. Even a scientifically ascertained individual ancestry does not determine patterns of behavior or preferences among humans.
3. Even the most racist biologists have failed to establish any link whatsoever between race or ethnicity and mental properties, behaviors, or even preferences for behaviors. . . .
4. Just as people emphasize different aspects of their language, body language, behavior, and style in different situations, so too do they emphasize or abjure the attributes of their ethnicity.[5]

Baumann later defines ethnicity as being "about the cultivation and refinement of all the possibilities first given by nature, but not finished by nature."[6] Despite these important statements about the problems with the concept of ethnicity, it is hard to find substitute terms as descriptors. And that means that those of us who claim to be social scientists fall into the same traps that racists do, if for very different reasons. Here I will try to use the term ethnicity in the sense that Baumann means it.

Identity and Diasporas

In recent years much scholarly attention has been paid to the concept of identity. Of particular interest has been the identity of diasporic peoples. Many of those who write on this subject have personal experience to add to their academic interest, making the theoretical work all the more interesting. However, little of this work has an empirical base.

Several authors have written about identity and the cultural "translation" that takes place for peripheral groups residing in nation-states to which they have migrated.[7] In Hall's terms, identity for diasporic groups and others in the postmodern age is not fixed or permanent. "Identity becomes a 'moveable feast'; formed and transformed continuously in relation to the ways we are represented or addressed" in postmodern societies.[8] This certainly fits the Turkish migrant in Europe. Neither Turk nor Dutch, they fall somewhere in the middle and move back and forth between both cultures, all the while creating a new place for themselves. Since the society in which they live can be hostile at times, and is certainly different in language, mores, and religion, many migrants find it important to try to hold on to the culture of their homeland and abide by their perception of its rules. At the same time they conform to certain conventions in the host society. In describing this aspect of the lives of the Turks in Germany, Tan and Waldhoff write:

> As long as the outside world they perceive as German appears to be hostile, there is little chance of individual families shrugging off the traditional notions of authority and ignoring its guardians. On the contrary, the guardians of tradition are all the more likely to put social pressures on families in order to make them comply with their claims of dominance.[9]

But the influences to preserve or change identity come from several directions. So the diasporic individual's identity is in constant flux. That is why Hall thinks that it is better to think of identity as a "production," a process that is never complete.[10]

> Cultural identities come from somewhere, have histories. But, like everything which is historical, they undergo constant transformation. Far from being eternally fixed in some essentialized past, they are subject to the continuous "play" of history, culture and power. Far from being grounded in a mere "recovery" of the past, which is waiting to be found, and which, when found, will secure our sense of ourselves into eternity, identities are the names we give to the different ways we are positioned by, and position ourselves within, the narratives of the past.[11]

Hall places cultural identification on two axes that operate simultaneously, an axis of similarity and continuity, and one of difference and rupture. The first of these provides continuity with the past and the second one demonstrates the discontinuities. Of course, for peoples who are part of true diasporas, created by forced expulsions, those discontinuities are painful to recall, and may have included slavery or colonization. Safran defines diasporas today as "expatriate minority communities." He has six criteria for determining diasporas. Those are that the people left an original center and were dispersed to at least two peripheral places, that they have a memory or vision or myth about their homeland, and their perception is that they are not completely accepted in their host country. They also believe that they will eventually return to their home country when the time is right, and they have committed themselves to the restoration or the maintenance of the homeland. Finally, their consciousness and solidarity are importantly defined by this continuing relationship with the homeland.[12]

While the Turks who live in Europe have no memories of slavery or colonization, they do fit the several criteria set by Safran. When they lived in Turkey, they were part of a relatively homogeneous society (unless they were Kurdish), where the common language spoken by the overwhelming majority of the people was Turkish and the common religion subscribed to by most of the citizens was Islam. They held a common cultural base and historical heritage, and they had the privilege of never having been dominated by a colonial power. To the contrary, the Turks were the rulers of the Ottoman Empire that controlled all the land in the Middle East, much of southern and eastern Europe, and even territories in North Africa. That rule lasted for more than four hundred years. Under Ottoman control, parts of some nations chose to covert to Islam, and others adopted cultural practices and even the cuisine of the colonial power. But times change and political power changes. Modern day Turks may have no personal memories of the empire, but they remain a proud people with a rich cultural heritage. And they carried this memory with them to their European homes. It came as a surprise to many of them that the Europeans did not share those glorious memories. Instead, many of them looked upon the Turks as barbarians and heathens. They held stereotypical notions about the Turks and their lifestyle. They were thought of as dirty, lazy, backward, and ignorant. And their religion was something mysterious and to be feared. No longer a part of a society that shared their beliefs and traditions, they took their place among the Dutch and Germans and Belgians and French as an oddity to be merely tolerated—as long as they did the work they were hired to do.

Though the Turks who migrated to Europe were not forced to leave their homeland, their departure from Turkey was not entirely voluntary. Despite their proud heritage, the reality of the time was that many of them were struggling to feed and clothe their families on the earnings from their village or small town employment. Others had no jobs at all. Still others were spurred on by the attraction of the possibility of building a nest egg that would be used to establish some kind of small business in Turkey upon their return. But no matter what the goal, the experience shook them to their cultural roots. And what they expected would be a temporary condition turned out to be a permanent one for most. Many of them were not reunited with their families for several years after their departure, so they experienced a profound loneliness in the alien culture. Many of them lived in inhospitable surroundings with several other migrants in cramped quarters. And all the while, who they became was different from who they were at the time of departure from the homeland. In Hall's framework, they were able to have continuity with the past through trips home, through letters from family and friends, and through the occasional film screened in their neighborhoods. But the discontinuities came from the experiences they had in Europe—few people around them who could speak their language; no place to practice their religion; food that was unfamiliar; and skies that were almost always gray.

Homi Bhabha uses the term hybridity to refer to the continual transformation of identity that Hall describes. Bhaba's view of hybridity is identity that occurs in the space between cultural borders.

> Terms of cultural engagement, whether antagonistic or affiliative, are produced performatively. The representation of difference must not be hastily read as the reflection of *pre-given* ethnic or cultural traits set in the fixed tablet of tradition. The social articulation of difference, from the minority perspective, is a complex, on-going negotiation that seeks to authorize cultural hybridities that emerge in moments of historical transformation. The "right" to signify from the periphery of authorized power and privilege does not depend on the persistence of tradition; it is resourced by the power of tradition to be reinscribed through the conditions of contingency and the contradictoriness that attend upon the lives of those who are in the minority. The recognition that tradition bestows is

> a partial form of identification. In restaging the past it introduces other, incommensurable cultural temporalities into the invention of tradition. This process estranges any immediate access to an originary identity or a "received" tradition.[13]

The Turks who migrated to Europe carried their cultural traditions, marked by the celebration of national and religious holidays, marriage customs and child rearing practices, family division of labor practices, etc., to the new environment. There they were adapted to the circumstances in their new home and re-articulated in the context of the dominant culture. To some extent, a process of cultural hybridity ensued. Some of them, for example, adopted Christmas holiday traditions, but exchanged gifts and put up a decorated tree in the absence of a religious context. And on high holy days in Islam, they were forced to plan around the European workday requirements to carve out a special time for family celebrations, very different from those they experienced in the homeland.

Hannerz prefers to look at the coming together of separate and distinct traditions in a global context as a process of "creolization." These traditions interconnect "in the shape of a relatively continuous spectrum of interacting meanings and meaningful forms, along which the various contributing historical sources of the culture are differentially visible and active."[14] In addition to interconnectedness, creolization is characterized by diversity and innovation in the context of global center-periphery relationships.[15] Hannerz sees this process as a continuum, perhaps even multiple continuums. From this perspective we would see the identities of the Turkish migrants shifting as they continued to interact with the Dutch in the Netherlands. And we would also see the Dutch majority changed by the culture brought in from Turkey. Parts of this study will examine those shifts. But Hannerz also acknowledges that it is possible for diasporic peoples to have such a strong allegiance to their countries of origin that they may remain relatively uncreolized. They are "in the nation but not of it."[16]

The common experiences Turkish families had in the new European setting brought them together as a community. But as Baumann illustrates in his study of Southall in London, community is also a complex and dynamic concept that has several interpretations and applications.[17] Although useful for both the majority and minority populations at particular times, the dominant discourse that places all members of an ethnic minority in a community is an inaccurate portrayal of culture, says Baumann. It is widely applied by both the majority and minority groups because "it is conceptually simple, enjoys a communicative monopoly, offers enormous flexibility of application, encompasses great ideological plasticity, and is serviceable for established institutional purposes."[18] Though members of the ethnic minority recognize that it is not an accurate reflection of the multicultural environment that defines their lives, Baumann found that by equating culture with community, the minority group could better negotiate for public resources, converse with political and media establishments, and legitimate themselves and their needs to authorities by essentializing themselves in this way.[19] In Amsterdam, for example, those Turks who sought to increase the number of mosques or to establish Islamic schools with public subsidies portrayed the Turkish migrants as a community of devout Muslims. Most Turks might call themselves Muslim if asked their religious affiliation. But there is wide variation in the nature of that affiliation, and the degree of orthodoxy to which they subscribe. Many Turkish migrants in Amsterdam do not go to the mosque or pray on a regular basis. Yet they are thought of as part of a community of Muslims (which could also include Moroccan migrants), as part of the hegemonic discourse. And certainly different types of Islam are practiced. In Amsterdam, as in other parts of Europe, there exist the Nurcus, the Suleymancis, the Milli Görüş, and the Alevis, each subscribing to a different version of Islam.

Ayşe Çağlar believes that we risk essentializing any group by referring to them in terms of creolization, hybridity, or hyphenated identities. She supports Friedman when she says that by describing people in these terms we create another way of creating "otherness, in which mixture is inscribed as essence."[20] She details her meaning with the example of the hyphenated group, the German-Turks living in Germany.

> It is assumed, for example, that German-Turks share common predicaments and aspirations regarding their status in German society. The stress is always on the hyphenation of ethnic (national and religious) identities to the exclusion of other forms of identification. Yet the latter may potentially cut across ethnic attachments and generate quite different forms of sociality and alliance, based, for example, on class, gender, lifestyle, religious zeal, political tendency, and so forth.[21]

Çağlar is equally concerned over the use of the term "community" when describing immigrant peoples as it tends to identify them as a "bounded and unified cultural entity,"[22] which they are not.

Appadurai would agree that community identity is an inaccurate concept, but his concern is that the reality of the diaspora is much more complex. Understanding the nature of global societies, according to Appadurai, can be accomplished by thinking of the "imagined worlds" of its citizens, or "the multiple worlds that are constituted by the historically situated imaginations of persons and groups spread around the globe."[23] Appadurai believes the global economy is sufficiently complex that it is useful to think of the disjunctures between its economy, culture, and politics in landscapes of global cultural flows. He describes five of these "scapes" as ethnoscapes, mediascapes, technoscapes, financescapes, and ideoscapes.[24] He thinks of them as the building blocks of the imagined worlds. The ethnoscape is the world of the migrants and other displaced groups who may be constantly on the move, forever having to adapt to new environments. These people become deterritorialized, and therefore consumers of transnational media, adopters of fundamentalist religious movements, and target populations for international travel agencies and other transnational businesses.[25]

Hall, Appadurai, Bhaba, and the others view the process of identity from a cultural perspective. Manuel Castells takes a sociological view:

> By identity, as it refers to social actors, I understand the process of construction of meaning on the basis of a cultural attribute, or related set of cultural attributes, that is/are given priority over other sources of meaning. For a given individual, or for a collective actor, there may be a plurality of identities. Yet, such a plurality is a source of stress and a contradiction in both self-representation and social action.[26]

Castells asserts that all identities are socially constructed, and that process takes place in a context marked by power relationships. He distinguishes between three forms and origins of identity building.

> *Legitimizing identity:* introduced by the dominant institutions of society to extend and rationalize their domination *vis a vis* social actors. . . .
> *Resistance identity:* generated by those actors that are in positions/conditions devalued and/or stigmatized by the logic of domination, thus building trenches of resistance and survival on the basis of principles different from, or opposed to, those permeating the institutions of society. . . .
> *Project identity*: when social actors, on the basis of whichever cultural materials are available to them, build a new identity that redefines their position in society and, by so doing, seek the transformation of overall social structure.[27]

Castells believes that each type of identity-building process leads to a different kind of society. Legitimizing identity generates a civil society, or one where a "set of organizations and institutions, as well as a series of structured and organized social actors, which reproduce, albeit sometimes in a conflictive manner, the identity that rationalizes the sources of structural domination."[28] Identity for resistance results in the building of communities, the most important type of identity building in his view. Here a collective resistance against oppression is constructed. Castells says that this type of identity building may result in religious fundamentalism, territorial communities, and nationalist self-affirmation—or it is the "exclusion of the excluders by the excluded."[29] This type of defensive identity building, says Castells, reinforces boundaries between the dominant institutions and the new ones. The example Castells provides for project identity is that of the feminist movement. When it first appeared it was in the form of resistance against the patriarchal society, but eventually developed to produce a different life for women, liberating them (along with men and children) and allowing them to form a new independent identity.

The Turks in Europe have been especially successful in forging new identities through resistance in religious terms. The first migrants to Europe from Turkey may have been religious, but could not be thought of as fundamentalist in their views. Over time some of them adopted such a position. This partially grew out of a resistance identity perspective. As they observed Dutch society and its mores, they determined that the Dutch were socially and politically overly liberal, dressed too revealingly, didn't appropriately value family relations, etc. So they built stronger barriers between themselves and the Dutch majority by taking more extreme positions on religion and the education of their children. This also led to more importation of spouses for their children—often choosing close relatives in Turkey.

Some scholars claim that Islamic identity has taken on more importance for the migrants than the identification with homeland, especially for the second generation Turks who have no firsthand memory of the geographic place other than what they have gained through summer vacations spent in Turkey. So the identification with Islam brings them together with other Turks in the diaspora, and provides the glue that holds the community together. This is one explanation for the brand of fundamentalist Islam that has become so popular in Europe of late. Castells says that the fundamental attachment for Muslims is not to *watan*, but to *umma*, or the community of believers. If Islamic teachings stress this in the European environment, it would add to the reasons for the strength of the religious identity. But it does not explain why, in Amsterdam, as in other European cities, Moroccans practice their religion in separate mosques from those the Turks attend. Likely the interpretation of Islam and the linguistic and cultural differences provide some of the explanation for the separation.

Castells believes that the spread of fundamentalist Islam is directly related to the "dynamics of social exclusion and/or crisis of nation-state."[30]

> Thus social segregation, discrimination, and unemployment among French youth of Maghrebian origin, among young Turks born in Germany, among Pakistanis in Britain, or among African-Americans, induces the emergence of a new Islamic identity among disaffected youth, in a dramatic transference of radical Islamism to the socially excluded areas of advanced capitalist societies.[31]

If he is right, then the future will hold less possibility for European Turks to increase their identification with Europe and with the dominant cultures that surround them. In this context, Castells claims the nation-state doesn't represent a powerful identity for the migrants, and may not provide room "for a coalition of social interests that empower themselves under a (re)constructed identity, a social/political force defined by a particular identity (ethnic, territorial, religious)."[32] He worries that the "excluded identity" formed under these circumstances may become powerful enough to take over the state where the migrants live.

Of all the influences on the lives of any migrant group, language predominates. Schudson writes that

> the importance of language as an aspect of culture can scarcely be overestimated. Language is the fundamental human mass medium. It is the mass medium through which all other media speak. No other medium is so deeply rooted, so emotionally fraught, so insistently the basis for political aspirations,

> or so much an impediment to the efforts of states to use modern media for hegemonic control.[33]

For the Turkish migrants, the learning of Dutch proved to be an important obstacle to cultural adaptation. Those who arrived in the early 1960s claimed a Dutch-Turkish dictionary was not even available for their use. And since the plan was for guest workers to stay temporarily, it didn't seem particularly important to learn this difficult language. They only needed to understand some words and phrases to get by day to day. Once they learned the routine in the factory, they could even manage their jobs without learning much Dutch. It wasn't until their children went to school that things began to change. And even then, the second generation's mastery of Dutch meant that their parents didn't need to understand the language in any depth. The children could serve as translators at the doctor's office, the tax office, and the unemployment office. Perhaps the importance of language in acculturation is the reason many scholars of multicultural environments say that it takes several generations for integration to take place. The residents in a new culture must have a command of the indigenous language that usually comes from attending school from an early age in that culture.

There are, however, problems in expecting the schools to bear the burden of managing cultural adaptation. In the Dutch system, parents are allowed to send their children to school anywhere in the system they please. Many of the participants in this study indicated that when they moved into a neighborhood, their children went to school in the neighborhood with a majority of Dutch children. But as more Turks and other migrants moved into that same neighborhood, more Dutch moved out or removed their children from the neighborhood school and sent them elsewhere. The result of that process can be seen across Amsterdam today where many schools have a high percentage of migrant children and others have few or none of these children. This means that though the language of instruction in the school is Dutch, the children interact on the playground, at lunch, and before and after school in their parents' native language instead. So it takes longer for them to be as fluent in Dutch as native children are and can create problems for making good progress in school.

All of these views on identity have importance for the Turkish migrants in Holland. And all of them point to explanations of the migrants' ties to Turkey and to one another. But nothing specifically explains why strong ties have not been forged to the Dutch culture, why "being Dutch" is not a state to which the majority of Turks living in Holland aspire. Even the second- or third-generation Turks in Amsterdam refer to themselves in hyphenated terms—as European-Turks or Dutch-Turks. It is hoped that the results of the study of this minority group will begin to explain why integration has not taken place, why identity formation is a dynamic process for these people, and why they are still perceived as "the other" in this environment where they have lived and worked for so many years. It is hoped that by detailing the views of a variety of men and women across a range of ages, socioeconomic, political, and religious groups that a more complete picture of the diversity in this "community" can be obtained. And it is also hoped that a more dynamic view of the role of imported television in the lives of the Turks who live in Amsterdam can be obtained.

Hannerz's notion that some people can be "in the nation but not of it"[34] applies particularly well to most Turks in Amsterdam who were part of the first generation. People who are in this position

> may be the real cosmopolitans, or they are people whose nations are actually elsewhere, objects of exile or diaspora nostalgia (and perhaps of other debates). Or they may indeed owe a stronger allegiance to some other kind of imagined transnational community—an occupational community, a community of believers in a new faith, of adherents to a youth style. There may be divided commitments, ambiguities, and conflicting resonances as well.[35]

In the 1960s, when I first began teaching in an urban high school in an African-American neighborhood in Cleveland, Ohio, I suggested to my students that they go see a film based on a play they had been reading in class, because it was playing "in town." The film was showing in Shaker Heights, then an upper middle class neighborhood of the community, only a relatively short distance by bus from their own neighborhood. They told me that this neighborhood "was not in town," and they would not be able to go. I then began to understand what it meant to be *in* a place and not *of* it. Those students didn't feel sufficiently comfortable to even think about venturing into the rich white neighborhood to view a film in a public theater. I believe that must be the feeling the migrants have about parts of Amsterdam.

Social and Civic Identity

Though the Turks have formed many social groupings among themselves in the city of Amsterdam—some based on religion, others based on political affiliations, still others based on the work place or the neighborhoods where they reside, few of these groups include Dutch members. Martin Castells believes there is some strong historical basis for that. In the 1960s when the first migrants came to Holland, the Dutch society was alien to the Turks who came largely from a rural environment in Turkey, and many were literally plucked from the village and set down in the midst of a culturally sophisticated populace, with whom they shared nothing. Castells also reminds us that Dutch society was going through a great change at that time, a change in the relationship between youth and their elders, a change in the social and work life of the women, a de-Christianization of society, and a move toward individualization, such that caretaking was being removed from the family setting and transferred to the state.[36] He also believes that the migrants chose to reject the Dutch ways of doing things, holding to their own traditions, rather than compromising, or carrying on a dialogue about why local values and religious beliefs were as they were.[37]

That attitude persists in the Turkish communities around Amsterdam to this day. And it is especially likely that the Turks who have strong ties to Islam reject the Dutch values across a number of issues, particularly those that relate to the family. Those attitudes, however, are frequently not based on much direct knowledge, but rather on the generalizations and stereotypes that have grown up over the years in the absence of social contact. Of course this is not as true for the second- and third-generation migrants, but even in those communities, people claim there is a lack of understanding of one another's values and social customs such that contact with other Turks is preferred over contact with the Dutch.

Within the Turkish population, there are numerous organizations. Of those registered with Dutch officials, more than 100 in Amsterdam alone are cited in various places. These organizations were founded around social, political, religious, and cultural differences in the Turkish migrant population. Some people would like to wipe out all of them and make a single Turkish organization that addresses all topics and presses all minority rights issues in the country. Others would like to replace many of them with a single lobby that tries to change the image of the Turk in the Netherlands. But that is not possible. There are major differences in this group of about 300,000 Turks or Turkish-Dutch who live in the Netherlands—differences of gender, age, education, income, religious belief, class, and likely many others. My husband, now an American citizen, who came to the United States from Turkey to study, has said that in the college towns where he lived it was not enough to be a Turk to form a community with other students who came from Turkey. He needed to have other things in common with those people before lasting bonds could be formed. He would often remark, "If I wouldn't associate with this person when I lived in Turkey, why would I want to do that here?"

This is also true in Amsterdam, where more than 30,000 people of Turkish origin make their permanent home. In that city, they join organizations, make coalitions, establish friendships, wear certain types of clothing, attend particular mosques, and celebrate holidays together. And they divide themselves from others who join other organizations, make different coalitions, become friends of other people, and so forth.

Perhaps Stuart Hall made this point most forcefully in a speech where he was defining what it means to be black in Britain and the difficulty of defining oneself vis-à-vis the white British majority.

> Has the moment of the struggle organized around this constructed Black identity gone away? It certainly has not. So long as that society remains in its economic, political, cultural, and social relations in a racist way to the variety of Black and Third World peoples in its midst, and it continues to do so, that struggle remains.
>
> Why then don't I just talk about a collective Black identity replacing the other identities? I can't do that either and I'll tell you why.

> The truth is that in relation to certain things, the question of Black, in Britain also has its silences. It had a way of silencing the very specific experiences of Asian people. Because though Asian people could identify, politically, in the struggle against racism, when they came to using their own culture as the resources of resistance, when they wanted to write out of their own experience and reflect on their own position, when they wanted to create, they naturally created within the histories of the languages, the cultural tradition, the positions of people who came from a variety of different historical backgrounds. . . .
>
> What is more there were not only Asian people of color, but also Black people who did not identify with that collective identity. So that one was aware of the fact that always, as one advanced to meet the enemy, with a solid front, the differences were raging behind. Just shut the doors, and conduct a raging argument to get the troops together, to actually hit the other side.[38]

So for Hall, "Blackness as a political identity in the light of the understanding of any identity is always complexly composed, always historically constructed."[39] And Turkishness in Amsterdam or the Netherlands or Europe is an equally complex issue. In this book I will try to illustrate the basis for understanding the people of Turkish origin in Amsterdam when they come together as some kind of community and when they stand individually or in smaller groups around special interests. Almost all of them watch television from Turkey—but in different amounts and under different circumstances and with different consequences. That is the behavior that holds this study together and to some extent holds these people together.

The Host Culture

Though this is not the story of the Dutch who live in Amsterdam, it would be impossible to write about the Turks who live there without discussing them in relation to the dominant culture of the society where they live. At the same time I don't wish to write extensively about the Netherlands and its cultural history. That has been done elsewhere. I also don't wish to spend a great deal of time writing about the issues of power relationships between the Dutch majority and the Turkish minority. That is not to deny that they exist. These relationships will surface in the discussion throughout the book, and I choose not to separate out a discussion of those relationships for special treatment.

However, it is important to understand a few things about the Dutch that make the situation for Turkish immigrants to that society different than they are for Turks who settled in France or Germany or Belgium during the same time period. Here I wish to emphasize the characteristics that have led to certain Dutch policies. The policies I will describe below are the ones that most affect the migrant peoples in their midst.

Most people who know little about the Dutch marvel at its tolerance of drugs and prostitution. Visitors to Amsterdam usually put a visit to a "coffee house" and a trip to the red-light district on their "must visit" list. But it is not so likely that they discover the underpinnings of policies that legalize activities that are considered immoral and corrupting in other locations. A book that helps understand the Dutch better is *The Low Sky,* written by Han van der Horst to help strangers to the Netherlands negotiate Dutch culture. He frames the notions of tolerance and acceptance of individual privacy and liberal policies to help readers understand their origins.

Here I will call on van der Horst and others to try to explain some of the features of Dutch society that particularly relate to the migrants in the country.

Until 1949 the Dutch ruled the third largest empire in the world. The Netherlands was a trading nation with important colonies in the Dutch East Indies (now Indonesia), and six islands in the Caribbean and Surinam (then called Dutch Guyana). The Dutch made their money from trading goods in Asia and the Caribbean. Amsterdam became one of the world's leading ports. During the colonial period most of the trade in goods from Asia came through the East India Company and from the Caribbean through the West India Company. The West India Company also obtained a monopoly in slave trade, transporting people from Africa to the Americas.[40] Van der Horst notes that the great reliance of the economy on trade led to the country's favoring international free trade with minimal restriction (while at home the Dutch have had a long tradition of government intervention in the economy). And the Dutch adopted neutrality policies that allowed them to stay friendly with as many nations as possible to keep business moving.[41] By the seventeenth century, or the Golden Age in Dutch history, the country, and particularly Amsterdam, had become a distribution center for goods from all over the world.[42] The policy of neutrality and openness to immigrants for business purposes was retained up to 1940 when the Germans invaded and the Dutch joined the allies. Following the war, the Dutch began to accept other kinds of immigrants. The first groups came from the former colonies for political reasons. Between 1946 and 1962, 280,000 Indonesians, many with Dutch nationality, arrived and claimed their right to settle. In 1951, 125,000 Moluccans who had been soldiers in the Dutch army came with their families. The end of the war brought immigrants from Dutch Guyana, who came in greater numbers in 1975 when the colony became Surinam, an independent nation. These immigrants were allowed to choose whether they would take Dutch citizenship on arrival.[43]

Van der Horst divides his book up in chapters, each titled with one of the five traits the Royal Tropical Institute[44] attributes to the Dutch. Those are egalitarian, utilitarian, organized, trade oriented, and privacy minded.

Tolerance, a characteristic we have long thought of as Dutch, was originally related to the interest in trading with all cultures and not making judgments about others' cultural traits. Immigrants who settled in Amsterdam were welcome as long as they brought money.

In his *History of Holland*, Mark Hooker says that tolerance should not be understood as the "indiscriminate acceptance of diversity; it is the recognition of someone else's right to be different, as long as that difference is not intrusive."[45]

And the Dutch government did not interfere in people's private lives, a tradition that continues today. Van der Horst says that was certainly true of the Calvinist government's treatment of the Catholics.

> As long as Catholic churches were not recognizable as such from the outside, the government generally turned a blind eye. In practice, in spite of clear legislation to the contrary, tolerance had become second nature for political leaders in the Netherlands. And just as then a Catholic church was tolerated as long as it looked like a barn or a house, small-scale entrepreneurs may sell soft drugs today, as long as the outlet looks like a coffee shop. In the same way, modern governments have tolerated organized prostitution since 1911, and occasional illegal gambling.[46]

The Dutch policy to be tolerant towards drug use and prostitution also grows out of their idea of tolerance. Hooker describes the drug policies as ones designed to reduce harm to youth, in particular.

> The Dutch recognize that in a certain phase of their lives, young adults will want to experiment with soft drugs. The de facto legalization of soft drug use makes this possible without forcing these young people into contact with the drug underworld, which is what would happen if both hard and soft drugs were treated equally. With soft drug sales essentially confined to coffee shops, the Dutch are able to regulate the market much the same way as they regulate prostitution and the sale of alcohol.[47]

Bound up with the practice of tolerance is the concept of pillarization. Though the term was applied after the fact of its adoption, it has been used "to describe cases in which worldview communities had been allowed to develop and operate their own, distinctive institutions of civil society. These side-by-side 'pillars' were presumed collectively to hold up a united state. 'Pillarization' was used to describe the social institutions in the Netherlands between 1917 and 1970."[48] Abraham Kuyper (1937-1920), a Dutch Calvinist minister, led this worldview community through his formal establishment of the Anti-Revolutionist Party, the first modern political party in the Netherlands. Succeeding Guilliaume, Groen van Prinsterer was the first to begin the movement that argued that a state shouldn't be absolutist but subordinate to divine will and should be based on antirevolutionary Christian principles. Both Groen and Kuyper argued that different societal spheres should be created. And the Christian principles should be able to tolerate various approaches in the different spheres.[49] Kuyper believed that religion and politics were bound up together and the state should recognize the rights of each societal sphere, no matter what its religious and social views were. This worldview was applied to all areas of public life. Hiemstra wrote, "For example, Protestant, Catholic and atheist families, schools, or businesses must be equally protected in law, and should one type be publicly funded, all should be funded equitably."[50]

Eventually Kuyper's views as having "sovereignty in one's domain," as van der Horst puts it,[51] became the policy of pillarization of the institutions of society. Hooker views the pillars as the building blocks of society, where everything was separate but equal. He said "the pillars kept society compartmentalized into small groups, in which the pressure of the group could maintain a certain order."[52] And though the policy no longer exists as instituted, it has left its mark on political parties, schools, and broadcasting—areas of concern for this study.

It is in line with Kuyper's belief that schools in the Netherlands today are all funded—whether public or private—by the state, as long as they abide by the state curriculum. Muslims have been able to get funding for their schools, too, so Muslim families can send their children to schools that teach religious principles along with the approved curriculum. This has allowed many Turkish Muslims to bring up their children in an environment where the home, the school, and even the social activity provided through the local mosque send strong religious messages. In 1999 there were twenty-nine Muslim elementary schools in the Netherlands.[53]

Broadcasting, which began in the 1920s in the Netherlands with the coming together of radio amateurs and the Phillips company, soon also developed under a system of pillarization.

> In 1930 the government made special rules for radio in which only broadcasting corporations with strong ties to these "streams in society" were allowed on the air: the VARA for the socialists; the KRO for the Catholics; the NCRV and the VPRO for the Protestants. The AVRO, originally born out of commercial interests, aspired to be a national broadcasting corporation, but in reality had strong links with the bourgeois-liberal sphere.[54]

Under this system, broadcasters were allotted an amount of time on one of the national radio stations or television channels according to the number of paying members supporting the religious or social group. The print press had ties to political parties through interlocking directorships with one of the pillars.

Donald Browne, who has written a history of the Dutch broadcasting system, says that the 1967 Broadcasting Act created major change in the system. It established a new body, the Netherlands Broadcasting Foundation (NOS) whose job it was to look after the affairs of radio and television. He writes:

> While the 1967 act didn't represent an attempt to create a new broadcasting system, it did weaken the "pillarized" concept in several ways: by encouraging the establishment of nondenominational, nonpolitical broadcasting organizations . . . by strengthening the centralized portion of the system (NOS); and by giving the other broadcasting organizations less control over NOS, even though they were its original creators.[55]

Brant and McQuail observe that the structure became depillarized toward the end of the 1960s as religious and ideological ties were loosened. At the same time pirate broadcasting was competing with the official system.[56]

Some of the features of the pillarized system remain that have affected a proposed challenge to the national Dutch broadcasting system. If a group seeks to have air time allotted to it, that group must collect membership fees and signatures from at least 50,000 people to obtain one hour a week on the national television system and a few hours of radio time. A second-generation Turk made an unsuccessful run at acquiring this status in 1999.

But the Dutch have been conflicted about the rights they have allowed the minorities in their country. While they believe that discrimination should not exist and have developed many policies to assure equality for minorities, public opinion polls have reflected a growing concern that the minorities have too many privileges and are too big a liability on the social welfare system. Van der Horst reports that in a 1993 survey by the Social and Cultural Planning Office, half of the respondents said there were too many people of other nationalities in Holland, while in 1991, 43 percent reported that attitude on the survey.[571] And according to Penninx et al., some discrimination occurs in an indirect way.

> One may speak of *explicit* negative position-allocation by government if immigrants and ethnic groups are designated in law and official regulations as separate lower-classified group. . . . In general such negative allocation has not taken place in post-war Dutch society. This would be in contradiction of the democratic foundations of Dutch society and of ideology of equality and equal opportunities for all in welfare states.
>
> *Indirect* negative allocation of the ethno-cultural position, however, does exist. Here we mean that in certain laws and regulations criteria for differential treatment are used, which frequently coincide with membership of a separate ethno-cultural group: nationality, religion, culture, language or mother tongue. Nationality or citizenship is the most important of these criteria. Being a citizen of another country formally excludes the foreigner from the national community, and in common language and thought this often carries the connotation of "not belonging here."[58]

However, it is possible for foreign residents to acquire Dutch citizenship, and increasingly Turkish migrants are seeking it. Since 1991, foreign nationals in the Netherlands have been able to carry dual citizenship. As of 1997, about thirty percent of Turkish and Moroccan residents had obtained dual nationality.[59] Of course, since a certain level of fluency in Dutch is necessary to obtain citizenship, many other foreign nationals will not be eligible until they become literate in Dutch. Individuals who are permanent residents of the Netherlands but who do not hold citizenship are also eligible to vote in municipal elections and to hold municipal offices.

Some of what the minority communities perceive as discrimination may be more directly attributed to cultural difference. One of the concepts at the core of running Dutch society is something called *overleg*. As van der Horst describes it,

> Foreigners will soon notice that the "holy" diary of Dutch friends and colleagues is full of appointments, meetings and what they call "*overleg*." *Overleg* literally means "consultation" but this is an inadequate translation of what has become an entire concept to the Dutch. It is closer to the English "in conference," an equally vague and discouraging phrase. Generally, you can get through to the person you are calling without encountering too many problems, even if you only succeed in making an appointment for a later date. But if you are confronted with a colleague or a department secretary who informs you that the person you wish to speak to is "in a meeting" or "in *overleg*" you may as well give up.[60]

The end of the *overleg* is a decision reached by consensus. Hooker claims that consensus is the glue that held Dutch society together.[61] This is usually the only outcome acceptable at the end of a meeting. Though the consensus may not result in much action being taken, and instead only lead to another meeting, that outcome is preferable to not allowing everyone to have his or her say in a meeting.

This must be particularly disconcerting to the Turks, who are used to waiting for officials to meet with them, but usually not bound to coming for specific appointments on particular days. In Turkish there is the phrase, "bugün git, yarın gel," meaning "go away today and come back tomorrow" for an appointment or to get what you seek, but that doesn't necessarily mean that when you return the next day the situation will be any different or that you will actually get to see the official in question. You may be indefinitely put off. And Turks are not used to pressing issues in this way. They have become used to having "devlet Baba," or Father government take care of their needs.

Van der Horst believes that foreigners' misunderstanding of *overleg* leads to being disadvantaged in school or the workplace. "These immigrant groups find themselves in a society based on *overleg*, where each group is left to its own devices and help is given only to those who ask for it."[62]

The utilitarian aspect of Dutch society may well derive from the fact that a large portion of the country has been reclaimed from the sea. Throughout the history of the Netherlands, the battle to hold back the sea has taken a prominent place in government policy. Later, protection of the environment also became important. So function over form, of necessity, grew to be a part of Dutch culture. I noticed that often on the streets of Amsterdam most Dutch people ride bicycles—to work, to shop, to school, for pleasure. The weather in the Netherlands is not always hospitable to being out of doors. But that doesn't prevent people from being outside and on their bicycles. So rain, snow, or shine, people travel about the cities and the countryside on their bicycles. That means that people are usually dressed for the occasion, in clothing that will withstand the elements. How they look is usually much less important than whether they are dressed to withstand the damp and cold. My experience with middle-class or upper-class Turks is just the opposite. How they look is extremely important. In Turkish culture, form is often chosen over function.

Organization, the last of the five characteristics identified as reflecting Dutch culture, is also apparent from observation on the streets of most cities. Tram, bus, and train schedules are posted everywhere, listing arrivals down to the minute. Though transport doesn't always arrive on time, deviations will frequently be announced to waiting passengers who view arriving late as a signaling failure and unreliability.[63] Van der Horst describes the appointment system and lives regulated by diaries as signs of Dutch near obsession with organization. Turks, on the other hand, tend to be more relaxed about time and schedules. Inviting people for dinner at a certain time may not ensure that the guests will arrive at the appointed time. It is not considered rude to arrive late for many appointments, though this custom has changed as a busier pace of life has demanded punctuality in Turkey. Most of the first migrants, however, came from villages and worked with the rising and setting of the sun.

Briefly here I have outlined some of the principles of Dutch society and policy that directly affect the degree of belonging felt by Turkish and other immigrant groups. A sense of fairness and adherence to the notion of equal rights for all usually, but not always, applies to migrant groups. Vestiges of pillarization allows religious groups to obtain schools and broadcast stations reflecting their interests. The Dutch use of *overleg* and other cultural practices may sometimes be misunderstood by migrant groups until they learn how to negotiate the cultural differences that may result in national or institutional policy. The extent to which the migrants learn the meaning and rationale for those cultural differences often determines how well they get along in the Netherlands. The next chapter will describe the experience of the first Turks to come to the Netherlands.

Notes

1. Gerard Chaliand and Jean-Pierre Rageau, *The Penguin Atlas of Diasporas* (New York: Penguin, 1995), xiii.

2. Chaliand and Rageau, *Penguin Atlas*, xv.

3. Chaliand and Rageau, *Penguin Atlas*, xvi.

4. Gerd Baumann, *The Multicultural Riddle* (New York: Routledge, 1999), 19-20.

5. Baumann, *The Multicultural Riddle*, 20-21.

6. Baumann, *The Multicultural Riddle*, 63.

7. See, for example, Stuart Hall, "The Question of Cultural Identity," in *Modernity and Its Futures*, S. Hall, D. Held, and T. McGrew, eds. (Cambridge: Polity Press in association with The Open University, 1992), 272-316; Ulf Hannerz, *Transnational Connections: Culture, People, Places* (New York: Routledge, 1996); Arjun Appadurai, "Disjuncture and Difference in the Global Cultural Economy," in *Global Culture: Nationalism, Globalization, and Modernity*, Mike Featherstone, ed. (Newbury Park, Calif: Sage, 1990), 295-310; and Arjun Appadurai, *Modernity at Large* (Minneapolis: University of Minnesota Press, 1996).

8. Hall, "The Question," 277.

9. Dursun Tan and Hans-Peter Waldhoff, "Turkish Everyday Culture in Germany and Its Prospects," in *Turkish Culture in German Society Today,* David Horrocks and Eva Kolinsky, eds. (Providence, R.I.: Berghahn, 1996), 137-156.

10. Stuart Hall, "Cultural Identity and Diaspora," in *Identity: Community, Culture, Difference*, John Rutherford, ed. (London: Lawrence & Wishart, 1990), 222.

11. Hall, "Cultural Identity," 225.

12. William Safran, "Diasporas in Modern Societies: Myths of Homeland and Return," *Diaspora* 1, no. 1 (spring 1991):83-84.

13. Homi Bhabha, *The Location of Culture* (London: Routledge, 1994), 2.

14. Hannerz, *Transnational Connections*, 67.

15. Hannerz, *Transnational Connections*, 67.

16. Hannerz, *Transnational Connections*, 90.

17. Gerd Baumann, *Contesting Culture* (Cambridge: Cambridge University Press, 1996).

18. Baumann, *Contesting Culture*, 30.

19. Baumann, *Contesting Culture*, 192.

20. Ayşe Çağlar, "Hyphenated Identities and the Limits of Culture," in Tariq Modood and Pnina Werbner, *The Politics of Multiculturalism in the New Europe.* (London: Zed, Ltd., 1997), 173.

21. Çağlar, "Hyphenated Identities," 175.

22. Çağlar, "Hyphenated Identities," 174.

23. Appadurai, *Modernity at Large*, 33. Appadurai adapted this concept from the "imagined communities" of Benedict Anderson. See Anderson, *Imagined Communities: Reflections on the Origins and Spread of Nationalism* (London: Verso, 1983).

24. Appadurai, *Modernity at Large*, 33.

25. Appadurai, *Modernity at Large*, 33.

26. Manuel Castells, *The Power of Identity* (Malden, Mass.: Blackwell, 1997), 6.

27. Castells, *The Power*, 7, 8.

28. Castells, *The Power*, 8.

29. Castells, *The Power*, 9.

30. Castells, *The Power*, 20.

31. Castells, *The Power*, 20.

32. Castells, *The Power*, 275.

33. Michael Schudson, "Culture and the Integration," in *The Sociology of Culture*, Diana Crane, editor.(Cambridge, Mass.: Blackwell, 1994), 29, 30.

34. Hannerz, *Transnational Connections*, 90.

35. Hannerz, *Transnational Connections*, 90.

36. Martin Castells, "Muslims in the Netherlands," in *Muslim Minorities in the West,* Syed Abedin and Ziauddin Sardar, editors, (London: Grey Seal, 1995), 86-96.

37. Castells, "Muslims in the Netherlands," 88, 89.

38. Stuart Hall, "Old and New Identities: Old and New Ethnicities," in *Culture, Globalization, and the World System,* Anthony D. King, editor, (Minneapolis: University of Minnesota Press, 1997), 56.

39. Hall, "Old and New Identities," 57.

40. Han van der Horst, *The Low Sky: Understanding the Dutch.* (The Hague: Scriptum, 1996), 184.

41. Van der Horst, *The Low Sky*, 185, 187.

42. Van der Horst, *The Low Sky*, 35.

43. Claire Frachon and Marion Vargaftig, "The Netherlands," in Claire Frachon and Marion Vargaftig, editors, *European Television: Immigrants and Ethnic Minorities,* (London: John Libbey, 1995), 200.

44. The Royal Tropical Institute (KIT) is an international knowledge institute. KIT contributes to furthering a better understanding between the nations worldwide. KIT plays a significant role in both Dutch society, as a window to other cultures, and internationally, as a partner in many collaborative development programs.

45. Mark T. Hooker, *The History of Holland,* (Westport, Conn.: Greenwood Press, 1999), 46.

46. Van der Horst, *The Low Sky*, 36.

47. Hooker, *The History of Holland,* 169-170.

48. John L. Hiemstra, *Worldviews on the Air: The Struggle to Create a Pluralist Broadcasting System in the Netherlands*, (Lanham, Md.: University Press of America, 1997), 4.

49. Hiemstra, *Worldviews on the Air,* 12.

50. Hiemstra, *Worldviews on the Air,* 25.

51. Van der Horst, *The Low Sky,* 50.

52. Hooker, *The History of Holland*, 144.

53. Geke van der Wal and Mathijs Tax, *De vele gezichten van Turks Nederland: een wie is wie* (Amsterdam: Uitgeverij Jan Mets, 1999), 80.

54. Kees Brants and Denis McQuail, "The Netherlands," in *The Media in Western Europe*, Bernt Stubbe Ostergaard, ed. (London: Sage, 1997), 154.

55. Donald R. Browne, *Electronic Media and Industrialized Nations* (Ames: Iowa State University Press, 1999), 168.

56. Brants and McQuail, "The Netherlands," 154.

57. Van der Horst, *The Low Sky*, 255.

58. Rinus Penninx, Jeannette Schoorl, and Carlo van Praag, *The Impact of International Migration on Receiving Countries: The Case of the Netherlands*, (The Hague: Netherlands Interdisciplinary Demographic Institute, 1994), 165.

59. Thijl Sunier and Astrid Meyer, "Religion," in *Immigrant Policy for a Multicultural Society*, Hans Vermeulen, ed. (Brussels: Migration Policy Group, May 1997), 119.

60. Van der Horst, *The Low Sky*, 133, 134.

61. Hooker, *The History of Holland*, 144.

62. Van der Horst, *The Low Sky*, 278.

63. Van der Horst, *The Low Sky*, 127.

Chapter 2

The Invitation and the Aftermath: Changing Policy in the Netherlands

This story begins in the 1960s with the migrants who were brought to the Netherlands and other west European countries to fill a labor shortage. Contrary to some people's belief, Europe was not a group of countries that contained relatively homogeneous populations before this migration occurred. We know that European cultural groups have adapted and changed from the immigrants who arrived over a long period of time. War, displacement, business, economic deprivation—all these led to movement by people of one or more national and ethnic cultures into a different culture in Europe. And though several European countries, including the Netherlands, do not consider themselves "countries of migration," in fact they are, and they have been for a long time.

Following World War II, the first major movement of peoples from one part of Europe to another was largely made up of those who were victims of the Nazis, while the Turkish migrants who are the subject of this book came to Europe in the second phase of postwar migration as a consequence of the expansion of European economies.[1] Panayi labels this the "Age of Labor Migration" in Europe, the longest lasting period of migration to Europe and the one likely affecting the largest number of people. Ironically, it was the first time since the Gypsies and the Ottoman Turks had come to Europe that such a large group of migrants had moved into Europe from beyond the continent and from one part of Europe to another.[2] A loss of population accompanied by war destruction, but particularly spurred by a period of unprecedented economic growth, led Germany, France, Belgium, Great Britain, and the Netherlands, and some Scandinavian countries, to seek labor beyond their national borders. Workers were especially needed in the low-end positions, in skilled and semiskilled—even unskilled jobs—jobs not easily filled with workers in the native countries. At the same time, workers in sending countries, like Turkey, Greece, Spain, and Morocco, had a problem of unemployment, low GNP levels and high population growth rates.

So the import of labor solved problems on both ends. The receiving countries brought in workers to fill the need in manufacturing and services, and the sending countries were somewhat relieved of the problem of unemployment. Meanwhile, the workers who left were expected to send back remittances from their earnings to help boost the limited supply of foreign currency in the sending country economies. Though initial remittances to Turkey were small, they eventually outstripped the expectations of the government. According to Ministry of Finance figures, the volume of migrant remittances in 1972 was larger than Turkey's national debt, some $740,000,000.[3] Since the men and women who left Turkey and other sending countries were young, strong, and single (or left their families behind), there was little need for the host countries to supply social services. Panayi details the situation in Turkey:

> This country has had one of the highest birth rates in the world since 1945, peaking at forty-four per thousand in 1960. In 1972 the country had a population of 36,500,000, which had increased to 55,000,000 by the end of the 1980s, when it was growing by one million a year. This rapid population growth resulted in the presence of a large number of children, dependents who could not play a full role in economy. In the early 1970s about 40 percent of the population was under fifteen, about twice the figure in industrial societies. However, between 1960 and 1970 Turkey's labor force only grew by about 1.9 percent per annum. Economic growth, although it took place on a scale comparable with the rest of Europe, did not expand quickly enough to keep pace with the population explosion, so that high rates of unemployment developed, which may have reached about five million in the early 1970s. A final element which constitutes a push factor, almost as important as the willingness of European states .to import labor, was the readiness of Turkish governments to export their population as part of a planned economic strategy.[4]

In Turkey the way had been paved for a large-scale migration with Article 18 of a new constitution that was passed in 1961 that conferred freedom of movement, including the right to a passport, to all citizens.[5] Before that time, Germany had begun importing Turkish workers in 1956 under a vocational training program. That program ultimately failed, but the men found employment at the dockyards of Hamburg, Bremen, and Lubeck.[6] Following a revolution in 1960 in Turkey, the new government wrote into the first five-year development plan a provision for encouraging worker migration. Though it was first envisioned as a one-year training program to supply Turkey with a highly skilled labor force, it never turned out that way.[7] Subsequently labor agreements were signed with several European countries—with Germany in 1961; with Austria, the Netherlands, and Belgium in 1964; with France in 1965; and with Sweden in 1967.[8]

Reflecting on the agreements and the deficiencies in the guest-worker programs, two political leaders later made the following points:

1. Turkey did not request the German government to establish a vocational training center in Turkey, similar to one it had founded in Italy.
2. Turkish workers, especially during those early years, when huge numbers of migrants were dispatched almost weekly by special trains or planes, were not offered any orientation course before their departure.
3. Due to multiple registration at various local branches of the Employment Office, the exact number of migrants was never properly established.
4. Turkey's migration policy provided for no definite priority for regions with high underemployment rate.
5. The problem of clandestine workers, usually defined as "tourist migrants," was never efficiently fought.
6. The special staff dealing with Turkish migrants abroad—personnel of the embassies and consulates—were mostly unsuited for the purpose.
7. The low level of political consciousness and legal information among Turkish workers has meant a high degree of ignorance about their social rights such as social insurance, child allocations, bonus for dangerous tasks, work accidents, etc.[9]

Despite the lack of attention paid to the guest workers, especially in the early years of the programs, Turkish men and women, but primarily men, applied to go to Europe to work in increasing numbers. Individuals were chosen to go according to their age, condition of their health, and skills. By 1974, more than a million were on the waiting list. The bulk of the workers who were selected went to Germany. According to the Turkish Employment Service, about 650,000 workers were sent to Germany in the years from 1961 to 1974. During the same period, about 25,000 workers went to the Netherlands. Of that number, fewer than 200 were women.[10] These numbers, of course, do not account for the unofficial migration that occurred in those years.

Though the benefits to the European businesses and governments and to the sending countries were substantial, the workers may have had fewer benefits. Of course they went seeking employment and they were given jobs. But there is some reason to believe that those who left Turkey already had work. They assumed that the work they would find in Europe would allow them to save money to buy a house or establish a business on their return. And they likely had little specific information on the nature of the situation they were going to—with respect to living conditions, work conditions, and details on the social and cultural environment. So they had no way to assess whether the benefits would outweigh the costs. To a large degree, the Turkish government, in political turmoil during the period of 1967 to 1973 when leftist terrorists were involved in continuous acts of violence, was not capable of providing the kind of information and establishing the kind of infrastructure to support its workers abroad. Onulderan and Renselaar put it this way:

> Their major concerns with regard to migrant workers can be grouped under two headings: efforts to attract the greatest amount of savings into the country in order to bridge the gap in Turkey's balance of payments; and fears of subversive actions which might involve Turkish workers abroad. Concern about the

> upbringing of Turkish workers' children was centered around the same ideas. The exceptional nature of these governments and the martial law regime which accompanied them did not promote greater discussions about long-term programs and the eventual adoption of a national migration policy. This kind of attempt could only begin to crystallize after Turkey's return to a multi-party democratic system.[11]

Some of those programs were established after 1973, despite the continuing political instability in Turkey.

Abadan-Unat summarizes some of the consequences for governments of the migration phenomenon, but also describes the difficulties individual workers experienced through her focus on one district in Turkey that sent a number of workers to Germany. She says that the indefinite employment abroad limited the socialization such that migrant workers, as a marginal group, were forced into political and social isolation. A second major negative impact was on families who were fragmented when the male head of household left to become a guest worker. The unpredictability of household remittances, the infrequent visits of the workers to their families in the village, and the differences between the life led in Europe and in the rural Turkish communities put great stress on families.[12]

More recently Peter Stalker conducted a study for the International Labor Organization of the impact of globalization on international migration. He summarizes the advantages and disadvantages for immigrants in the new environment. While the worker finds employment, a larger income, new cultural and social experiences, he or she may also have bad working conditions, longer working hours, lower status work, and encounter racism or discrimination along with the personal suffering that results from separation from his or her family.[13]

What the Migrant Found in the Netherlands

The movement of Turks to Europe can be divided into three periods, according to Faruk Şen, who heads the Center for Turkish Studies in Essen, Germany. Writing in 1993, Şen says that the first phase ran from 1961 to 1973, when workers were recruited by the European countries. He characterizes this period as a "workers-only society." The second period ran from 1974 to 1981 when workers were no longer being actively recruited. This was a time of family reunification, where spouses and children joined the workers to make their homes in Europe. The last period, from 1982 to 1992, is characterized by efforts to stop further migration and European encouragement of remigration to the home country. Since 1992, most countries have been experiencing migration in terms of "family formation," where second- or third-generation Turks born and/or raised in Europe return to Turkey to find a spouse and bring the husband or wife back to Europe to live.[14] The last period also has included migration by a number of refugees, mostly of Kurdish ethnicity, who have fled Turkey for political

Table 2.1 Advantages and Disadvantages of Migration

	Emigration from Sending Country		Immigration to Receiving Country	
	Potential Advantages	Potential Disadvantages	Potential Advantages	Potential Disadvantages
For migrants, or for individuals in receiving country	Employment	*Bad working conditions*	Services that free women to enter labor force	*Competition for jobs*
	Greater income	*Long hours*	Cheaper goods and services	*Lower local wages*
	Training or education	*Lower status work*	Opportunities to move up to supervisory jobs	
	New cultural experiences	*Racism or discrimination*	Richer cultural life	*Strange languages and customs*
	Meeting new people	*Separation from family*	Learning about other countries	*Creation of immigrant ghettos*
For enterprises	Skills of returning migrants	*Losing skilled work force*	Meeting labor shortages	*Need to give language or other training*
		Labor shortages that drive up wages	Cheaper, more flexible labor	*Dependence on foreign labor for certain jobs*
	Extra business for communications and travel firms		Larger markets and economies of scale	
For society	Lower unemployment	*Coping with sudden returnees*	Lower inflation	*Slowing technological innovation*
	Knowledge and skills of returnees	*Brain drain and loss of better workers*	Gaining people already educated	*Costs of language and other training*
	Building transnational communities	*Culture of emigration*	More diverse and energetic population	*Social friction*
	Foreign currency remittances	*Increasing inequality*	Capital brought by immigrant investors	*Loss in balance of payments from remittances*
			Tax income from younger workers	*Cost of social services*
	Reduced population pressure	*Losing younger people*	Rejuvenating population	

reasons and seek asylum in European Union countries. And still others have arrived on tourist visas to visit family members in EU countries in the hopes of finding jobs and securing permanent resident status.

Rinus Penninx and his colleagues, writing about the Netherlands, divide the Dutch policy governing immigrants into two periods—before and after 1980.

But roughly the same general demarcations Şen describes can be found in the Netherlands too. Though the Netherlands discussed offering incentives for migrants who wished to return to their home countries, specific bills were never introduced in Parliament.[15]

Workers arriving in the first period came under an understanding, if not a policy, that the Netherlands was not an immigration country, and that the time they would spend there was somehow limited to the period during which their work was needed. Most came with employment contracts in the first period.

Personal Experience in the Early Years

To understand conditions during the first period of migration to Amsterdam, perhaps it is good to hear the voices of those who lived it, rather than rely only on the description of host country policy.

Ömer was one of the early migrants, and his father came before he did. His father arrived in Amsterdam in 1963, while Ömer was still in vocational school in Turkey. He joined his father and mother after he finished his military service in 1970. He says there was no dictionary when he came in 1970 and that he learned Dutch by listening in the factory. He remembers that the first guide to Dutch for the Turks had a lot of mistakes in it.

> But many of us didn't learn much Dutch because when we came we had only one thought—to stay for five years and then go back. If I had been able to go to a Dutch course for six months, I would be fluent. But I couldn't because I had to work all day and then come home and do cleaning and other chores. And on weekends, it is vacation and you need the time for rest.

His job was at the Ford plant, where many other Turks worked, and which is now closed down. Ömer lost his job there in 1982, getting early retirement benefits.

Haci Karar Er, thirty-eight, press spokesperson for the *Milli Görüş* mosque, Aya Sofia, came at the age of eight. His father, who arrived in 1969, brought him. Though Er is educated and has plans to educate his own children as much as is possible, he remembers what a hard time his father had in the beginning.

> My father had no education, but learned to read and write in the Turkish military. He had to make the sound of a chicken in order to buy eggs in the grocery store here. That's how difficult life was for him then. He bought me a small dictionary when I arrived. Since he wasn't educated himself, he thought this

> would be enough for me. But that was all there was to help me learn the language at that time. Now there are several Dutch-Turkish dictionaries.

Hayri came in 1971 thinking that his stay would be a short one.

> The value of money was great and the attraction was money. I thought I would save 25,000 or 30,000 Turkish Liras and return to open a shop and work in it. I thought I could do that in three to five years. My father was working in the fields in the village. I was the oldest child in the family. So I kept sending money back to help with the family—to get married, to go to school, to eat and drink. Then suddenly many years had passed and it was more comfortable to stay here. I had work. I got up every day and went to work. I could come home at night and look out for my own comfort. When it is like that, we decided to stay. There was a decision. Should I go there or stay here? Now I can take my children to Turkey. I couldn't educate them there. They got used to this system, to this kind of discipline.

Mehmet came as a guest worker to Germany in 1965, and two years later was recruited by a Dutch company and settled in Amsterdam. He is bitter about many of the experiences he had when he first came, but doesn't think the situation has improved much for Turkish people in the Netherlands.

> The people who brought us here did not want us to stay. They did not want us to live here as people. They just wanted us here as workers; and in that capacity, they wanted us just to work hard. They worked us twelve to fourteen hours a day. After that many hours in those working conditions, how would you be able to learn Dutch?
>
> I knew German, had studied it in high school. And I took some university courses in Germany, so I knew it pretty well. And I had worked in my father's store in Turkey. At the time I thought about studying and working at the same time, but it didn't work out in Germany. The work was too hard for me to be able to handle both.

After two years of factory work in Amsterdam, Mehmet opened his own store in the city center, selling gift items and imports. As a foreign entrepreneur, Mehmet had difficulties gaining the trust of local authorities.

> I was the first Turkish store owner here in 1969-70. I would have so many visits by the police with their dogs. I would say, "Is there anything you are looking for here?" And they would answer, "No." "OK," I'd say, "Who complained about me?" And they would not want to tell me anything in response. And my customers would be frightened away by the presence of the police. In the end, they would look around and finally leave without saying anything. This negatively affected my business.

I ask him if they weren't concerned about drugs at the time, since his store was located in a district where drugs are now frequently sold. He answered, "This was in 1969 and 1970 when they needed workers in this country. They were inviting us to come here." His answer implied that the Dutch should be treating him well, since they needed the immigrant labor. But likely Mehmet was unusual in owning his own business at that time and Dutch authorities were suspicious of a store owner who was a migrant.

Banu, a woman in her fifties who went to school only through the fifth grade, came as the wife of a worker when she was eighteen. Her husband worked in a factory in a small town outside of Amsterdam, and there were not many Turks there at the time. She spent her days mostly alone and people treated her as if she came from an alien civilization. After a few months she decided she couldn't tolerate it in this strange place and returned to Turkey. Her mother told her she had to go back, that her place was beside her husband, no matter how lonely it was.

> When I first came I had a new coat and the people asked if it came from Holland or Turkey. "Oh, do they have such things in Turkey?" they asked. If I couldn't explain, my husband would tell them. And I had a nice pair of shoes and when people were told they were Turkish, they were surprised. When I first came, the people heard that my husband had brought a wife. They looked at me through the window to see what kind of a person a Turkish woman was. The people told him they wanted to see me. I asked "Why? Do they want to know how I dress or what?"

Banu came from Ankara, Turkey's capital, so she had a certain sophistication she found lacking in the other women who came from rural areas and were illiterate.

> They came from the villages and didn't know anything. Then they began to adjust their clothing a little according to the place they now lived in. Or they should have. They didn't need to call attention to themselves. Since some people looked at Turkish women as if they were something to eat, some of the men told their wives to cover themselves. But not my husband. He used to go to work at two in the afternoon. When I first came I was alone and had no language skills and didn't know the environment. My husband would take me out in the area so I wouldn't get bored—or tell me to go out on my own when he wasn't there, to go places I could figure out how to get to. I'd go out on the street and see strangers who were Turks and think of them as my mother or father and want to hug them. My husband and I would walk around until 1 o'clock and then eat lunch. Then he'd go to work. Then I'd fill the time walking around until he came back. Yes, I suffered my first year here.

Of course these are memories, not exact accounts of history. But they reflect the difficulties the first migrants encountered. They worked hard in a strange land side by side with people who spoke a language they didn't understand and apparently didn't have the energy to learn. If they viewed the Dutch in stereotypical terms, the Dutch evaluated them similarly. They were seen as strange, suspicious, as the "other." And they seemingly didn't know how to cross the divide. All the while they were imagining a return to Turkey with money in their pockets—a return that never happened.

In the first period there wasn't really an established policy toward the workers. They were to be in the country only temporarily. But once the spouses and children arrived, there was a need to provide social services. So education of the children was conducted in Turkish, and teachers were imported to provide that education. Eventually, some provision was made for religious needs by bringing Islamic clergy from Turkey, too.

The men who arrived as guest workers in the 1960s of course required housing. But the government didn't get involved in this problem, since the stay was meant to be temporary. So employers took the responsibility. Citing his earlier study, Penninx says, "The foreign workers found accommodation in communal barracks, rented rooms and boarding houses. In the private sector in particular, the housing was very poor, and during this period boarding houses were often in the public eye because of overcrowding, lack of facilities and fire risks."[16] This situation did not change much until the second phase when families joined the workers, and even then, workers only had access to less desirable housing.

Families who brought their children in the 1960s had no special services offered to them in the Dutch schools, but a lot has changed since then. In 1974, a program known as Immigrant Minority Language Instruction was introduced in elementary schools. This program called for providing schooling for the migrants in their mother tongues. So during regular school hours, minority students were removed from the classroom for instruction in the native language. In a comparative study of European policy toward migrants, this program is critically appraised.

> In 1974, IMLI (then known as OETC in Dutch, and today as OALT) was introduced for large groups of pupils in primary schools without any preparation, counseling, curriculum, or supervision, and even without any legal basis. IMLI was originally introduced in primary schools with a view to the remigration of migrant families.[17]

Van der Horst writes that teachers were recruited from the home countries of the migrants, "partly induced by some vague idea of sovereignty in one's own domain, but was also a response to the desire to return home: the generations that grew up in the Netherlands would also have to be able to survive if the dream ever came true."[18]

Once the remigration position was reassessed at the end of the 1970s, IMLI developed in a different way, to focus on socioeconomic deficits. Under this perspective, schools with a large number of students from disadvantaged families (which included immigrant families) were given extra resources to help make the pupils achieve at a more equal level with advantaged ones.

Turkish workers arrived in a largely Christian country with no place to practice their Islamic faith. But they did find a hospitable policy to help them establish places of worship. They were able to take advantage of provisions under the Church Construction (Subsidies) Act (1962-82) to build mosques. Though the act was written to target Christian churches, the Social Democrats added an amendment to allow it to apply to non-Christian religions.[19] However, it wasn't until 1975 that the first mosque appeared in Almelo, the Netherlands. The first mosque in Amsterdam was not established until 1977 in a converted Catholic chapel. Many mosques followed. As of 1995, between 150 and 200 mosques had opened around the country, many of them in storefronts and former warehouse-type buildings—wherever Muslims could find available space. Of course these mosques serve the religious needs of Moroccans and other ethnic groups in the Netherlands too.

The Aya Sofia mosque, established by the *Milli Görüş* Islamic group in Amsterdam, is one of the larger mosques in the city. Established in a group of garages, the members said there was a court battle over the use of the space for their activities. They said the municipality told them to find a place and they would help finance it. But once the 10,000-square-meter space was located, the *Milli Görüş* members thought the officials became frightened of having such a large facility with so many people involved. Eventually they were able to occupy the space and received a bank loan to pay for it. But the municipality told them they could not use the space for sports (which they planned for the young members of the congregation), and only part of the facility for a mosque. The building also houses a grocery store, and a tea and coffee house and restaurant where the men gather and play backgammon and talk. There are prayer rooms on two levels with room for the 1,000 to 1,500 who come to pray on Fridays. There are also separate rooms for the women. The building is also used for youth groups and classes in martial arts for boys. Members of Aya Sofia, named after the Istanbul mosque that was once a Byzantine church, view the mosque as a center for the *Milli Görüş* community.

Myth of Return and Change of Policy

Safran discusses the "homeland myth" and the dream many migrants hold of returning. He first discusses this myth in terms of the Turks in Germany. He reports on a survey of the Turkish community in Germany at the end of the 1980s where more than half of the Turks said they were hoping to return to Turkey in the next few years. Safran partially attributes this response to the policies of German authorities who promote the myth of return and who see citizenship as conferred on someone by descent rather than birth or length of stay in the country.[20] The homeland myth was also perpetuated in the Netherlands, however, and it had a base in reality. Contracts between guest workers and employers delineated the length of stay for Turkish workers, and they planned to return to Turkey when the work was completed. Even though that didn't happen, the workers, the employers, and the Dutch government all entered into those agreements under that assumption. But despite the agreements, the Turkish families were not deported, and they had no wish to return immediately since they had become settled, and their children were enrolled in schools in the Netherlands. Many of the workers who lost their jobs found new ones or joined the ranks of the unemployed on welfare.

As time went on, the situation had changed from what everyone intended. Safran says host governments, home country governments, and migrants have reasons to perpetuate the "myth of return," after all parties have accepted that return will not occur.

> It is a defense mechanism against slights committed by the host country against the minority, but it does not—and is not intended to—lead its members to prepare for the actual departure for the homeland. The "return" of most diasporas (much like the Second Coming or the next world) can thus be seen as a largely eschatological concept: it is used to make life more tolerable by holding out a utopia—or *eutopia*—that stands in contrast to the perceived *dystopia* in which actual life is lived.

The Dutch government did face up to the permanent stay of the migrants at the end of the 1970s when they began to address the visitors as permanent residents and potential citizens. Penninx et al., report that the "Ethnic Minorities" report prepared by the Scientific Council for Government Policy in 1979 marked the turning point. It led to a new more comprehensive policy in 1980, which eventually became adopted as the Minorities Bill of 1983.[21] The bill had two specific purposes under which all measures would be drafted. The first was to create a "tolerant, multi-cultural or multi-ethnic society in which cultural and ethnic differences would be accepted and appreciated." The second was to solve "the arrears of the immigrants' social position in Dutch society, and fight discrimination (institutional or otherwise) which leads to unequal chances and sustains these arrears."[22] Policy changes in labor and income, education, and housing were set up to improve the social position of minority groups. And organizations of immigrant groups were to devise plans for preserving their cultural identity. Funding for minority-targeted programs increased from 595 million guilders in 1981 to 800 million guilders in 1988.[23]

No matter the goals of the bill in the area of employment, many migrants remained unemployed. Many saw this as an effect of the restructuring of the sectors in which migrants had previously found work.[24] But if migrants were out of work or sick, or were of retirement age or needed allowances for their children, the government did pay for the social services they needed, just as they paid native Dutch people under the same circumstances. Unemployment among migrants, particularly the Turks and the Moroccans, remains a problem today. Many of the unemployed in these populations will never obtain work. Kloosterman cites statistics released by the Dutch Central Bureau of Statistics that show that the rate of unemployment in the Netherlands among Turks in the years between 1989 and 1994 was consistently more than three times that of the indigenous workforce. In 1994 that rate was 36 percent, the highest among any ethnic group.[25]

Kloosterman explains why he believes that this high unemployment rate among migrants is not likely to drop in the current political and social environment of the Netherlands. In a corporatist welfare state like the Netherlands, "traditional family-oriented welfare policies, a high minimum wage and a concomitant high level of social benefits, combined with labor market policy aimed at reducing the labor supply by, on the one hand, hindering women from working, and, on the other, offering smooth exit-routes (high benefits, low thresholds) to disabled and older workers, among others," prevent many workers who previously held low-end jobs to find work in the postindustrial economy.[26] Though job growth has been stronger in the service sector than might have been expected in the 1990s, the less well educated, long-term unemployed migrants have not found work. That has happened, according to Kloosterman, because employers have been hiring better educated women and other nonstandard workers in part-time positions or other new entrants to the labor market.[27] In Amsterdam, the head of household in at least a third of the participant families in this study was out of work. Sometimes he had taken very early retirement; other times he was out of work on extended sick leave; and other times, he had simply lost his job. Very few women with whom I talked were unemployed. Several talked of having jobs in the past, but had since quit those jobs. The younger participants in the study also reported difficulties finding and keeping jobs. Of course I am not referring to the professionals in this study. Lack of educational achievement was holding back several of the young people I talked with.

Tolga, a young man finishing his education to be a computer engineer, says he makes it his job to try to encourage his friends in a youth group at the mosque to stay in school and complete their educations. "I kept pushing them to stay in school. Some didn't make it. Now there are twenty or twenty-five students in the organization who are still studying," he said proudly. But he understands that the welfare system can be an attractive alternative if these young people don't get good jobs.

> I work part time so I can support my wife and our baby, who is soon to arrive. I get a subsidy from the state to study. Some young people drop out because they get married—3,000 guilders a month they get. Many people take the money for subsidy, then work illegally and get much more. I'm an engineer and get 3,000 guilders—an uneducated person could get 4,000 from combining sick pay, unemployment and illegal job earnings. Many people get sick pay and work elsewhere.
>
> One person I know gets 2,400 guilders from the factory. He gets another 1,900 from social security. He also gets an apartment subsidy and some other help, so he gets 2,500 in total from social security, while I will get 2,500 as a new graduate). My father, who is unemployed, gets 2,500.
>
> I study and study and will get about the same thing as my father does for not working. My father never wants to work. He gets a subsidy for the apart-

> ment, return on taxes, other perks—so why should he want to work? I don't like the income policy of Holland. Those who work should get more for their labor than those who don't. I think they should either drop the social security or increase the salaries.

The welfare system also helps women with small children who are single parents or who need to work. Gaye, thirty-three, who has a school-aged daughter and a preschool aged son, is happy for the services she receives. Her husband, who is an illegal alien in Amsterdam, isn't much help at all to her, so she might as well be a single parent.

> I will speak for myself. As far as the health of my children is concerned, I wouldn't have had this much support if I stayed in Turkey. And I would not have been able to get things for them that I thought they needed. Sure, they would have had clothing, but not like they do here. And I would not have as much information about child rearing as I do here. The only thing I regret is having to work and placing them in a crèche for long hours. I wish I didn't have to, but I wanted to provide for them and that was the only way.

As for the changed policy regarding the schools, compulsory education for all children up to the age of sixteen continued, but the goals of the foreign language teaching programs and the intercultural education programs had changed. Now that migrant children were to be accepted as permanent residents of the Netherlands, they continued education in their native tongues, if they wished, but it was for purposes of enrichment and cultural preservation under the new philosophy. At the same time, greater emphasis was placed on Dutch language teaching to children who were from non-Dutch speaking backgrounds, and greater attempts to bring together children, parents, and educators was made. All of this was meant to improve the quality of education for migrant children, but while this was happening Dutch parents were removing their children from schools where minority children predominated and enrolling them in schools largely attended by Dutch. Such choice is possible under the Dutch educational system. So children who speak a language other than Dutch at home and who share that language with many of their classmates have less opportunity to learn Dutch like a native.[28]

Housing also remained something of a problem despite the changes in the law. Part of the problem had to do with the lack of resources among unemployed migrant families. And more widespread unemployment occurred in the Netherlands and across Europe following the 1973 oil crisis. Minority families of Moroccan and Turkish heritage also tend to have larger families, so finding housing with enough rooms in this very densely populated country is always a problem. In the years since migrant families have lived in the Netherlands, ghettoization has increased in the cities. Kloosterman reports that in the four largest Dutch cities, including Amsterdam, ethnic minorities made up more than 30 percent of the population in a quarter of all neighborhoods in 1995. Only 10 percent of those neighborhoods had that many ethnic minorities in 1986.[29] These neighborhoods had relatively low levels of socioeconomic development, high levels of unemployment, greater numbers of disabled workers, and higher crime levels. As more Moroccan or Turkish families move into a neighborhood, the Dutch who live in these neighborhoods begin to move out. Some Turkish families in this study expressed a preference for living in predominantly Turkish neighborhoods. When that happens, the local grocer and green grocer, baker, coffee shop, travel agent, and other businesses are more likely to be owned by Turkish entrepreneurs. This makes shopping easier. First, the products in the stores are ones that fit their diet and lifestyle. Second, the owners and clerks in the stores speak Turkish to them, so there is less need to speak Dutch. But not all of the Turkish residents of these neighborhoods are happy when their environment is so homogeneous. Nizam, a chauffeur for a private hospital, said he isn't all that happy in his neighborhood because there are few Dutch people.

> We moved from another neighborhood because of the large foreign population, and the same thing is happening here. The biggest number is of Moroccans and their children are less well mannered than Turkish children. Lots of foreign people came here directly from villages and they don't know how to live in this European city.

Voting and citizenship rights also followed the change in policy. As of 1986, all permanent residents who have lived in the Netherlands for at least five years can vote in municipal elections. And after five years residency (or three years if the individual has a Dutch national for a spouse) he or she can apply for citizenship. The allowance for dual citizenship came in 1991.

From Multiculturalism to Integration

Throughout the 1980s the term multicultural society became increasingly popular to describe the Netherlands. In the 1990s there has been more concern for integration, reflecting the nagging problems in the work force and in education. These problems are seen to have their roots in the lack of proficiency in Dutch. So today the Integration Policy for Newcomers requires all new residents to enroll in language courses to become proficient in Dutch, and also to take vocational training courses.[30]

Haluk Bakır, a journalist for NPS radio, doesn't see the move from multiculturalism to integration as a positive one. He believes it opened the door for the Dutch to express their prejudiced views about the Turks more freely.

> In the 1980s in every report published by cities or government agencies, they were always stressing maintaining your own identity, but later in the nineties there has been a sort of shift. Why should we consider it a taboo to criticize minorities, they think. And some politicians broke that understanding. And they started talking about how the foreigners shouldn't exploit our social welfare system.

If migrants are to be integrated into Dutch society, it means also that the Dutch must accept the minorities as one of them and not constantly focus on their differences. One young professional woman, Meryem, says she is constantly being reminded that she isn't Dutch.

> When you are in a public place, and people know you are Turkish, the conversation always moves to the issues of foreigners. If they want us to be integrated, why do they always focus on our being foreign or Turkish. The Dutch want us to turn into Dutch and assimilate into the Western culture. But they forget that Turkey has Western culture too, and it is older. But the Dutch people should also show an effort to learn about me and my culture. They ask my brother if he has four wives. They don't know that the Turkish Republic has been in existence for seventy-five years and polygamy has been illegal all that time. Stereotypes exist because of the lack of knowledge about the country.

The participants in this study have a mix of views on the ways they have been treated under Dutch policy directed toward them. Many see the Netherlands as a place that is far superior to Turkey in terms of social policy. In Turkey they would not have all their medical, unemployment, and schooling costs covered by the state. And retirement benefits would not be nearly so good. They believe the safety net in the Netherlands allows them to survive in less than ideal conditions. All of these things lead Turkish people to stay on in the Netherlands, despite the strong pull from Turkey.

Some Turks who live in Holland are in the business of helping make the policy that minorities live by. Nevin Özütok is one of those people. Özütok is an Amsterdam municipal council member for the Green Left Party. She has worked to solve problems of discrimination and exclusion for Turkish people here for a long time. But she has also had her own encounters with discriminatory policy. Arriving in Amsterdam as a middle schooler, she studied organizational and labor sociology in university. She worked for the municipality as a specialist in labor issues for about six years. Then she experienced personal discrimination in her job. She asked for privileges that all the other colleagues in her workplace had. She discovered that the Dutch personnel were given those privileges and she was not. She filed a report, saying that an injustice had been done to her. Though it was settled in her favor, she was never comfortable in that office again and left the job. Later she ran for office and was elected as a representative from the Green Left Party. And she works as a policy officer for ethnic minorities in Amsterdam. Though she fights to eliminate discrimination in the workforce, she is also concerned about those who take advantage of the system. She calls the Turks who have come to depend on the welfare in the Dutch system lazy—and characterizes them as living an "Arabesque lifestyle—if we don't get it today, it will come tomorrow. If God doesn't give it to us, the government will give it. There is this attitude here," Özütok said.

Özütok has her supporters in this view. When speaking separately from their husbands, some of the wives who participated in this study confided that unemployment support was too good. When the money comes on a regular basis, it doesn't provide any incentive for the men to keep looking for work, they said. And though they can get by on the money, their lifestyle never improves. Besides, they really don't like the idea of having their husbands hang around the house much of the day.

Ahmet, a musician in his late thirties who speaks Dutch and supports himself and his family in Amsterdam, also resents that people who are unemployed get so much money. "The biggest issue in Holland is that there is no difference between those who work and those who are unemployed in their salaries, so those who work are unhappy. It is the difference between 2,000 guilders or 2,200 guilders and 1,800 guilders in salary. So lots of people don't work here. We never get ahead. The Dutch are given promotions over the Turks and we cannot get the best jobs."

Yusuf is thirty-three, has lived half his life in the Netherlands, and is already "integrated," in that he is literate in Dutch. But he believes that the Dutch employment policies, designed to make everyone equal in the workforce, don't work as well as they might.

> Job preference is for the Dutch, but it is hard to tell about discrimination, because it isn't obvious. It doesn't come from neighbors and acquaintances. I asked for a promotion on my cleaning job for three years, and never got it. But when a Dutch person comes along, he is always promoted over a Turk.

When such discrimination occurs, the Dutch employers have a different view of the situation. Frequently the employee who has the best language skills, all other things being equal, is selected for the promotion. But even with extensive language training, it may never be possible for a worker to achieve fluency on a par with a native.

Süheyla and Mithat are a young couple with a baby and a three-year-old. Süheyla was born in Turkey but educated in Amsterdam. Mithat came as a young adult and is being trained for a job under the newcomers policy. He is more pleased with the Dutch system as it affects minorities. He thinks that Holland is in the best economic position of all the countries in Europe. He says he knows this from the news he listens to. He thinks that will benefit him when he seeks a job. "There isn't a real problem with unemployment here. Especially if you have a profession, but we hear there is a lot of unemployment in Germany. Here, even if you want to start your own business, the government will help you get started."

When he thinks about problems in Holland, he points to diminishing rights for migrants. "We see that. There are more controls on bringing spouses from Turkey and the need to have established a household and have work and prove that to the authorities before the spouse arrives. The difficulties are not insurmountable but are greater than they used to be," Mithat said.

And Mithat said he heard that there is talk of legally stopping the reuniting of families. Süheyla thinks that is not a good idea, especially because she married Mithat in Turkey and brought him to the Netherlands as her spouse. "You should be able to marry somebody from Turkey if you want to. You shouldn't have to marry someone from Holland," Süheyla said.

Marrying someone and bringing that person to the Netherlands means that there will continue to be a first generation of migrants. Any children who come from this union will have one parent who is likely less fluent in Dutch. Şeref Acer thinks this is a problem.

> There is a constant problem of starting over with a new first generation. And the children of the marriage are always a second generation. And if at home the family is only speaking Turkish, the cycle continues. The children who speak Turkish at home start school not knowing any Dutch, or very little. This puts them behind in school. And it takes a long time for the spouse who comes from Turkey to get adjusted to life here and learn enough Dutch.

Separation in Schools

The Dutch policies that allow parents to send their children to the school they want and to support the existence of Islamic religious schools may cut both ways in both benefiting and disadvantaging minority children. Semiha has exercised her option to send her daughter and son to Islamic school. She wanted to have the strong religious values her children learn at home be reinforced in the school. But lately she has had second thoughts about the decision she and her husband made.

> All the students in my kids' school are foreign because it is an Islamic school. I was discussing this with my husband the other day. He said, from one side we did the right thing, but from another perhaps we did the wrong thing. The kids have very little contact with Dutch kids. They are learning Dutch more slowly. And they think of themselves as Turks. But I think that if the kids they spent time with were Dutch, they would learn to speak Dutch with a Dutch accent, not a Turkish one.

The Islamic schools are not populated only with Turkish children, meaning that they must speak Dutch to communicate with the other pupils. But on the playground and before and after school, children tend to associate with others who speak their native language. Semiha thinks it would be better for them to associate with Dutch children more. She is probably reflecting on her own experience. Semiha came to Germany with her family when she was five years old, entering the German educational system with other German students at a very young age.

Pınar and her husband, Yusuf, have chosen to educate their three daughters in Catholic school, even though they are Muslims. That choice was made on the basis of their assessment of the educational quality in that school.

> The educational system here is very good. It keeps their interest and attention. They used to go to a school with a lot of foreigners—Moroccans and Turks. I took them out of that school and now they get a better education. They are in a Catholic school, so they can get a more disciplined education. There are only four Turkish kids in the school. They get along well with the teachers and others at the school.

Still other views are held by the participants in this study. Akşit, a man who has been retired since his late forties and who now works much of his time for the Islamic political party in Turkey, favors a separate, but equal system, where Turkish people would not be "contaminated" by the Dutch values.

> There are problems with education too. Of the 900 kids in the local school, there are no Dutch. Though all of our children completed middle school, at least, we didn't like what they learned in the schools. They want to teach their own culture in the schools and they want us to be Dutch because they aren't having any kids.

Discrimination

Though Dutch policies have evolved to attempt to redress inequalities and to provide more opportunities for minority families, it is impossible to legislate tolerance and understanding on a personal level. Jessika Ter Wal and her colleagues write of the schizophrenic attitude the Dutch have taken regarding the minorities in their midst.

> In spite of widespread xenophobia, the Dutch still see themselves as a tolerant people and point to the fact that in the Netherlands racism and prejudice are not as prominent as in many surrounding countries. As a result of the Second World War the Dutch people are very strongly opposed to anything that resembles Nazism or fascism. The discourse in the Netherlands reflects this attitude. Blatant racism is difficult to find; racist jokes are usually found non-acceptable.
>
> Existing xenophobia is usually expressed under a layer of common sense, making the speaker sound reasonable: "I have nothing against Turks, but you must agree that they are very different." In the expression of "sensibility" toward ethnic minorities and asylum seekers the slogan "The Netherlands is full" is often used as a justification.[31]

The view that the country is already full of minorities is supported in the 1977 Eurobarometer survey. Respondents were asked whether they agreed with the statement "Our country has reached its limits; if there were to be more people belonging to these minority groups we would have problems." Of the Dutch people surveyed, 60 percent agreed with the statement.[32] Ter Wal said the Dutch are also resistant to mixed schools on racist grounds.

> It is not uncommon for indigenous Dutch parents to refuse to send their children to schools with a large percentage of ethnic minority pupils because they

think that these would negatively influence the attitudes, norms, values, and achievement of their own children. This "white flight" phenomenon causes segregation: some schools have become increasingly "black" whereas others remain "white."[33]

In the Eurobarometer public opinion poll, cited above, Europeans were asked to assess their own racist feelings. Of the Dutch who responded to the survey, 24 percent characterized themselves as not at all racist, 46 percent said they were a little racist, 26 percent said they were quite racist, and 5 percent said they were very racist.[34] That was similar to European responses overall, as one-third of them said they were very racist or quite racist. In the same survey, respondents were asked whether they agreed with the statement "People from minority groups are discriminated against in the job market." Of the Dutch respondents, 74 percent agreed with the statement. This means that in spite of Dutch values of tolerance and respect for equality, those values don't preclude racist attitudes, and the racism translates into overt employment discrimination. In 1998, Europeans were asked about their perception of the number of foreigners living in their countries. Of the Dutch responding to this survey, 40 percent said there were too many, 51 percent said there were a lot, but not too many, while 8 percent said there were not many.[35]

A story of problems Hayri's family had in their mixed cultural neighborhood illustrates the differences in attitudes of some Amsterdammers. Hayri's wife, Sevgi, describes their encounter with a racist neighbor.

We had an older man who was our neighbor, a man of sixty or seventy. We all have property lines. And on each property is a place to put our garbage. When I would take out my garbage, he'd come up to me and swear at me [she uses the Dutch curse words here]. He said we should go back to Turkey. He said we didn't belong here. This went on for a whole year. People said I should be careful of this man, especially since about four years ago a Turkish girl in the neighborhood had died following an incident where a Dutch boy hit her on the head. He too might decide to hit me and kill me. Then one day after I had just been to Turkey for the summer, I was putting out my garbage and he came out again cursing at me. "Why did you come here? What are you doing here? Why don't you go home?" he said to me. Then my son came out and said I should get away from there. The man ran off. Later that night—about 1:30 in the morning, he came out shouting things about us and ringing all the neighborhood doorbells. He wanted to collect signatures on a petition for us to leave. He woke the whole neighborhood, and finally a Dutch woman came out and told him that we had as much right to live there as he did and drove him off. "The one who should go is you," she said to him. There are good and bad among all nationalities. Not all Dutch are bad or good. That woman came to see us many times afterward—for our children's birthdays and other days. She was a good person.

I asked Sevgi if she called the police. She said the Dutch woman had told her to call the police. She said the woman told her to tell the police that this is our home and he can't do that to us. Though Hayri claimed you shouldn't call the police for small things like this, he insisted that all people should be treated the same. "We are all human beings," Hayri said..

Few of the participants in this study related stories as extreme as this to illustrate examples of discrimination. Most people said they had never experienced any discrimination. Others spoke of subtle things, like people whispering when they encountered them on the street. Others talked about comments made about women who wore head scarves. And still others just alluded to the difficulties they had when they tried to make friends with Dutch neighbors. Semiha related her attempts to make friends with her Dutch neighbors.

> I am friendly with all of them, but we don't visit one another's homes. I invited one friend for tea and she came and spent some time with me, but she never invited me back. I suppose I could drop in on her, but I'm waiting for her to invite me. I am shy about just showing up at her house.

Semiha's Turkish friend Özgü said she has one neighbor that she's invited for dinner and that person did accept, but never returned the invitation. "Mostly we talk on the balcony," she said. Semiha wonders whether it is cultural—whether they expect her to just drop in. But other of Semiha's neighbors are not so nice to her or her son.

> I have two neighbors who always frown when they see me. They never say hello and don't want to. One of them has a son my son's age and she doesn't want him to play with my son. When we pass by her, she gives us an evil look, draws her son up close to her and grabs his hand. And when my son and others are out playing, she calls her son in. One time he asked if he could play with my son and she didn't permit him to do it.

Other participants in the study believe discrimination is not uniform. It depends on the individual and the experiences that person has had with Turks. Mesüt, an educational and labor consultant for the Dutch government in his late thirties, also thinks that sometimes the Turkish people live up to the stereotype, too.

> When you ask some people, they would say that the Turks are all criminals. But others talk about what Turks bring to the culture from their own backgrounds that contributes to Dutch society. Others think Turks are those who are quick to pull a knife on you. There have been many incidents here of that kind. A Turk gets agitated in a coffee shop about the discrimination he has suffered at the hands of the Dutch. All at once he pulls out a gun and kills seven people. That's an example of what happens too. The Turks here are people who are quick to anger. I see them that way. When you think about it, everyone has experienced discrimination here. Who among us hasn't? On the other hand, I am very comfortable here. If I have to go to a village for work or some other reason, on my return, I think, "This is my city, Amsterdam."

Stereotypes, misperceptions, discrimination—these attitudes and behaviors come easier when people have little knowledge of one another. And despite programs of intercultural education in the schools, the Dutch and the Turks and other minority groups don't get to know one another very much. Language difficulties head the list of reasons why they don't spend more time with one another. But even if all the Turks, Moroccans, and others spoke fluent Dutch, the cultural barriers would remain. Because there is a societal-level taboo on discrimination, it is difficult to get to the real sources of the problem. Van der Horst provides a hypothetical example of how intolerance gets expressed when the person knows that a racist statement is taboo.

> They are often preceded with disclaimers as "I don't like to discriminate, but..." People who protest about the building of a mosque at the end of their street, tend to base their arguments on the lack of parking space or the extra noise. They will even claim that the mosque will lead to a concentration of Moslems in one area, providing fertile feeding ground for racism and discrimination, which they themselves—of course—abhor.[36]

Role of the Media

In a later chapter I will detail the media that are targeted to minorities, but here I'll describe what the mainstream Dutch media (television and newspapers, mainly) do to promote multiculturalism and avoid discrimination, or when they are part of the problem. Penninx et al., summarize the research of media images of minorities. They say that the content analyses of media over the period 1963 to 1978 indicate that the media were more negative in their portrayal of immigrants up to 1972. After that time, the media were less negative, but still tended to distort the view of immigrants.[37]

Journalist Bakır thinks that Turks may be driven to watch more television and read more newspapers from Turkey when the Dutch media don't treat them fairly or aren't sensitive to their characteristics.

> Minority groups are too stigmatized also in the press. They take some Moroccan groups and say the minorities cause problems. You have this whole fury in the media and everybody takes up the subject and people feel frustrated. It is the same phenomenon as the way media treat African Americans in the United States. The Turks don't like to be lumped in with the Moroccans because historically they have had quite different experiences. Turkey was never a colony. Turks don't want to be treated as inferiors. On the other hand, there is also hope because some of the Dutch people see these media problems.

In general, there appears to be media for the majority and media for the minority and little crossover of the two. A project financed by the Dutch public broadcasters, the Ministry of Culture, and the European Union, called More Color in the Media, represents an effort to try to achieve balanced representation of ethnic minorities in the Dutch media. The goal of the project was to get at least twenty jobs in the Dutch media for minorities. And the longer term goal was to achieve proportional representation in the media by minorities for all functions and at all levels. That would be about 8 percent of all jobs.[38] The specific project is part of the work of *Stichting Omroep Allochtonen* (STOA), which is a cooperative group of migrant organizations in the Netherlands. Its purpose, with regard to the mainstream Dutch media, is to get enough minority participation in the Dutch media so that it truly represents the multicultural nature of the society, and also to make programs for migrants in their own languages.

Bakır doesn't think this program may be working as well as its organizers would like.

> The undersecretary for media affairs says beautiful things about increasing the number of minority journalists working in the media, like for NPS (*Nederlandse Programma Stichting*, the Netherlands Program Foundation), and so on. So but when you look at the practice, of the way we are treated in the NPS. [I say, You mean you are not a real journalist?] That's right. It's not true. We have enough experience. I mean I speak five languages. What is a minority? I work for the BBC and *Cumhuriyet* (a respected Turkish national daily) and I interview their prime ministers. They don't know that maybe. And they think we are just doing some programs in our corner. And nobody ever comes to ask what we think. They have their own opinion. They always pick the persons who tell things the way they want to hear them. And that makes you frustrated.

Whether it is the separate pillar-type arrangement for minority and majority broadcast media or whether different cultural groupings naturally separate themselves from other groups is unclear. Bakır doesn't think it is healthy and that it probably leads to further marginalization of journalists whose native culture is not Dutch.

> There are sometimes people we have worked with for ten years and we pass by each other in the halls and we don't know each other's name. We never talk, except in maybe in some reception we exchange a few words.

Participants in this study who watch both Turkish and Dutch television frequently cite the lack of program content for them on the Dutch channels. The absence of attractive programming doesn't serve the policy that promotes integration. Sibel, a homemaker in her late thirties whose husband works as a chauffeur for a hospital, spends most of her time watching Turkish television, because she finds little to interest her on Dutch television. She is literate in Dutch, so a lack of understanding is not the problem.

> Dutch TV doesn't discuss our issues or us much at all. We say that they should talk about the good things in the Turkish community, but I'm sorry to say that there isn't anything good to say. And when they show programs about Turkey it is always about the backward areas, the villages. The Dutch then think that all of Turkey is like that.

Atilla Arda, city council representative in Amsterdam who came from Turkey before he entered elementary school, works hard to change policies that might be discriminatory or develop ones that will help solve the problems of migrants. But he doesn't think the Dutch media do much to help improve the perceptions of the Dutch about the migrants.

> The media need to consider whether when a murder occurs in a café, the murderer is identified as a Turk or not. I think that is wrong. The media must consider the impact on society and how they contribute to that. If every night on TV, they keep identifying problems as "Turks did this," or "Moroccans did that," then I would wonder what kind of people these are. It's debatable whether that identification should occur.
>
> All of the news regarding Turkey is negative–Ocalan, the PKK, etc. The day a Western country had elected a woman as their leader, it was on the news here, but the fact that Tansu Çiller (the first female prime minister in Turkey) was elected the same day, and they didn't mention it, was not showing good judgment. Maybe Çiller's election was not good for Turkey, but they should have reported that a woman was elected prime minister in an Islamic country.

Dutch newspapers aren't really much of a factor in the Turkish community. The Dutch press is generally considered a serious press, and that likely makes it more difficult to read when Dutch is a second language. There is no tabloid press in the Netherlands, nor do Sunday newspapers circulate. Of course many Turks don't read Dutch at all, so it would be impossible for them to read any publication. Cost of the newspaper is another issue. Turks are generally avid newspaper readers, so if the newspaper is available, they will pay some attention to it. Many families talked about reading the free newspaper they receive midweek in Amsterdam. It is basically an advertising supplement. But very few of the families I talked with subscribe to any paper—Dutch or Turkish. Turkish papers are usually read at local coffeehouses, mosques, or centers for organizations to which Turkish people belong.

Whither Integration?

Over the years, the Turks and other migrant populations in the Netherlands have been the beneficiaries and the victims of changing policies. Though the changing European economic situation could not have been predicted at the time the workers were invited to the Netherlands and other European countries, once the government did become aware of the problem, they didn't act quickly enough to respond to the changing needs of the migrants. Now the government finds itself in an uncomfortable position. On the one hand, it seeks to do right by the migrants who were invited to work and live in the Netherlands. But on the other, officials see that too much money is going out to people on welfare and want to put an end to it. So since 1996 all newcomers are required to abide by a different set of rules concerning their admission and extended stay in the country. Herman Vuijsje describes the untenable position in which the government had placed itself.

> While the Netherlands was mobilizing for battle with the racism bacillus, social problems and deprivation continued to grow rampant. This is how the paradox of the Netherlands' good reputation in the area of racism, but the poor social prospects for *allochtoons* [literally, nonindigenous], came into being. The government promoted relatively peaceful racial relations in the Netherlands by "handing out" things. When, however, it came down to prescribing and requiring, the government dodged the issue.

The media have not contributed much that is positive to the issue. Though space has been set aside for migrants in the form of special programs, the migrants are always outside the mainstream—as journalists and as a subject of news and public affairs programs. And migrants resent being referred to only in terms of their ethnicity when it comes to criminal acts some of their members may have committed.

So while the Dutch would like the Turks and other minority groups to accept Dutch ways of doing things and to fit into Dutch society by learning the language and becoming educated and skilled for available jobs, there is the feeling that even if they did all these things, they would still not be integrated into Dutch society. Many Turks wonder why they would want to give up their cultural traditions and religious practices if it would not lead to greater benefit as Dutch citizens.

The next chapter will deal with the way Turks have perceived their situation over the years.

Notes

1. Panikos Panayi, *Outsiders: A History of European Minorities* (London: Hambledon Press, 1999), 119, 120.
2. Panayi, *Outsiders*, 129.
3. Nermin Abadan-Unat and Artun Unsal, "Migration through the Eyes of Political Parties, Trade Unions, Employer Associations, and Bureaucracy," in *Migration and Development*, Nermin Abadan-Unat et al., eds. (Ankara, Turkey: Ajans Turk Press, 1975), 100.
4. Panayi, *Outsiders*, 132, 133.
5. Abadan-Unat and Unsal, "Migration through the Eyes," 47.
6. Ersin Onulduran and Herman van Renselaar, "International Relations, Legal and Political Dimensions," in *Migration and Development*, Nermin Abadan-Unat et al., eds. (Ankara, Turkey: Ajans Turk Press, 1975), 27.
7. Onulderan and van Renselaar, "International Relations," 29.
8. Onulderan and van Renselaar, "International Relations," 29.
9. Abadan-Unat and Unsal, "Migration through the Eyes," 48, 49.
10. Rinus Penninx and Herman van Renselaar, "Evolution of Turkish Migration before and during the Current European Recession," in *Migration and Development*, Nermin Abadan-Unat et al., eds. (Ankara, Turkey: Ajans Turk Press, 1975), 11.

11. Onulderan and Renselaar, ""International Relations," 54.

12. Nermin Abadan-Unat, "Summing Up," in *Migration and Development*, Nermin Abadan-Unat et al., eds. (Ankara, Turkey: Ajans Turk Press, 1975), 375.

13. Peter Stalker, *Workers without Frontiers* (Boulder, Colo.: Lynne Rienner, 2000), 27.

14. Center for Turkish Studies, *Migration Movements from Turkey to the European Community* (Brussels: Commission of the European Communities, January 1993), 17.

15. Rinus Penninx, Jeannette Schoorl, and Carlo van Praag, *The Impact of International Migration on Receiving Countries: The Case of the Netherlands* (The Hague: Netherlands Interdisciplinary Demographic Institute, 1994), 160.

16. Pennix, Schoorl, and van Praag, *The Impact of International Migration*, 142.

17. Peter Broeder and Guus Extra, "Language," in *Immigrant Policy for a Multicultural Society*, Hans Vermeulen, ed. (Brussels: Migration Policy Group, May 1997), 79.

18. Han van der Horst, *The Low Sky* (Nuffic, The Netherlands: Scriptic, 1996), 279.

19. Thijl Sunier and Astrid Meyer, "Religion," in *Immigrant Policy for a Multicultural Society*, Hans Vermuelen, ed. (Brussels: Migration Policy Group, May 1997), 118, 119.

20. William Safran, "Diasporas in Modern Societies: Myths of Homeland and Return," *Diaspora* 1, no. 1 (spring 1981): 86.

21. Penninx et al., *The Impact of International Migration*, 161.

22. Penninx et al., *The Impact of International Migration*, 161.

23. Jan.Lucassen and Rinus Penninx, *Newcomers: Immigrants and their Descendants in the Netherlands 1550-1995* (Amsterdam: Het Spinhuis, 1997), 148-149.

24. Penninx et al. *The Impact of International Migration*, 162.

25. Robert Kloosterman, "Migration in the Netherlands and the Emerging Post-Industrial Social Divide in Urban Areas," in *Immigrants, Integration, and Cities: Exploring the Links*, OECD, ed. (Paris: OECD, 1998), 76.

26. Kloosterman, "Migration in the Netherlands," 77.

27. Kloosterman, "Migration in the Netherlands," 77.

28. Penninx et al., *The Impact of International Migration*, 132-141.

29. Kloosterman, "Migration in the Netherlands," 73.

30. Arrien Kruyt and Jan Niessen, "Integration," in *Immigrant Policy for a Multicultural Society*, Hans Vermeulen, ed. (Brussels: Migration Policy Group, May 1997), 45.

31. Jessika Ter Wal, Amy Verdun, and Karin Westerbeek, "The Netherlands: Full or at the Limit of Tolerance," in *New Xenophobia in Europe*, Bernd Baumgartl and Adrian Favell, eds. (London: Kluwer Law International, 1995), 242.

32. "Racism and Xenophobia in Euope," Eurobarometer Opinion Poll no. 47.1. First results presented at the Closing Conference of the European Year Against Racism (Luxembourg, 18-19 December 1997), 5.

33. Ter Wal et al., "The Netherlands: Full or at the Limit," 243.

34. Eurobarometer Opinion Poll no. 47.1, "Racism and Xenophobia in Europe," 1997.

35. Eurobarometer Survey no. 48, EC Eurobarometer, 1998.

36. Van der Horst, *The Low Sky*, 283.

37. Penninx et al., 175.

38. Myriam Sahraoui, "Putting More Colour into the Dutch Media," *Media Development* 45, no. 3 (1998): 22.

Chapter 3

Life in a Strange Land: Different People, Different Lifestyles

In the previous chapter, I focused on the policies and practices of the Dutch regarding the arrival and continued stay of the Turks in the Netherlands. From the Dutch perspective, the migrants became a problem to be managed. The country had settled into a set of policies and attitudes regarding the influx of peoples from former colonies about the time the new set of guest workers arrived from the Mediterranean countries. Then, of course, policies had to change to reflect the new immigrants, which was somewhat unsettling for the Dutch.

As one of the targets of the changed policies, the Turks had to make adjustments in their own lives. They had arrived in a country where almost everything was foreign. The weather was cold most of the time. It often rained and the sun appeared only infrequently. Most of these people came from parts of Turkey where precipitation occurred only in the winter and spring. The other months were sunny and warm or even really hot. Then there was the food. Used to a diet rich with a variety of fresh vegetables and fruit, they found the Dutch food bland and limited. Turks, especially those who are not very well-off, use meat to flavor dishes of eggplant, green beans, leeks, artichokes, etc. But in the Netherlands they found vegetables expensive and much scarcer than at home. Of course many of the migrants came from villages where they raised their own food, limited only by the availability of water and good soil. Here, they had no land, no space for growing anything. A video that was included in a television series on the Turks in the Netherlands (described in chapter 4) showed one of the early arrivals explaining how hard they found it to cook and eat. The men cooked what they remembered from home, but said they couldn't locate all of the ingredients and were not used to doing the cooking themselves in the communal kitchens provided for them. At home women did the cooking.

In the villages when men have free time, they usually congregate at coffeehouses, passing the time by drinking tea and small cups of Turkish coffee and playing backgammon with other men. There were no coffeehouses similar to those they were used to at home—no open-air cafes where they might be free to sit around for hours without ordering anything under the shade of a tree on a warm summer's day. Many of the first people to arrive had never spent any time in a large Turkish city, much less a European city, so negotiating the institutions, services, businesses, and the public transportation system in Amsterdam was bewildering to most of these people. The language barrier was also significant.

Turks' conception of time is different from that in northern Europe, too. It is not that Turkish people don't work hard. They do. But work in the village, where most of the men lived, was scheduled around the natural cycles, not time clocks. And if the work doesn't get finished today, it will be waiting tomorrow. Even in the cities, time is not kept so exactly. So the men had difficulty making those adjustments. The men who came on their own must have missed the women in their lives. Several men report having worked twelve hours a day in the early years. So when they returned to the boardinghouses or barracks, there was nobody to welcome them, and no familiar food prepared and ready for them.

Later, when the women joined their husbands, they had their own set of problems. Women in the villages have a hard life. They work in the fields in groups by day, but also do all of the household work and the child rearing. Women frequently gather at harvest times to prepare food for the winter together. Such times are social events for women; they chat with each other while they work.

Other issues arose when the wives and children arrived. Customs for women were different in Europe. The men felt a need to protect their women from the evils of the world. In towns and cities in Turkey in the 1960s, women generally didn't go out alone at night, and single, widowed, or divorced women were frequently escorted by fathers and brothers or other male family members. Women's gatherings were more often limited to afternoon tea parties or luncheons. And though many women in cities held full-time jobs, more often married women with children were full-time homemakers. In general, they had much less freedom than the men. In Turkey it was not uncommon for men to gather in the evenings in restaurants or coffeehouses, leaving their wives at home with the children.

In Holland, though few Dutch women held full-time jobs outside the home in the 1960s, they did enjoy a lot of personal freedom. And their dress was different. Village women dress modestly, often wearing a colorful dress over baggy pants with a scarf on their heads. The Turkish men who brought their families to Amsterdam, fearing they would not be safe, or that they would want to be more like the Dutch women, were generally more protective in this environment than they were at home. In the mid-1980s, a Turkish filmmaker, Tevfik Başer, depicted the extreme case in *Forty Square Meters of Germany*, about a guest worker who tells a young Turkish girl that by marrying him she will be able to have a wonderful life in Germany. After the wedding and the trip back to Germany, he locks her in their small apartment, refusing to ever take her out. Though this story is not typical of what happened, the experience in the new country must have been frightening for everyone when the language, the culture, and surroundings were all so strange. And it is easy to understand why a man might want to keep a woman locked up to protect her.

In the last chapter, I talked about Semiha who spoke of her Dutch neighbor who didn't return her invitation to tea, and her concern for why that hadn't happened. Turks are very friendly people who welcome friends and even strangers into their homes for a visit, always offering food and drink. In fact, in the course of conducting this research, I was very well fed. Not a single family I visited failed to offer me tea or coffee and cookies or cake. Usually the food was made especially for me. One of the participants, a divorced man, even cooked dinner for me and my colleague one evening. If you meet friends on the way home from work in Turkey, you might invite them to dinner without giving advance notice to your spouse. So it must have come as a big surprise to encounter people who might not accept your invitation, or didn't return it if they did come to your home.

When the Turkish participants in this survey made comments about the Dutch, it was often about their cool manner and their more formal behavior. However, a few of the participants had lived for extended periods of time in Germany before coming to Amsterdam, and all of them said that the Dutch were warmer and more relaxed than the Germans. That helped them feel closer to the Dutch culture than they might have. Most people said they had not experienced any discrimination, but very few said they had made close friends with Dutch people. That was true of people of all ages. Sometimes that was attributed to changes in the neighborhood when the Dutch moved out, and they lost contact with them. Sometimes it was noted that the Dutch were just too different from them. More often it was about their own failure to learn to speak Dutch. Tülin, a young woman in her thirties who heads a Muslim women's organization, expresses the contradiction in attitude toward the Dutch I heard occasionally from Turkish women who were practicing Muslims.

> It is good to live here in Holland. The Dutch are good people. I think they think well of us. Of course it depends on the individual. It is easier to live in Turkey than here—everything is different here—the culture, the language, the religion. I am opposed to the concept of integration, because everyone should stick to their own language and culture. That way we can respect one another's ways of doing things.

Tülin's feeling that the cultures should live separately stems from her strong religious beliefs. She sends her children to Islamic schools and would not want them to learn the ways of the Dutch, as she perceives those ways to be sinful. That is also a reason why some people avoid Dutch television. They see the programs as being too "open," meaning that women are scantily dressed and inappropriate sexual behavior is depicted. Many see this as offensive, especially to their young children. Since Turkish television has come to their homes, however, they have a chance to compare programs for their relative openness.

Özlem, a woman in her early forties who is generally critical of Dutch ways of doing things, said she had to admit that Dutch television was better than the recent programs she saw on Turkish television. "At least the Dutch show these programs late at night after the children have gone to bed, while Turkish television will show them all the time."

These days, one of the functions of the television programs from Turkey is to serve as a reality check on how things really are in Turkish society. The young people, whose parents came to the Netherlands twenty to thirty years ago, have to continuously hear stories about customs and ways of doing things in Turkey. And these are held up to them as standards of behavior for the current time. The television programs frequently put the lie to that discussion, since the children can point to examples on the television programs as evidence that times have changed considerably. Of course, it has always been true that immigrants remember the home country as they left it. It gets fixed in time as it really was or as they remember it was, not as it is now. The globalization of television allows people to maintain some contact with the home country and watch it as the country experiences cultural change.

Gurinder Chadha portrayed the fixing of time idea well in her 1993 film *Bahji on the Beach*. The film depicts a group of Asian British women having an outing to Blackpool Beach in England. All of them are first- or second-generation migrants except one of the women, who was visiting from India. The older migrant women are dressed in saris, while the visitor wears stylish Western clothes. A discussion ensues of the difficulty in maintaining the morality of "back home" when trying to raise a family in the foreign country. The Indian woman who is visiting, Amrik, tells Asha that this is impossible. "Home? What home? How long is it since you've been home? Look at your clothes, the way that you think," Amrik says condescendingly. She tells Asha that she is twenty years out of date. Pushpa, another older lady who works full-time in a shop, supports Asha's position. Commenting on one of the young girls who has become pregnant by her black boyfriend, she says that she has never seen such a deplorable situation in the thirty years she has spent in the country. The first and second generation talk about the differences between their ways of life there and what the first generation brought from India. But Amrik provides a reality check on the situation. Nobody in this film is shown watching contemporary television from India, however.

Very few of the participants in this study who had children in school had made close contact with the schools. That is often due to their inability to speak good Dutch or their lack of understanding of the educational system. It is also the way they might have remembered it in Turkey, where their parents sent them off to school and the teacher was in charge of that part of their lives. But since school is a place where the core values of a culture are passed on, children encounter the cultural differences firsthand. Mark-Jan de Jong believes the school system will help the integration process along by orienting children more toward Dutch culture.

> Attending Dutch schools will bring them in contact with Dutch pupils, unless the school has become a so-called black school, that is a school with only migrant children from different minority groups. It will certainly bring them into contact with Dutch teachers, the Dutch language, and Dutch teaching material which contains explicitly and implicitly a lot of the dominant Dutch norms and values. When this is added to all the other influences they consciously and unconsciously undergo during their stay in the Netherlands, by playing in the streets, visiting shops or looking at television programs, their socialization process will contain more elements of Dutch and western culture than the culture of their parents, because they spend more time in direct and indirect contact with it than the culture of their parents. In this way the western Dutch culture is drip-fed into them and becomes internalized.[1]

De Jong is assuming that integration through the schools is a good thing, and that it will take place naturally. However, the fact is that most migrant children do attend "black" schools. And in the schools, the children often spend their time on the playground and in other social settings with other children from their own ethnic group—where they speak the language of their parents. Other children are sent to the Islamic schools, so the core values of their families' culture are included in the daily socialization that takes place in the educational process. Yet some Turkish parents still worry that their children may be getting the wrong instruction in the schools. Özlem is a mother who worries about the lack of respect for adults that children have in the Netherlands and she attributes this attitude to an overly permissive school environment.

> In Turkish schools, the teachers decide a lot of things for the children, from what length your hair could be, whether you had shaved if you were male, down to checking your fingernails to see if they were clean. Everything is permitted here. If you want to dye your hair twenty colors, you can go to school that way. The only big difference is that here you can wear your headscarf. Otherwise it is better in Turkey.

Moving between Cultures

The sons and daughters of first-generation migrants are often torn between wanting to stay in the Netherlands or returning to Turkey to spend their lives. Several people in this study had siblings or parents who moved back and forth between the two countries or who had gone to Turkey permanently. It is hard to make such a decision when there are aspects of both cultures you like and other things you don't like.

Tolga, a student finishing his studies to be a computer engineer, now lives in Amsterdam with his wife, Serap, who spent all of her life in Turkey until her marriage to him. He has moved between Turkey and the Netherlands for his education and plans a return to Turkey to work and live, once his education is complete. But he sees positive and negative aspects of that decision.

> Serap: It scares me that you never know what tomorrow will bring in Turkey. Doesn't it scare you Tolga?
> Tolga: In Turkey there is no freedom of expression, ideas. Here, if you are open in saying something to someone, it stays where you discuss it. Not so in Turkey—but are we going to remain distant from our countrymen because of this? I know that the quality of education in Holland is much higher than that of Turkey. When the choice between the two came, I decided to do my degree in Holland. We are comfortable here. The people look at your brain, not the way you are dressed. My wife is covered, but they don't hold that against her or us. The universities in Turkey will not take covered women. This is a very sad thing for us. Do I ask you, "Why are you covered?" That's the way you believe. And this is the way I believe. In Turkey there are many things to be sad about. To change them is not something for a single person—it requires a systemic change in the political system. It can't be changed from Europe. We are too few here. It can't be done from here.

Perhaps Tolga's desire to change Turkish society is his reason for a permanent return. But he also did an apprenticeship in a Turkish company and really enjoyed it. "I will go back to Turkey when I finish. I love it here, but I have a closer attachment to Turkey. I have gone back fifteen to twenty times in the last five years," Tolga said. His parents live in the Netherlands now, but he said the whole family would return to Turkey upon his graduation.

Lale, a twenty-three-year-old student, had a very different reaction from her apprenticeship in Ankara. She chose Ankara because many of her relatives live there—including her mother. Her parents are separated because her mother could not survive the life in the Netherlands and her father's work was there. But Lale discovered she was more comfortable in Amsterdam, following the work experience.

> Since I left Turkey at a very young age, I didn't learn enough about Turkish culture and my parents didn't explain enough to me. And me and other Turkish kids like me have a problem knowing who we are. Are we Dutch, are we Turkish or what? We have an identity crisis (she says in English). So I said, what if I go to Turkey and see if I can do it. And I wanted to find out if I could learn more about Turkey that way. So I did an apprenticeship that was six months here and six months there. Of course I knew Turkey since we go to Turkey pretty much every year for vacation and I always enjoyed that time in Turkey. My parents always go to Ankara for vacation and then to the seaside.
>
> But I found it to be a very bureaucratic system. Many people are working and there is little work to do. The tempo was not very fast, not fast enough for me. Nobody told me what to do. I looked around and figured out what to do.
>
> They wondered why I came to Turkey to do my apprenticeship when it should be a lot better in Holland. I did enjoy the time there, but I didn't learn anything new there from a business perspective. But the culture was so different there and people's attitudes and ideas were so different. The people's daily lives were taken up with the political situation in Turkey mostly. Here you pay little attention to politics because the country's situation is mostly

> stable and doesn't change much. In Turkey the government wants to be involved in everyone's daily lives. It was hard for me. Then I came back and asked myself where I feel better about myself and where am I better off. I decided that Holland was the answer to that question.

Many of the participants share the view that neither culture is perfect and that it comes down to making a decision based on which place is most compatible and most advantageous for them and their families. Frequently that has less to do with any cultural advantage. The concern that they would not be able to survive, to find a job, and to educate their children is what they say keeps them in Amsterdam. But perhaps de Jong is right about the socialization process. The longer they stay in the Netherlands, the more accustomed they become to the way of life there. And some of that has to do with embracing a part of the Dutch culture. Sure, it is good to live in a place where you don't have to worry about meeting expenses related to unemployment or illness. And it is also good that children have free educational opportunities and subsidies. But this is not just government policy. The policy springs from a cultural attitude about caring for those who may not be able to care for themselves. It derives from a concern to provide for the educational development of all of the residents of the country—not only the native-born citizens.

In 1992, when Turks were able to adopt Dutch nationality without losing their Turkish citizenship, many of them did so. Now more than 30 percent of Turks in the Netherlands have dual nationality.[2] From my interviews in Amsterdam, I did not perceive that anyone opposed the idea of becoming Dutch citizens. In families where some members were dual nationals and others had not applied for Dutch citizenship, it was usually the inability to speak Dutch that prevented the adoption of Dutch nationality. It is also true that the majority considered themselves Turkish in a cultural sense, even if they planned to live in Amsterdam the rest of their lives and had taken Dutch nationality. In his research of attitudes toward plural nationality in the Netherlands, van den Bedem says that most of the respondents in his survey felt more of a sense of belonging to their country of origin.

> The acquisition of Dutch nationality does not change the feelings of belonging to a certain group, nor is it an indication of assimilation (or even integration) in the receiving society, as is shown by the study. Respondents who are naturalized do not have less contact with their own community, and in some cases (Moroccans and Turks), those who have opted for Dutch nationality are even more often members of associations of their own community than those who have not.[3]

A Home Away from Home

Though it is true that the first guest workers found everything strange—climate, food, language, music, religious practice—it didn't take them long before they set up "little Turkeys" around the city of Amsterdam. One I'll describe in a little detail is located on Kinkerstraat. In a two to three block area on this street there are many Turkish-owned shops. Two grocery stores that have a variety of vegetables and fruit displayed outside, a butcher, three different Turkish bank branches, a video rental store, a bakery, and a coffee shop are located here. A few blocks away is the Aya Sofia mosque operated by the *Milli Görüş* Islamic group. Of course, many Turkish families also live in this neighborhood. But the shops also are patronized by the Dutch, as they find the products good, the produce fresh, and the prices generally lower than equivalent Dutch shops. I spoke with the shop owners of several of these stores. The owner of the largest grocery store, who imports many products directly from Turkey, also operates a wholesale business at the central market. In this store, he sells all manner of food that Turks would be used to in Turkey. The fruits and vegetables were very fresh and appealing. The man who owned the business spoke fluent Dutch with his customers. His daughter-in-law, who worked in the store, had only been living in Amsterdam for about two years, but spoke little Dutch. He thought she would learn like he did—by waiting on customers. So far, however, she had learned only the most basic Dutch.

A second grocer up the street specializes more in canned goods and also sells fresh meat, which has been butchered according to Islamic rules. He is comfortable here in his Turkish community in the middle of Amsterdam. But he is skeptical of the Dutch wish to integrate him. "If they mean by integration I have to give up my culture, then I'm opposed to it," he said. To do that, he shields his family, particularly his children, from immoral Dutch television programs by only allowing them to watch the Muslim-owned channels on television.

As my colleague and I sit in the pastry shop sipping tea and eating baklava, I feel as if I have been transported to Ankara or Istanbul. The shop sells only Turkish pastries, and most of the people who come and go while we are there are Turkish. When I ask if he has a satellite dish, he responds with, "What Turk doesn't have one?" He tells me that he and his Dutch-born Turkish wife are able to watch as many as 200 channels with his fully automatic system, but they only watch Turkish channels now.

The video rental shop owner said he opened his store in 1983, before satellite television came to town. His business was great then, because it was the only form of Turkish entertainment available at the time. Turkish films, subtitled American and European films, tapes of concerts by Turkish pop and folk music stars, and even specially made-for-video news magazine tapes were all available in his store. But he said that once the cable started to carry Turkish public television, and then the privately owned stations could be received on the satellite dishes, people stopped renting. Many video shop owners went broke. He turned his business into music audiocassette and CD sales. Though the walls were covered with video boxes, he said most were empty and there just for show. "There are alcoholics and videoholics, but those folks now watch television," he said of his former clientele.

Any Turkish family living in this neighborhood could find most of what they needed for daily life without having to speak Dutch or change their daily habits and routines. And if they were not happy with the products and services they found here, they could go to one of the open-air markets in a neighboring area. In Turkey, open-air bazaars travel from place to place on different days of the week. So this custom is very familiar to the migrants. In these markets too—the most famous of which is the Albert Cuyp, not too far from this neighborhood—Turkish vendors can often be found. There are also many Turkish restaurants, from döner kebab hole-in-the-walls to full-fledged restaurants that can be rather pricey. Turks are generally good at entrepreneurial activity, so their establishments can be seen in all parts of Amsterdam.Turkish entrepreneurs in the Netherlands exceed the percentage in the nation (12.2 percent as opposed to the national average of 10.2 percent). The total number of Turkish entrepreneurs in 1997 was 7,453, according to data collected by H.G.M. van den Tillaart and E. Poutsma and cited by Rath and Kloosterman.[4] The Center for Turkish Studies in Essen, Germany, found that there were about 42,000 Turkish-run businesses in that country, accounting for about $20 billion annually.[5] Of course there are fewer Turks in the Netherlands, but Rath and Kloosterman believe that migrant entrepreneurship has received less attention than it should have in urban economics.

The Kinkerstraat shopping area is only one example of a Turkish business enclave. But not everyone sees these places as good for the Turkish community, since they may allow the residents to avoid Amsterdam culture and life altogether. Not everyone sees this strong attachment to the culture of Turkey as a good thing. Nevin Özütok, Amsterdam city council representative from the Green Left Party, used to live in the neighborhood of the Albert Cuyp market and had time to make observations about the people who watched only television from Turkey and shopped only in Turkish stores.

> The women who watch television all day don't have time for their kids either. It isn't just that they are taken out of the Dutch culture, but that is a problem too. To be part of a culture you need to interact with it every day and the satellite dish helps keep that from happening—though the neighborhoods full of Turkish stores have the same function.

Speaking the Language

Everyone in this study agrees that speaking Dutch is essential to having a satisfactory life in the Netherlands. Of all the influences on the lives of any migrant group, language predominates. So without Dutch, the Turkish migrants are confined to the organizations, services, and institutions that conduct business in Turkish. It seems simple to say that the answer is to get language instruction. But it is particularly daunting for people who may not even be literate in their native language to suddenly try to learn a foreign language.

Though courses in Dutch are much more accessible than they were when the first migrants arrived in the Netherlands, there is reason to believe that long waiting lists for language courses still exist. According to Vuijsje, in 1992, the waiting list for Dutch language courses was 11,000, of whom 80 percent were foreign. And even after a plan to eliminate the problem by the ministers of education and domestic affairs, the problem has increased, rather than disappeared. In Amsterdam in 1994, Vuijsje reports that there were four times as many adults waiting as there were spaces in the courses.[6] Vuijsje is critical of the Dutch government for not providing free language schools wherever immigrants live in the country.

In this study, most of the participants who said they could not read or write were women. Women are the ones who spend the least amount of time interacting with the Dutch, since they also are the least likely to be employed. Indeed, the women who were illiterate in Turkish in this study were also not able to read and write Dutch—and very often spoke no Dutch at all.

Afife, a woman in her late forties who came directly from a village to Amsterdam, is typical of this group. She has lived in the Netherlands for more than twenty years and keeps to her Turkish neighborhood when she ventures out of the house. "When we first came here our life was not easy. I mean, as a foreigner, it was hard to shop and do other things. But now it is good; now we have a lot of Turkish shops and if I need to go to a place where I can't communicate, the children can come with me and speak." As a result of her linguistic isolation, she believes that change is difficult. "It is impossible for us to break off from our own culture. Some (Turkish) families can change, but I think that is very few. Culture is very powerful and it is very difficult to break ties with it," she says. Other women who also did not speak Dutch talked of dependence on their children for assistance with reading official documents, explaining symptoms of their illnesses to doctors, and serving as translators when called to the school by the children's teachers. Their children come to function like Seeing Eye dogs for the blind, always negotiating the foreign territory so that no dangers befall the parents.

In this kind of environment it becomes impossible to learn much of anything about the host culture, much less adopt its ways. Wicker refers to language as one of the barriers to integration, using the example of the Turkish migrants in Switzerland.

> At best—following the praxiology of Bourdieu—culture is expressed in and through those durable dispositions which form the habits of people and which, as linkages of objective structures and subjective thinking, give expression to social fields. In this sense, it is not *the* Turkish culture that determines the

> integration process of Turks in Switzerland but, on the one hand, the migrants' social field of origin (rural, urban, social class, degree of literacy, etc.) which generates and naturalizes durable dispositions in the form of action strategies and world-views, and on the other, the social fields in the country of admission into which the migrants are to be integrated and whose residents, obviously, have equally naturalized habits. Dispositions permit the search for alternative action strategies, and enable individuals to participate in processes of integration and creolization, respectively. However, since dispositions are inert—*hysteresis* is the term Bourdieu uses in this context—and the dynamics of adaptation are thus reduced, the change from one field to another—and from lower to higher social stratum, from country to city, from one country to another—is characteristically slow. It is not cultural persistence, therefore, that is responsible for the typical formation of field-related or field-ethnic enclaves—particularly among first-generation immigrants—but the dialectic of existing barriers of integration and the staying power of habits.[7]

So in Wicker's view, a whole variety of habits that people bring with them when they migrate to a new location, not the concern to hold onto their cultural heritage, is the cause of the ghettoization of migrants in their new location. By clinging to one another, they are able to establish a buffer between themselves and the new social field that is so different from theirs. Thus, it is not unusual for women like Afife, whose field of origin is so dramatically different from the social field where she finds herself, to be the most unable to overcome the barriers. And it follows that the Turkish migrants in this study who were the most insistent that migrants need to learn Dutch, spend time socially interacting with the Dutch, and consume Dutch media began their lives in a place that was closer to the new social field. Most of them were educated in the Netherlands or they came to Amsterdam having completed a relatively high level of educational proficiency. They had some orientation to an urban environment in Turkey before they came to Europe. They were more likely to hold professional positions of employment where they interacted with Dutch people as colleagues. And they tended to mix socially with the Dutch outside of work. So it may be easy for them to say that what they did is what everyone should do. Though some of the people in this group may have had a parent who is illiterate, they did not experience this for themselves, and therefore have a difficult time understanding how difficult it might be to break out of the life habits of the illiterate, village-born, and lower-class immigrants. Since the Dutch didn't require language training of newcomers for a very long time, there wasn't a lot of incentive to break those habits.

People who move between the Turkish and the Dutch cultures in Amsterdam develop a more nuanced view of the Dutch. Ayfer spends her days teaching Turkish in the Amsterdam schools, and has much opportunity to interact with Dutch teachers. Like others who have continuous interactions in both cultures, she is able to make comparisons about what she likes about the habits of each culture.

> I'm so glad to be far away from that competitive spirit I see in Turkey. You don't have to deceive others here. You appear as you are. You don't have to carry a second mask around to cover yourself. Interpersonal relations are the same—direct. But in Turkey it is necessary to cringe with embarrassment over this distressing habit.
>
> I can think of other examples from the school where I work. Here, you are sitting in the teachers' lounge and there is no room to sit down. Nobody gets up to give the principal a seat when he comes in. That would be impossible in Turkey. You would have to give him or her a seat. Or the principal would come in and have something to say to you. She'd come over and kneel beside you, say what she wanted and leave. When I first came here, this surprised me a lot. I was embarrassed by it. After I observed this behavior for awhile, I decided it was a custom, a way of life here. I shouldn't be bothered by it.
>
> People look you straight in the eye here when they want to say something to you, even when there is a difference in status, like a professor and a student. They think they can't trust you if you don't look straight at them. In Turkey, it is a matter of respect. If the student looks the teacher in the eye, it is considered disrespectful.

When I tell Ayfer that other people I have talked with see this directness as rudeness, she acknowledges that may be so, but she thinks they reach that conclusion from lack of interaction with the Dutch.

"I am in contact with the Dutch on a daily basis—all day—and they may not be. They do their shopping in the street markets, the flea markets—where the storekeepers tend to be Turkish or from other nationalities, not Dutch," she said.

Gaye, a woman in her thirties with two small children, is trying to understand better what the Dutch culture is about and what the Dutch intentions may be. She has been taking intensive Dutch lessons for more than a year and she now finds that she mistook the nonverbal signs from passersby.

> We say hello, or we look at each other, or we laugh as we pass one another because we don't understand what they say. Since I have learned a lot more Dutch in the last year, I have begun to see things that my Dutch neighbors do that are discriminatory. I personally see it.

Of course she is disappointed that the Dutch do not always think positively about her, but learning the language better has also helped increase her confidence that she will be able to find a job and support her children on her own here eventually.

An Often Unacknowledged Heterogeneity

The group of migrants who are like Afife—illiterate in both languages, unable to navigate Amsterdam without their children, whose social network is confined to other Turkish families in their neighborhood—have certain ideas about the

Dutch that may have little to do with the complexity of Dutch society. They form these ideas from their limited observation and from what they hear from other family members and friends. In other words, they describe the Dutch in generalities that may be little more than stereotypes. But the Dutch, many of whom are educated and who consume information from multiple sources, may be equally ignorant of the Turkish community. That is why the portrayal of the Turks as undesirables exists. Rath describes the ideological construction of the minorities in the Netherlands this way:

> To pick some of the characteristics ascribed to them: they show insufficient respectability, neatness and hygiene; they don't housekeep properly; they are noisy; are a nuisance to their neighbors; are difficult socially; settle conflicts by violence; show criminal tendencies; go in for alcohol or drug abuse; run into debt; do not have a sound work ethic and are often unemployed; are dependent upon the state and hardly capable of standing on their own feet; have enjoyed little education; don't speak proper; don't care much for parliamentary politics; don't base marriage on romantic and affectionate relationships; give a low status to women; don't bring up their children properly, letting them stay up late and not being supportive of their education, *etcetera*. The predominant ideological representation of these collectives on the whole revolves round real or alleged *socio-cultural features* of human beings. That's why the Others are not represented as *races apart*, but as *minorities apart*.[8]

Women like Afife don't have many resources to be able to understand the Dutch on most any level. The same is not true of the Dutch. They may be drawing their conclusions on the basis of a stereotype of the migrant that appears in the press, or on some government statistics that lack a social context. What many Dutch don't do is have any personal contact with the migrants in their midst. And when they don't make friends or venture into the Turkish neighborhoods to meet the Turks, they describe the Turkish community as a homogeneous group that shares a set of general characteristics.

In fact, the Turks are quite heterogeneous. And that is true even of the first generation. I have said that those folks came from villages and towns, had little education, believed in the tenets of Islam, and had few job skills. While that is so, such a description masks the differences in the people who arrived in the Netherlands between 1960 and 1973, recruited by Dutch companies to work in the factories. For one thing, they came from different parts of Turkey. Most of the participants in this study originated in central Anatolia, where the winters can be quite harsh and the summers are hot and dry. The villages in this part of the country may have some trees planted by local residents, but in general, the terrain is hilly and rocky with little vegetation. Life is difficult in this relatively infertile land. Another large group originated in the Black Sea coastal area, which is lush and covered with green pine forests, but suffered serious financial setbacks at the time of the recruitment of guest workers in Europe, because of a failure of the hazelnut crop that is one of the region's primary income sources.

This area is mountainous and the climate more humid because of its proximity to the sea. Even the architecture of the houses built here is different, made from wood and generally two stories high, while in Anatolia they are usually constructed of mud bricks and a single story. A few of the participants in this study came from the south or southwest part of Turkey where citrus grows and at least two crops a year can be grown. There the local culture, as depicted by the regional folk dances, is more colorful and male-female relationships more open and women less concerned to cover their bodies completely than in the other parts of the country. This is a broad-brush description of these regions, but it is provided to indicate that though all of the migrants from the several regions may have come from Turkey, they may have experienced Turkey very differently depending on the part of the country they lived in. (See map in front of book.)

Role of Religion

Though I will discuss religious affiliation in more detail in chapter 6, it is important to say here that forms of Islam practiced by the migrants may be as varied as the geography in Turkey. Diversity in Islam seems to be an alien concept in most people's minds. As a religion, it has been characterized stereotypically by even the most educated people. Often, even the difference between Sunni and Shiia is glossed over. Jan Rath and colleagues describe that view in an article about social reactions to Islam in several European countries.

> According to the prevailing opinion encountered in our research, Muslims have an excessive tendency to cling together and resist becoming a part of modern Dutch society. They are neither willing nor able to integrate into it, and have an irrational preference for traditional, i.e. non-democratic forms of political leadership. They do not treat women as equals to men, adhere to old-fashioned views on bringing up children, and are extremely susceptible to influence by international powers, particularly arch-conservative ones. In the Netherlands, they undermine the separation of church and state. In these views, Islam is a conglomeration of pre-modern and culturally alien elements. Whether or not there is any truth to this is irrelevant. These are widespread notions about Islam and its believers that condition actions. They are also related to Dutch society itself, and its non-Islamic residents. The features attributed to them are a mirror image, as it were, of the features felt to characterize Muslim.[9]

Here I would like to describe some of the differences between the Turkish Islamic groups in the Netherlands that run counter to the Dutch stereotype. What distinguishes some of these is not so much specific differences in belief, but political affiliations of the several groups. Several of the Islamic groups in the Netherlands and across Europe have expressed opposition to the secular government in Ankara as their key organizing principle. Others are distinguished by their specific approach to religious doctrine. But they differentiate their own brand of Islam from that of the other groups, and may even be in serious opposition to the other groups.

The *Diyanet*, or Turkish religious affairs directorate (*Diyanet Işleri Türk-İslam Birliği*), has the authority to appoint imams for most of the Turkish mosques in the Netherlands. But these mosques have a direct relationship with "official" Islam as it is related to the Republic of Turkey, not to any of the groups listed below. The *Diyanet* approach to Sunni Islam would be consistent with maintaining a secular government in Turkey. Originally this organization provided the religious scholars for the mosques in the Netherlands, and they all originated from Turkey. The *Diyanet* is a union of mosques that is coordinated by the Turkish government through the religious attaché of the Turkish embassy.[10]

One of the largest groups, the *Milli Görüş* (*Avrupa Milli Görüş Teşkilatı*), on which I will focus in a later chapter, is affiliated with the Fazilet Partisi/Virtue Party (formerly the *Refah* Party) in Turkey. Its goal is to bring Islamic law (Shariah) to Turkey. Begun in 1985 in Cologne, Germany, the group has branches in several European countries. In the Netherlands it is referred to as the *Nederlandse Islamitische Federatie* or Netherlands Islamic Federation, and has more than twenty mosque communities across the country.[11] A 1996 publication claims it has 262 member associations in Europe.[12] It is a Sunni Moslem group that opposes the Turkish state-supported Islamic organization in Europe. It sponsors a newspaper, the *Milli Gazete* (National Newspaper). The organization finances its activity from cooperatives, where goods are sold (like the groceries in the stores inside the mosques). Dassetto and Nonneman say that the main activity in this group is from young fathers who came to Europe as adolescents and received some of their education (and therefore language training) there.[13] My own conversations with men in their twenties and thirties supported this view. They called themselves "Dutch-Turks" or "European-Turks" and were critical of those who were more oriented toward Turkey than Europe. One of these young men, İbrahim, said:

> From my point of view, it is like this. The first generation came about thirty years ago when they were between thirty-five and forty years old. They knew no language. They couldn't learn the customs of this place. They came; they passed. Most of them are now retired here. They couldn't return. Even though they came here when they were forty years old, they could never get used to this place and they could never return. Now I look at the third generation or the second generation. They were born and raised here. And I wonder if the first generation couldn't return, how we could possibly go?
>
> But I have a wish. It is settling into my heart, but it also has to be a little bit of reality—I mean if they could not return, we will never return, I think. So for that reason, I am preparing my needs and my activities for that prospect. They didn't go, we will never go.

It is fair to say that this group's political agenda is what defines it and separates it from some of the other groups. Though one goal of the organization is to bring more religious freedom to Turkey and more Islamic law into the now-secular Turkish government, most of the members don't talk of returning to Turkey to live. How they reconcile this issue in their organizational discussions is not clear. Perhaps it works as an organizing principle to have a goal for the group that is outside their own geographic environment. I doubt that most of the *Milli Görüş* members plan to return to Turkey to live, even if the country became an Islamic state.

The *Nurcu* group is also a Sunni Moslem group that had its beginnings in the 1920s with Said Nursi, a Kurd who opposed both Kurdish and Turkish nationalism. He is said to have written down his views on the Koran as the only guide to developing natural laws. He did not establish a religious order, but his followers have used those writings to guide them. Nursi, who believed that individuals are constantly torn between desire and reason, can only manage this tension by developing a complete relationship with God. Islamic scholar Hakan Yavuz explains why Nursi was opposed to the secularization of the state under Kemal Ataturk, founder of the Turkish Republic.

> Nursi sharply criticized positivist epistemology and its desire to control simultaneously, nature and man. Since religion is innate to human nature, Nursi sees the lack of religion as the source of many conflicts and wars. He extended this concept of tension to the societal level, where the absence of God in public space is the source of man's problems. His goal, therefore, was to bring God back to the public space. This required a response to the dominant positivist epistemology. Connecting to God, for Nursi, meant introducing new conceptual resource tools, to shape and lead human conduct. Nursi's project offered a new "map of meaning" for Muslims to guide their conduct. He did not offer an "Islamic constitution" or an "Islamic order" but rather a mode of thinking about reconnecting with God.[14]

Fethullah Gülen, a follower of Nursi, is the recognized leader of one of the Nurcu groups today. Gülen's community is separate, however, from other Nurcu groups. Though the *Fethullahcilar* have become popular in many countries, they do not have a large base in the Netherlands. Gülen's community owns several publications, a television station, and a radio station, so his influence in the Netherlands may come more through the media than in organized religious groups.

The *Alevis* are Shiia Muslims who have almost no relationship to the Shiites in Iran. Described as an "unorthodox, universal and mystical belief system with its faith, morality structure, love for God, mankind and nature, equality and fraternity covered by a thin gauze of Islam" on the *Alevi* Web site, this group generally does not pray five times a day nor attend prayer services at the mosque.[15] They claim to have been misunderstood and even persecuted in Turkey and this is the reason so many of them chose to work abroad when the opportunity arose. In Turkey they have been associated with free speech and pro-democracy movements. Many Kurdish people are Alevis.

The *Süleymancis* (also *Süleymanlis*) were the first organization of Turkish Muslims in Europe. According to Shadid and van Koningsveld, the group is an offshoot of several mystical orders. They say that Süleymancis believe that the "religious aspects of education and the intensification of personal piety" are of great import.[16] Because they oppose the secular state, they do not recruit imams through the *Diyanet.* Shadid and van Koningsveld say that this group is connected to a federation of Islamic groups with its center in Cologne, Germany, called *Avrupa İslam Kültür Merkezleri Birliği* (The European United Cultural Centers). They produce a weekly publication called *Anadolu* (Anatolia). In the Netherlands, its base is Utrecht, where it is called *Stichting Islamitisch Centrum Nederland*, and was founded in 1972. The group reportedly supports the separation of church and state. It is strongly oriented toward Koranic instruction and mystical meetings in the mosque.[17]

In trying to understand the differences between the various groups, I asked two young women about what distinguishes them from some of the other Muslims in Amsterdam. They tell me that their own group, the *Milli Görüş*, has a mosque in each part of Amsterdam. They say that their Islamic practice is different from that of some others. Ferrah, a young woman trained as a midwife, says:

> For example, we tie our head scarves differently than the *Suleymancis*. That is how we identify one another. I wish there was only one practice and that was the *Milli Görüş*. The *Milli Görüş* accepts everyone, whether they cover their heads or not. That is why we chose the *Milli Görüfl* because it was the most open religion, accepting of all types of religious practice. The *Suleymancis* won't accept anyone who doesn't do as they do. And I don't approve of *Alevi* ways—they can even chew gum during the month of Ramazan when we fast. We have lots of disagreements with them over doctrine.

There are other Turks who are athiests or agnostics. Many would claim they were Muslims only because Islam and Islamic traditions are part of their culture. And the Dutch classify most all Turks as Muslim, despite the relative religious inactivity of a large number of them. These are people who have a more Western approach to life—in dress, values, lifestyle. Yet they get lumped in with all the rest of the people of Turkish origin when they are described by most of the Dutch. To those who would equate being an ethnic Turk in Europe with being Muslim, I would describe Hayri, a forty-five-year-old man who came from Sivas, one of twelve children. Hayri gets angry when he starts thinking about the mosques and the political Islam that is practiced here. He begins his history lesson to me about the Ottoman Empire and its relationship to Islam by saying he is not religious. After about ten minutes of explanation of how religion and state were united under the sultans and Ataturk formed a secular state, he gets to modern times.

> Here it is happening again all over (the attempts to have Islamic law rule the state). The mosques are brainwashing the people here. They call me a Communist for not following their way. They say that anyone who doesn't fast during Ramazan [this is the Turkish word for Ramadan] is a communist. They closed Refah [the Turkish political party headed by Necmettin Erbakan that had close ties with Islamic leaders] but they didn't kill its roots. Here the people from the mosques collect money for everything [including the Islamic political parties in Turkey]. The ones with the beards come to our doors. This money they collect is 60 percent in their pockets and 10 percent for religious purposes.

Hayri gets more agitated as he speaks. He believes that the members of the mosques in Europe are trying to bring a jihad to Turkey. Hayri may have been religious when he lived in Turkey but has been turned away from the practice of Islam as he has seen it become politicized in Amsterdam. He says he has not been in a mosque in more than ten years.

Education

There is an incredibly wide range of educational achievement among the Turkish population in the Netherlands. And it doesn't necessarily correspond to the age of the individual or the time of the arrival in Holland. I have said that the early arrivals were largely uneducated and unskilled. But some of those who came in the late 1960s or early 1970s, for example, were political activists in Turkey who were university educated and fled the country before they could be arrested during the political turmoil. Some of those people (mostly men) can never return to Turkey because they never served in the military, and would likely be tapped at the border and taken off to do their service should they decide to go back. Turkey keeps active files for military service until men reach the age of fifty.

One indication of the range of education comes from statistics collected by the City of Amsterdam on the people of Turkish origin who are unemployed and looking for work. At the other end of the spectrum is a group of young men and women who have been brought from Turkey to marry and find work in the Netherlands. Usually these are arranged marriages, and these newcomers often have very little education and their job prospects may be limited in Turkey, too.

It is true, however, that the majority of the Turkish migrant population in the Netherlands is not particularly well educated. A 1985 survey indicated that 65 percent of the adult Turks in the country had a primary school education or less. Another 12 percent had a low- to mid-level secondary school education. An additional 4 percent had completed secondary school, while only 1 percent had completed some form of higher education. At that time, 11 percent were students.[18] In 1987, 100 percent of the males and 92 percent of the females aged twelve to fourteen were in school. That number dropped to 90 percent of the males and 77 percent of the females in the fifteen to seventeen-year range, however.[19] Unfortunately, more current data could not be found.

Though far too many Turkish children still do not get sufficient education, many Turkish students today do stay in school and pursue higher education. In June 1999, I attended a meeting of young Turkish professionals who were organizing a lobby group to improve the image of the Turks who live in Amsterdam. Virtually all of the more than 100 men and women who attended the meeting had university degrees, and many others, with similar educational backgrounds, were unable to attend. One indication of the range of education in recent times comes from statistics collected by the City of Amsterdam on the people of Turkish origin who are unemployed and looking for work. Of the total of 5,133 people looking for work in 1998, 1,593 had been educated at a level less than middle school. Another 1,545 had some form of secondary education (including vocational), sixty-five had completed three years of university, and eight had some kind of university or graduate degree, while the educational level of fifteen people was unknown.[20] The people in this group ranged from age nineteen to sixty-four and were about half men and half women.

Vuijsje blames the Dutch for their lack of political will to enforce attendance policies among migrant youth for the poor educational achievement. From the mid-1990s on, the Compulsory Education Act increased the penalties for parents who did not make sure their children went to school, but the results of the tightening of the law may not be seen for awhile.

> The Netherlands offered young *allochtoons* [nonindigenous] an antiracist subsidy and classes in their own language and culture, but measures to increase their participation in school and in the job market and to open ways out of a life of crime were not forthcoming. In the early 1990s, things became more open, but by then it was too late for part of the second generation.[21]

Travel

I don't know how typical the Turkish migrants in Amsterdam are when it comes to where they spend their summer vacation, but I do know that most of the participants in this study who leave the city of Amsterdam for their summer break choose to return to Turkey. Perhaps foreign travel, or even travel outside the city of residence, is strongly correlated with the educational level. I did not collect data on that for this study. I did ask how frequently people had returned to Turkey in the previous five years. It was rare to hear that they had not made any trips to Turkey at all. More than 75 percent of the families in the study had gone back two to three times in the five-year period and stayed for five to six weeks when they went. Limited finances or lack of time were the reasons given for not returning. They did not choose to go somewhere else for the summer vacation instead. Only one mother and daughter talked to me about the time they spent in the summers camping in various parts of Holland. Banu, a woman now in her late fifties, who married and came at the age of eighteen and had little education, thought it was important for her three children to understand something about the country where they lived and worked. Of course, they returned to Turkey on some of their vacations as the children were growing up, but they also traveled around the Netherlands once they were able to buy a car.

Banu's story was unusual. When people said they couldn't go back for any reason, they expressed sadness or regret. One woman who hadn't returned in eight years because of her legal problems with obtaining permanent residence asked me what it was really like there and how it had changed in the years since she had been in the country.

If anything, the professionals who participated in this study traveled more often to Turkey. But that was usually because business took them there—and it was for shorter trips. However, these people also traveled around Europe on business.

These days most families are able to get reasonably priced flights to Turkey, and that means that they don't even pass through the countries between the Netherlands and Turkey as they drive through. Those people with large families and limited resources tend to pack the family in the car and save money by taking a road trip.

Perhaps it is because the home country is so close to where they live. It must also be because the summertime climate makes it an ideal spot for an escape from the rain and lack of sunshine in Amsterdam. And of course it is related to the need to reunite with family at home. Finally, if they have limited skills in speaking foreign languages, it is one of the few places they can travel where they can speak the language. For all these reasons, Turkey is the country of choice when the migrants have time off. So the participants in this study are more homogeneous when it comes to travel than on the other dimensions discussed here. Some participants had actually returned to Turkey to live and work, thinking they would stay permanently. And those who had done that were not all first-generation immigrants. Some of them came to think that life would be better there, and they would fit into Turkish society better than they did in Dutch society. Once they spent an extended period of time in Turkey, they decided that Amsterdam was a better choice.

However, there is an important difference in travel in the participants in this study. And that is usually in where they chose to go when they get to the home country. Those who came from villages returned to those villages and stayed there or in a nearby town. A study I did of Turks who lived in a squatter settlement in Ankara in the mid-1970s found that guest workers from this settlement returned from Europe to the houses they used to live in for the summer holiday, despite the slum-like conditions there. Parents in this study complained that their children didn't like making the summer trips. They were bored and not accepted by their cousins or neighbors in Turkey. People remarked about their accents and their lack of firsthand knowledge of Turkish pop musicians or other cultural figures. So they were anxious to return "home" to Amsterdam. I would ask if they took their children to the seaside or to museums or places of historical or cultural interest in Turkey. Many people said they did not. If they were more affluent they did rent or own a summer house by the sea. But most could not afford that. And those who grew up in central Anatolia didn't have any personal experience of summer vacations on one of the Turkish coasts, so they didn't think it was important to take their children there. In other words, they didn't expand their own worldview and didn't provide those experiences for their children.

The families who had higher educational levels with whom I talked were different in this regard. A trip to Turkey for them meant that most of the time was spent on the Mediterranean or Aegean—or maybe the Black Sea. And the children had fond memories of that time. Some of the second generation who decided to try to live in Turkey had done so based on the pleasant memories from those summer vacations. It wasn't until they lived there year-round that they realized that there was more to living in Turkey than spending summer days swimming and eating outside.

Cultural Orientation

In earlier research, I examined the concept of cultural orientation. I argued that whether a person is oriented only towards the culture of birth or whether that person is instead oriented outside that culture to a wider cultural sphere is based on several factors. Those factors include a person's general educational level, proficiency in foreign languages, socioeconomic status, and amount of foreign travel. I also suggested, and found some support for the idea, that the more people were oriented outside their cultures, the higher their consumption of foreign media (films and television programs).[22] The idea of cultural orientation is pertinent to this study. I am arguing here that not all the Turkish migrants can be placed in a particular homogeneous group. And the degree to which they are educated, have higher income, have traveled extensively, and speak foreign languages (Dutch, in this case), the more likely they are to be integrated into this foreign society (The Netherlands). They are also more likely to be reading the Dutch press and watching Dutch television and other foreign television. In the earlier studies, I did not consider religious practice as a variable, but I believe it needs to be taken into account in this research. I believe that the more religious (in belief and practice) the participants in this study are, the less likely they are to be integrated into Dutch society, and in fact choose not to be a part of that society at all where cultural values are at issue. I am willing to concede that the depth of one's faith would not always figure into cultural orientation, but that for this group of migrants, it becomes a key variable.

In fact, Dassetto and Nonneman, who tried to form a typology of religious orientation of Muslim movements in Belgium and Holland, believe it may be more complex than just examining the depth of religious belief. They conclude that there are three axes of classification. The first relates to religious orientation and discourse.

> Along this first axis, three classes are theoretically distinguishable: (1) that of a discourse which we will call "traditionalist," and which restores in a fairly rigid manner the classical interpretation of the fundamental "facts;" (2) a "modernizing" class which reshapes this discourse in a new form but one drawing considerable inspiration from traditional attitudes; and (3) a "remolding" class, which is embarking on a new exercise but does not yet appear to have taken organized shape, being instead limited to the work of individual thinkers.[23]

The second situates the Islamic organizations on a continuum ranging from private to public. "In other words, these movements can be classified according to the extent to which they tend overtly towards spiritualization and individualization of the religious or towards bringing the latter into the public domain."[24] The *Milli Görüfl* would be an example of a public organization.

The last axis differentiates the organizations according to the positioning of the organization. At one end of the spectrum, they are satellites of organizations in their home country, and at the other end of the continuum, they are part of a transnational vision of the type of Islam they practice.[25]

The authors are placing organizations within their typology, but their classification illustrates the complexity of Islamic religious orientation, whether for the organization or the individual.

The variables that make up cultural orientation can be placed on scales. One end of the scale would place the migrants closer to the culture of their birth or their family with as little involvement with Dutch culture as possible. People who are situated at the other end of these scales would be able to move freely between Dutch and Turkish cultures, being as comfortable in one as the other. Those people with a cultural orientation that is most expansive and outer-directed might have trouble answering the question "To which culture do you feel closer?" In this survey, the participants who were outwardly oriented would usually answer that they were closer to the Dutch culture and were more comfortable living in Amsterdam than in Turkey. But many of those oriented outside their culture of origin also acknowledged a closeness to Turkey in the friends they keep, the television programs they might watch, the food they eat, and the spouse they chose.

Though it is good to try to place people on some kind of cultural orientation scale, made up of the several variables, of course not everyone is going to fit neatly into any particular place on the scale. Take Narin, for example. She is Banu's daughter—she grew up in a household where her mother and father felt it was important for her to learn something about the country where she lived. Narin was born in the Netherlands and educated through college—though she left before finishing. She is fluent in Turkish, but writes more in Dutch than Turkish. And she prefers Dutch television to Turkish. She also speaks English, as that is a requirement in the Dutch schools. She is not particularly religious. All these things would suggest that she would be on the far end of the cultural orientation scale—feeling more comfortable in Amsterdam and among the Dutch than many of the other participants. Yet Narin says that most of her friends are Turkish—just like her mother's and her sister's, she says.

> You can have work friends who are Dutch, but you look for people from your own culture when you want to be close to someone or tell your problems to someone. The Chinese and Surinams are the same. You can't tell your innermost thoughts to a Dutch person. They'll think, "Oh, you're Turkish. Your customs are like that." When the problems may really have nothing to do with the culture. They don't understand. They're looking at it from a different point of view.

Yasemin, a young woman in her late twenties, who has a university degree and has worked in a variety of professional jobs, has tried to move between Turkish and Dutch friends and communities without finding a satisfactory place for herself. She constantly weighs the advantages of trying to be in both places.

> When I'm here, I think about how great it would be to live there. But once there, for example, I look at all the dirt around me and think—I wish I were back in Holland. You are always of two minds about it. That isn't necessarily a negative thing. It brings more color to your life. People today are not from a particular place; they are from a lot of places. In the future, perhaps more people will be like me—from several places at once. You know that people who go back to Turkey from here are not necessarily happy. But if they stay here they cannot become completely integrated into this society. And the society doesn't change here. You would think each group would be affected by the existence of the other and both groups would make a change to evolve to something new. But that doesn't happen. They don't come closer to one another here because neither side is open to the other culture. There is only an attempt to get to know one another's culture. And that doesn't really happen, because neither side has real interest in learning about the other.

There are things she dislikes about both cultures, so she isn't always thinking that a person can just pick and choose the best traits of both cultures.

> But there are lots of problems in Turkish culture. You can't say what you think. You aren't free. Here [in Dutch society] you are free, but you still can't say what you think. You have to self censor. There you have no choices to make. Here you have all kinds of choices, but the outcomes can be manipulated. There, there is a lot of physical aggression. Here there is none of that, but manipulation (or subtle control) exists. The system is like that. But here women are free to come and go as they please and to live alone—but in Turkey there is a lot of social control. Male-female relations are not normal there. There are still a lot of things that make no sense in Turkey.

In many ways Yasemin perceives invisible barriers to entering one another's cultures in Amsterdam. She sees this as a problem, as the Turkish and other minorities are growing in population relative to the Dutch. Ultimately, the Dutch will have to face the problem and figure out a way to solve it—to achieve real integration, she thinks. But she can't do it on her own.

> As an individual it is difficult to cross into Dutch society. At home you live a Turkish life. And my parents were never able to enter it [Dutch culture]. You can't do everything by yourself. You need to have connections to be able to get the right job, for example. It is not enough to just have the qualifications. It isn't easy for people to find work here. And if you cut the social welfare, you'd see more criminal activity, since people would have no recourse when they lost their jobs.

The Role of Media in Cultural Orientation

In general, media reinforce the values in a particular culture, rather than oppose them. And those who produce news and entertainment for print, broadcast, and on-line media are often unaware the extent to which what they produce reflects their own cultural orientation. In Herbert Gans's classic study of the sociology of journalism at CBS, NBC, *Newsweek*, and *Time*, he notes that all news is based on a set of enduring values—values that are American, but that journalists may not even be conscious of espousing in their day-to-day accounts. Those values in U.S. news include ethnocentrism, altruistic democracy, responsible capitalism, small-town pastoralism, individualism, and moderatism.[26] So when consumers of U.S. news read or watch the daily news, they also get a heavy dose of these enduring values underlying the news stories. Of course, these are also values that pervade other parts of the daily lives of Americans and that are supported by the institutions in society, so they are comfortable to Americans.

But imagine yourself as an immigrant to the United States coming from some culture that has a very different set of enduring values. You might find the U.S. media discomforting and alien—and as a result find yourself trying to locate the media from home, which is cast in a set of enduring values with which you grew up.

The next two chapters raise the implications of this issue, and examine what happens when the Turkish migrants have the opportunity to easily choose whether to consume Dutch or Turkish media.

Notes

1. Mark-Jan de Jong, "The Immigration of Immigrants: A Challenge for the Netherlands," in *Democracy, Civil Society, and Pluralism*, C. G. A. Bryant and E. Mokrzycki, eds. (Warsaw: IfiS, 1995), 405.

2. Geke van der Wal and Mathijs Tax, *De vele gezichten van Turks Nederland* (Amsterdam: Uitgeverij Jan Mets, 1999), 20.

3. Ruud van den Bedem, "Towards a System of Plural Nationality in the Netherlands," in *From Aliens to Citizens: Redefining the Status of Immigrants in Europe*, Rainer Baubock, ed. Aldershot, U.K.: Avebury, 1994), 106.

4. Jan Rath and Robert Kloosterman, "Outsiders' Business: A Critical Review of Research on Immigrant Entrepreneurship," *International Migration Review*, 34, no. 3 (fall 2000), 658.

5. William Drozdiak, "Citizenship Debate Divides Germans: Dual Nationality is Proposed for Offspring of Immigrants," *Washington Post*, 5 November 1997, 28(A).

6. Herman Vuijsje, *The Politically Correct Netherlands since the Sixties*, trans. and annot. Mark T. Hooker (Westport, Conn.: Greenwood, 2000), 26.

7. Hans-Rudolf Wicker, "From Complex Culture to Cultural Complexity," in *Debating Cultural Hybridity*, Pnina Werbner and Tariq Modood, eds. (London: Zed Books, 1997), 29-45, 41.

8. Jan Rath, "The Netherlands: A Dutch Treat for Antisocial Families and Immigrant Ethnic Minorities," in *The European Union and Migrant Labour*, Mike Cole and Gareth Dale, eds. (Oxford: Berg Publishers, 1999), 21.

9. Jan Rath et al., "The Politics of Recognizing Religious Diversity in Europe: Social Reactions to the Institutionalization of Islam in the Netherlands, Belgium, and Great Britain," *Netherlands' Journal of Social Sciences* 35, no. 1 (1999), 86.

10. Yasemin Karakasoğlu and Gerd Nonneman, "Muslims in Germany, with Special Reference to the Turkish-Islamic Community," in *Muslim Communities in the New Europe*, G. Nonneman, T. Niblock, and B. Szajkowski, eds. (Reading, U.K.: Ithaca Press, 1996), 257.

11. W. A. R. Shadid and P. S. van Koningsveld, *Religious Freedom and the Position of Islam in Western Europe* (Kampen, The Netherlands: Kok Pharos Publishing House, 1995), 47-48.

12. Yasemin Karakasoğlu and Gerd Nonneman, "Muslims in Germany," in *Muslim Communities in the New Europe*, G. Nonneman, T. Niblock, and B. Szakowski, eds. (Berkshire, U.K.: Ithaca Press, 1996), 257.

13. Felice Dassetto and Gerd Nonneman, "Islam in Belgium and the Netherlands: Towards a Typology of 'Transplanted' Islam," in *Muslim Communities in the New Europe*, Gerd Nonneman, Tim Niblock, and Bogdan Szakowski, eds. (Berkshire, U.K.: Ithaca Press, 1996), 210.

14. M. Hakan Yavuz, "Towards an Islamic Liberalism? The Nurcu Movement and Fetullah Gülen," *Middle East Journal* 53, no. 4 (autumn 1999): 589.

15. See the Web site at http://alevi.org.au.

16. Shadid and van Koningsveld, *Religious Freedom*, 47.

17. Van der Wal and Tax, *De vele gezichten*, 38.

18. Rinus Penninx, Jeannette Schoorl, and Carlo van Praag, *The Impact of International Migration on Receiving Countries: The Case of the Netherlands* (The Hague: Netherlands Interdisciplinary Demographic Institute, 1994), 131.

19. Penninx et al., *The Impact*, 133.

20. Het Amsterdamse Bureau voor Onderzoek en Statistiek, *Amsterdam in Cijfers: Jaarboek 1998* (Amsterdam: O+S, 1998), 240.

21. Herman Vuijsje, *The Politically Correct Netherlands*, 26.

22. Christine Ogan, "Media Imperialism and the Video Cassette Recorder: The Case of Turkey," *Journal of Communication* 38, no. 2 (spring 1988): 93-106; and Christine Ogan, "The Audience for Foreign Film in the United States," *Journal of Communication* 40, no. 4 (autumn 1990): 58-77.

23. Felice Dassetto and Gerd Nonneman, "Islam in Belgium and the Netherlands," 211.

24. Dassetto and Nonneman, "Islam in Belgium and the Netherlands," 211.

25. Dassetto and Nonneman, "Islam in Belgium and the Netherlands," 211.

26. Herbert J. Gans, *Deciding What's News: A Study of CBS Evening News, NBC Nightly News, Newsweek, and Time* (New York: Random House, 1980), 42-52.

Chapter 4

Media for and about Turkish Migrants

Most ethnic groups who feel a need to sustain their identity in a place away from the one they might consider home usually look to the broadcast and print media to carve out a space for themselves. They view the dominant media in the culture where they live as unfair in their coverage of ethnic issues and stereotypical in their portrayals of the ethnic group.

Such feelings predominate in the Turkish community in Amsterdam today. And the perception that the Dutch media have not met the needs of the Turkish immigrants and their children and even their grandchildren has led most people of Turkish heritage in that city to install satellite dishes on their apartment balconies to bring them an alternative—television from Turkey. More than ten Turkish television channels can be received throughout Europe today. The existence of these dishes may have been a source of joy to most viewers, but they have concerned policy makers and media producers in every country where they are in common use.

This chapter will first discuss the problems Turks find in the mainstream Dutch media. Then it will examine the broadcast and print media created for the Turkish minority in Amsterdam, analyzing sample programs and issues of newspapers and journals. Next it will explore reasons why the Turkish community has decided to largely reject the media designed for their use in the Netherlands. Finally, it will discuss what the future might hold for the media mix in the Netherlands.

Problems with Dominant Media

It may be that all minority groups have disaffection with the dominant media of a nation or even a local community. Reasons for that disaffection include: stereotypical portrayals of the group; lack of producers and presenters of content who represent the group; lack of content that addresses the needs and interests of the groups; and portrayal of the group as the "other," rather than as included in the majority or welcoming their minority views in the community or nation.

I found all of these reasons cited by the people I talked to. However well meaning the Dutch broadcasters and print journalists may be, they fail to satisfy the needs of the minority interests of the Turks in Amsterdam and likely all of the other ethnic minorities who live there. The Dutch approach to multiculturalism is backed by "the state sponsored habit of religious communalism" called pillarization.[1] Baumann claims that for about a hundred years (from 1850 to 1950) the Dutch state elite dealt with its citizens as religious communities, interacting with the people according to their religious identity. The spillover into the current policy of multiculturalism is to treat the Turkish and Moroccan communities as Muslims rather than as heterogeneous groups.

Selma, a seventeen-year-old girl who was born and raised in Amsterdam and who is fluent in both Turkish and Dutch, believes there exists an enormous cultural divide and that the Dutch look down on the Turks in their midst. "I'm tired of the way Turks are portrayed on television—always as if they had just arrived as immigrants and always in terms of problems and stereotypes—as criminals, as kids who don't go to school, as people whose language skills in Dutch are bad."

Şenol, an artist in her forties who came to Amsterdam to study and stayed on to make her life there, agrees. "Dutch television always shows Turks as immigrants. They even look at artists as immigrant artists. I don't feel that way about myself. I feel like I am a native here. I am not an immigrant artist. We are doing contemporary art, not immigrant art." This concern about her own portrayal on television has not led her to install a dish for receiving television from Turkey, however. She believes it is not a good idea to orient herself too much outside of Dutch culture. But she would like to see Dutch television reflect the place she feels she has in that society.

The news and public affairs programming carried by the Dutch media frightens some other people. They begin to see Turkey as a country so backward and so riddled with problems that they feel they can never return. Betül, a thirty-year-old woman married to a Kurd, has lived in Amsterdam for seven years and has inadvertently lost her legal right to stay. Now she is struggling to regain legal residency. Television doesn't allay her fears about the possibility of being deported.

> On Dutch television Turks are always shown as foreigners—people who are always fighting or who play the zurna [a type of musical pipe played with the drum in Turkey]. When I see the foreign press cover Turkey, it is always about who did what to whom, who tortured whom, who denied whose rights. The press always focuses on the lack of human rights. I worry that I can't take my children back to Turkey—a person like me without a profession—because I would have no rights. I would only be a housewife and the foreign press has scared me about going back to Turkey.

Narin came to the Netherlands as a young child from Turkey with her family and is now married and settled in Amsterdam. Her family was particularly concerned that she and her sisters adjust to the Dutch culture. In chapter 3, I spoke of her mother Banu, who thought it was important for the family to learn about the Netherlands, so she and her husband took the children on family camping trips in the countryside. With that kind of background, it is particularly disconcerting to her to see Turks characterized as fitting a particular model and not being able to become a part of the majority.

> Ten years ago they used to show things on television about us—and it was always about villages; they never showed a city. In recent years they have been showing more about how Turks live in Holland—whether it is the first or second generation, but again it is, "Oh look, it is a Turk. He too goes to a disco or he also goes to the cinema." I think this is a type of discrimination. But Chinese, Dutch, Turks—all of them could go to the movies. There isn't any difference. I studied Italian at the university and people would say, "Ah, you study Italian. How is that?" Shouldn't I be able to be interested in studying Italian?

Narin's examples show the ways the Dutch choose to generalize about a group of people they know little about. Others think that since some of the early migrants who came directly from villages brought with them some customs educated city dwellers found odd, that all Turks fit that model today. Ayşe, a teacher of Turkish in the public schools, articulated this view.

> Thirty years ago the people who came from the villages had never seen the cities of their own country and they end up in the center of Europe. They encountered cultural shock. Then the Europeans looked at them and said, "Oh, since this Turk is like this, this must be the way all Turks are." But that was a mistake and that view has persisted. The Turkish villagers washed sheep's wool on their balconies and the water dripped down on people's heads—they slaughtered lambs in their bathrooms on the Sacrifice Holiday. The things they did. The Dutch saw and heard about these things and they looked at us. They wondered since we didn't dress and act the same, "Are you really a Turk? Are you really from Turkey? But you aren't like the others," they'd say.

Jerome Bourdon classifies the various traps media fall into when portraying the minorities in their cultures. In general, says Bourdon, whether it is openly stated or merely suggested, a person's ethnic origin is "usually associated with a conflict, problem or difficulty."[2] Ethnic minorities are characterized as individuals who are criminals or victims. They may be the cause of all crime or they live in abject poverty, or are the victims of the image of their homeland, says Bourdon.[3] And as long as they are described in one or the other of these categories, the ethnic group in question remains always as the other. One young man, Ahmet, who was born and raised in Holland, is a Dutch citizen and is tired of being cast in the role of permanent minority, said, "But sometimes I tell the Dutch, I mean in the midst of friends we joke—you Dutch, what do you want, I ask as intentional joke. I have a Dutch passport. I speak Dutch. I go vote in your elections when the time comes. And yet, you still don't accept me. What do I have to do—have blond hair and wear blue contact lenses?"

Other participants who talked of this problem expressed their feelings with less humor. These are people who would like to be considered "integrated" in Dutch society on one level. They noted that learning the language, acquiring a good education, and even marrying a Dutch spouse did not qualify them for entry into the majority culture. They talked of constantly being reminded of their minority status and told of their "difference."

Still others struggle to preserve Turkish identity in this Western and Christian society. They fight for separate schools where Islam is a central part of the curriculum and provides guiding values for the children. They fight for new mosques that also serve as cultural centers for their communities. They seek out television programs that are broadcast in Turkish and stress issues and topics of concern to only people like themselves. So there is not a single direction to take for the mass media or for any policy making organization in the country. As Ayşe Çağlar has so well put it, when focus is placed on the hyphenated identity, it masks the differences that exist between various transnational groups.

> The notion of a "hyphenated" identity, instead of resolving cultural essentialism, tends thus to highlight the problematic nature of collective attachments: the clash of interests experienced by translocal groups which arise from their multiple and multilocale attachments and commitments. It is assumed, for example, that German-Turks share common predicaments and aspirations regarding their status in German society. The stress is always on the hyphenation of ethnic (national and religious) identities to the exclusion of other forms of identification.[4]

So as we examine the various media for Turks living in Amsterdam in this study, it is important to keep in mind that whatever might suit one individual or group may be unsatisfactory to another. That said, nobody with whom I talked was totally satisfied with the print or broadcast options serving Turkish minorities in the Dutch city. And all were concerned about the overly stereotypical view of Turks and Turkey, prompting most everyone to say that they seldom see "people like me" on television or read about "people like me" in the print media. Part of the problem, of course, is in our definition of what constitutes news. Journalists are always looking for information that is out of the ordinary, that illustrates conflict, that is unusual. However we may disagree with such criteria for news, they have become standard. And these standards may lead to reporting what is perceived to be "bad" about a group of people or a set of events—or even what is perceived to be exotic about that group of people.

Dutch Media Response to Minority Interests

Dutch media officials, particularly those in broadcast media, saw the need for programming that would interest the minority groups in their society. But it took a long time for them to recognize that need. When the Dutch government first brought guest workers from Turkey and other countries, officials didn't think about what went on in their lives outside work. After all, these people were just coming to fill the labor shortage for a while, they thought. Then they would return to their countries of origin. Most of the early workers were single or left their families behind in Turkey, so the Dutch government had little responsibility to them—for education and other social services or even for their health, since they were relatively young and strong.

Later, when the Dutch government realized that the workers would likely not be returning to their homelands, a decision was made to begin programming for migrants. But it was created in a separate space from mainstream broadcasting: a radio program of news and pertinent information useful to migrants; a television program filled with public affairs information broadcast in multiple languages. But such programming was always presented in top-down format and filled with content that producers thought was good for the ethnic community. Perhaps that is why almost every person expressed his or her resentment about the way Turks are described in the context of majority media. Instead of being integrated into the messages and entertainment delivered to everyone in society, they were criminals and victims in the public space for the majority. And in the special space reserved for them exclusively, they were people who needed to be taught how to live in Dutch society

Television first began to allocate some specific time to migrants in 1984 with the establishment of four cable channels for minorities in Amsterdam, Rotterdam, Utrecht, and The Hague. In fact, these stations were the first of their kind in Europe.[5] But radio broadcasting to Turks and other minorities dates at least to 1963, according to Ahmet Azdural, general broadcast manager for Radio 5, who produces a daily news and public affairs program for the Turkish listeners in Amsterdam. Azdural said that the first programs were aired less frequently in the early days than they are now.

> The first program was music. And it wasn't only for Turks. Each week they'd pick several cities and play music from those places. It was on one half hour a week. In 1972-1973 the broadcasting expanded to include a magazine show for one half hour for each of several groups. Finally, the three largest groups—Turks, Chinese, and Arabs—got their own space on the radio on a weekly basis. They are aired on middle wave and can be picked up in surrounding countries—as far away as Spain. We also broadcast on cable and live on the Internet.

Despite the radio and later television programs for minorities, the Dutch didn't make media a part of official policy to promote integration until 1991, when the then minister of well-being, health, and cultural affairs, Hedy d'Ancona, published a document on media's role in a multicultural society.[6] D'Ancona also promoted the February 1994 law giving NPS, *Nederlandse Programma Stichting* (Netherlands Programming Association), a central role for programming to and about minorities. Part of its mission is to devote 20 percent of its 650 annual air hours to programs for ethnic and cultural minorities. But the rest of its time is devoted to a variety of cultural and public affairs programs.

The concept of integration as used by the Dutch government has never been particularly clear. As described by Kruyt and Niessen, the first articulation of the concept was in a 1981 memorandum in which the government promoted the goal of integration alongside the preservation of cultural identity. Later that goal was modified, but "cultural identity" was never precisely defined. During the 1980s the terms "pluriform" or "multicultural society" became popular.[7] Then in 1996 in the Memorandum Outlines for the Newcomers' Integration Bill, the government operationalized the term, saying that integration requires that "newcomers rapidly learn to find their own place in society" through learning of Dutch, and taking other courses in social and vocational orientation, career planning, social guidance, and a follow-up course to help the newcomer enter the labor market in the Netherlands.[8] Perhaps the Dutch government thought that integration meant teaching the minority groups civic and cultural lessons so that they could speak the language, become gainfully employed, and even adopt Dutch citizenship. But it didn't go so far as to mean that individuals from these minorities could actually become one of them. They would always be hyphenated citizens, in the way Çağlar describes.

In the Frachon and Vargaftig account of minority television programs in Europe, the authors divide their broadcast programs for immigrants into magazine programs, mainstream programs, and cable and local channels. While most of the programs they describe still exist in some form, it might be more useful to look at media for migrants in another way. The purpose of this classification system is to determine why the various television programs and available print media may not be sufficiently addressing the needs of the Turkish community in Amsterdam, and consequently why so many people prefer print or broadcast media from Turkey to the available options in the Netherlands.

New Categories for Migrant Media

In reviewing most of the available programs and print publications targeted to people of Turkish origin in Amsterdam, it seemed more important to examine their content in relationship to the producers of that content. At least four types of producers were analyzed.

1. Television programs produced by the Dutch (with the help of Turkish consultants) to promote better understanding of the Turkish people who live in the Netherlands. The audience for these programs is mostly Dutch, but the goal is to reflect the diversity in Dutch society and celebrate that diversity to the Dutch. These programs usually appear as single programs or as a series on *Het Allochtoon Video Circuit* (The Nonindigenous People's Video Circuit). These programs are about a variety of minority groups in the country.

2. Television programs produced by multicultural groups employed by the Dutch NOS broadcasting authority (*Nederlandse Omroep Stichting*). The Turkish journalists produce their programs for *Migranten-TV Amsterdam* on the cable to the municipality. A second such program used to be produced in Utrecht and a third in The Hague. Only the Amsterdam program remains. It is a mixture of news and public affairs, cultural topics, and entertainment.

3. Programs on the Amsterdam municipal channel produced by local religious leaders to the Islamic community. These are generally aired in Turkish or Arabic about topics related to religious affairs.

4. Programs by Amsterdam youth of Turkish origin to other youth. These are on topics of interest to youth by a group called *Alternatif,* and aired on A2, an Amsterdam television channel, and also on Zandam FM radio. The organization gets a state subsidy to cover salaries and rent, but the greater part of the financing for the organization's activities (including the television and radio programs) comes from hosting bands for dances on Friday evenings in the building where *Alternatif* is housed, sale of cassettes of programs, donations, and grants from foundations for the health programs they produce.

5. Print publications that come and go. These are usually weeklies or monthlies that are produced in Turkish and carry news and public affairs, information about cultural events, and interviews. They are usually circulated in stores that carry Turkish products and services to the Turkish community and are funded through advertising only. The latest of these is a monthly titled *İkibinbir* (or 2001).

6. Print publications for youth that offer a creative outlet for their poetry, photography, and editorial perspectives. *Alternatif* produces one of those called *Duvar* (Wall).

7. A proposed channel on Dutch television by a Dutch broadcaster who has Turkish parents. He wants a space on one of the national public channels for programs that would be in Dutch but that would have appeal to all the people living in Holland. "I'm here to make the gap between the two groups of people disappear. Eventually I want to see as many Dutch viewers as Turkish viewers. Dutch viewers can also be members of the organization and they can work there," said Rıza Şeref, the broadcaster who was organizing the petition for this channel. Though Şeref's attempt failed, it will be discussed as a media option.

This analysis of the types of programs and publications will be different from the usual way of classifying such media, but examining the content based on the producer and the intended audience for that content should offer a better vantage point for the purposes of this research.

Another frame for examining the media for the Turkish community is from the insider/outsider perspective. Are the producers always the insiders and the audience the outsiders? Or is there some other combination of identities at work here? Finally, the analysis of the content of all of these programs must be understood in the context of the pull of the news and public affairs programs, but more importantly the entertainment programs in the television that arrives by satellite dish in the homes of the Turkish community from Turkey. This is media produced for Turks in Turkey, and in a way, the audience in Europe for these channels is an "outsider" audience that eavesdrops on the programs mostly intended for a very different audience.

First I will describe the producers of the various programs or media and their perspectives on these programs. In doing so, I will try to place them in their relative attitudes toward the Turkish community and the Dutch employers for whom most of them work. For each type of program I will also provide some analysis of specific program segments.

NPS Radio

I spoke with three people who worked at this station in June 1999. They produce a daily news program that is forty-five minutes long in Turkish.

Ahmet Azdural, general broadcast manager for NPS-Turkish radio, is the most optimistic of the NPS producers. He has been working at the station, located in Hilversum, for sixteen years. In addition to doing a lot of freelance writing for the Turkish press and some television production, he works with other Turkish journalists to produce the radio program for the Turkish community.

> The daily radio program is live—at least the first half when we give the news. Some of the reporting is on tape. But they have some problems with the live feed, because the technicians are Dutch and can't follow the Turkish to know when exactly the show ends, starts, or has breaks. Every night we broadcast for forty-five minutes—thirty-five minutes of background, reportage, and so on, and the other ten minutes of late breaking news. They also ask a broad question and have a call-in part to the show.

In addition to the daily news program, some special programs are aired occasionally. These are often more popular with the public.

> Sometimes we have a complete live program once a month that will be based on a social issue. We also have another one that relates to a point of law that is relevant to the Turkish community. And they call in with their questions. If

> there is a lot of interest in the topic, we continue as long as it lasts. If no interest, we change to another topic. We measure interest with the number of telephone calls, the reaction to the program. If it is a legal issue, the telephone doesn't stop ringing for a second. On average, we get between 700 and 4,000 calls. For Holland, this is a huge number.
>
> There are a lot of people interested in matters related to their Turkish roots—houses or land that they might own over which there might be some ownership dispute. Others are interested in matters related to their military service. If there is much interest in a topic, we continue it to another week.

Despite the good response to the legal issues, overall listenership is down. In a 1999 survey of minority audience's use of NPS, 63 percent of the Turkish respondents said they never listen to radio at all. That was up from 52 percent in 1995 and 29 percent in 1992.[9] When asked about whether they listen to Radio 5, the station that broadcasts the news in Turkish, only 4 percent said they did. The survey only samples 150 people in each minority group and Azdural does not trust the accuracy of the results, but the over-time analysis indicates a steady and steep decline as the satellite television from Turkey has become more popular. He sadly accepts those results. Fortunately, however, the ratings do not determine whether the program gets to continue or not. The Dutch government has made a commitment to maintaining this public service

Part of the problem, from Azdural's perspective, is that the Turkish community has many factions. That can be seen in the number of different organizations of Turkish people in Amsterdam. According to a recent count, about 150 social, political, cultural, and religious organizations related to the Turkish community in that city are active. And Azdural would like to include the various perspectives of these organizations in his broadcasts.

> But the Turkish community breaks down to many smaller social units, and all are not interested in the same things. For political, ethnic, ideologic, and other reasons they break up into groups. And each of these groups wants us to be the spokesman for their interests. We don't see it that way. We want to represent them all. We want to give each group a chance to express their point of view. When we do, the people who oppose a particular position get angry with us. I like it that people oppose what I do. I don't want to keep them all happy.

Azdural's dream is to start a multicultural station, one where all ethnic groups would speak in their own languages and from their own perspectives. Otherwise, he said, there will be no way to pull people away from the barrage of television programs they can view in their native languages. And he believes that happens because people lack trust in the leaders and institutions of Dutch society.

> Everywhere you go, every institution you relate to, you are told that you are not a part of that, you are a foreigner and don't belong. So you never feel you can trust those groups, that society, and retreat to where it is safe, where you trust

> people . . . you look for places where you are comfortable and accepted and media is one of those places.

Haluk Bakır, bureau editor at NPS, said in June 1999 that there were only four Turks, each working three days a week for seven hours each day to produce this show.

> Our resources are limited. But we do have a certain percent of broadcast time for minorities and that is nice. And we also have on Dutch broadcasting a certain amount of time to produce programs about minorities. We work hard to produce each day's broadcast and we have to do that with fewer people than we need because of financial limits. And we can't go to a conference unless we bring something material from there. We started having fights with one another. One of our colleagues was fired because he worked for *Andadolu Ajans* because it was a state agency [this was seen as a conflict of interest for the employee].

Bakır's concern about the flight from Dutch-based media to Turkish media is not based on statistical analysis, but rather on the many interviews with Turkish people living in Amsterdam that he conducts for his work.

> You know it is also the atmosphere. People have to hold onto something that is familiar. It is really that the look in people's eyes has changed lately. It gives me the chills sometimes. Maybe it sounds like exaggerating it. But you know I see little signs and I see them as symptoms of something. Manifestations of something latent. It is not everywhere. It worries me sometimes. It is a distance, a polarization. Before it wasn't like that. It was more relaxed, the relations. Also the Kurdish question has entered it. And the Turks are a little too hard-headed compared to other minorities. The first generation, yes, they did all the dirty jobs, and accepting all the jobs that they were given in the workplace, and they couldn't react. When you talk to them, they all tell about these things.

He agrees that the second generation is less willing to tolerate the treatment.

> Whereas the first ones say, we came here to work and they gave us work, and we were guests. The other ones say we were raised here or born here. Why are we still seen as foreigners. There is always a name or a term. They are *allochtoon* [or nonindigenous people, a term that has been frequently criticized].

I analyzed the programs for a week during the time I conducted the interviews with the NPS radio producers. Each program lasts about forty-five minutes and follows a fairly regular format of presenting European news, then news from Turkey, followed by a more in-depth look at a particular issue or two related to public affairs issues in Amsterdam or the Netherlands that affect the Turkish community. Features can also focus on topics of cultural interest or interviews with Turkish musicians or artists who may be presenting their work or scheduling concerts in Holland.

During the period from June 4 to June 11, 1999, the following topics were discussed in the in-depth pieces:

1. An extensive interview with a Turkish pop singer who has aspirations to cracking the European market with an English-language CD. She was in town to give a concert.

2. An interview with a Turkish folk musician who comes from the Black Sea region and who was performing in a concert in Utrecht.

3. Two pieces on the European Parliament elections. Both related to the need for the Turkish community to vote. One of the programs preceded the usual forty-five minute evening news. Both included interviews with opinion leaders, in particular the Turkish representatives holding seats in the Dutch Parliament and the Amsterdam municipal council.

4. Another feature following the elections that featured interviews with voters on who they voted for and why and what the value of the elections is for the Turkish community in the Netherlands.

5. A news feature on the meaning of a new law affecting workers that included an interview with a representative from the government agency that will implement the law.

6. A news feature focused on the meeting of the foreign language teachers' union meeting in Amersfoort. Several interviews with teachers of Turkish indicated that there was a variety of goals for the meeting, including the establishment of national standards for language instruction for the children of immigrants.

7. Two features based on a vacation service organization based in Cologne, Germany. Interviews with the director of the new organization featured discussion about transportation, travel conditions, and visa requirements for people traveling from Europe to Turkey (or elsewhere) during their summer vacations.

8. A weekly report on an organization. This one featured a support group for immigrants and their rights based in Belgium.

9. A feature on the Federation of Democratic Social Organizations. This group was meeting in Rotterdam and the journalists interviewed people about the goals of this organization and its value to Turkish residents in the Netherlands. The announcer claimed that there are 1,125

organizations of Turks or Kurds or that have Turkish interests in their titles. The federation would like to bring together the various social organizations to obtain more power for the minority group.

10. A report of a new organization meeting for the first time in Amsterdam, called *Netwerk*. It is composed of young, mostly second-generation professional Turkish men and women. And it is organizing to create a lobby to improve the image of the Turkish migrants and their families in the Netherlands.

11. A news feature on the implications of a new law related to unemployment and migrants. In this case, the producers invited an expert on this law to come to the studio to be interviewed.

12. An extended explanation of the actions of the defense attorneys in the Ocalan case in Turkey. [Abdullah Ocalan was the leader of the Kurdish revolutionary organization who was captured in Africa and returned for trial in Turkey. He has been sentenced to death for murder, but the case is still working through the appeal system.] It was separated from the rest of the news for detailed discussion. That likely happened because many of the Turkish people in the Netherlands don't believe that the Dutch press provides an accurate account of the Turkish government's position.

Het Allochtoon Video Circuit (The Nonindigenous People's Video Circuit)

This is a documentary magazine program. Frachon and Vargaftig report that the subjects of this program have included "how to use medicines, parental involvement in schools, immigrants returning to their home countries, retirement homes, violence against women, sterility, drug dependence, AIDS, racism, home workers, love, divorce and Muslim schools."[10] They also describe these programs generally as ones that are part of a larger information campaign. They are copied to video and circulated to interested groups at cost.

For this research I will focus on a particular magazine program, *Inburgeren in Nederland* (Acclimatizing in the Netherlands), a twelve-part television series on the Turks in Turkey and in the Netherlands in the current era, beginning with a history of the migration from Turkey to Europe. The series also includes a critical examination of how the first migrants were treated by the Dutch and other European host countries. In addition to a discussion of major Turkish organizations in the Netherlands and eighty-five portraits of individuals of Turkish origin, the project also produced a book that includes brief summaries of those portraits and also an Internet site.

Dick Oosterbaan, producer of the series, said the goal was first to show the diversity in ethnic Turkish politics and culture in the Netherlands. The series tried to show through the individual portraits what was happening in economics, religion, politics, and culture. Though hardly any of the Turks with whom I talked watched the program—and few had even heard about it—Oosterbaan thinks the opinion leaders in both the Turkish and Dutch communities watched it. Oosterbaan believes that to change attitudes, you need to start with the elite and move down. And one of the obligations of public broadcasters is to get more people in Holland acquainted with what their neighbors are doing. The series aired in May and June 1999 on N-3 (one of three national public television channels), an NPS-sponsored program.

Oosterbaan was very concerned that the production "get the series right," so he drew on the talents of both Dutch and Turkish broadcasters and they sought out consultants who have knowledge about the situation in Turkey from all major universities in the Netherlands. He also drew on research from IMES, the University of Amsterdam-based Institute for Migration and Ethnic Studies. Ahmet Azdural assisted in the production.

The series was produced in multiple languages so there would be "little or no possibility for people to provide an incorrect interpretation of what was meant." Oosterbaan thought that people wouldn't trust the broadcasters if they made a mess out of it. That means that some of the profiles of individuals were based on interviews conducted in Turkish and others were in Dutch. I wondered how the profiles in Turkish were received by the Dutch who believe that the language of the country should be Dutch. It is possible that this approach reinforced the stereotypes of Turks as people who don't learn to speak the language despite living in the country for many years.

I believe that the target audience for this series was primarily Dutch, but it is odd that so few Turkish people I talked with had any knowledge of it. Of course, if they always watch Turkish television, there is little chance for them to find out about it. But also, the program aired at an unpopular time on the weekend. The series was scheduled to repeat late in 1999. I don't know when it was scheduled, but if a better time were chosen, perhaps a larger audience of Turks and Dutch would have watched it. Turkish people might have been surprised to find this positive treatment of the accomplishments of their friends and acquaintances selected for portrayal.

Of the eighty-five people featured on this series, sixty-three were men and twenty-two were women. Though all details were not provided about the individuals' backgrounds, at least fifty of those interviewed had some sort of post-secondary education. This means they are not at all representative of the group of Turks in the Netherlands. But since the point of the series was to show that many Turkish migrants were movers and shakers in the communities where they live, it is understandable that these people would have more specialized educational backgrounds. The portraits were based on their involvement in one or more of the Turkish organizations, in the religious institutions, in the arts, or in sports. It was not unusual for the people to be members of several organizations. More than twenty of the group worked in public administration for a migrant-related organization or at a foundation that had migrant interests as its goal. Others were elected officials at the municipal, regional, or national parliament level. Still others were volunteers for a variety of organizations that supported migrants in the problems they confronted in their everyday lives—everything from illiteracy to homosexuality to discrimination in the workforce. Overall, the series made a powerful statement about the major contributions made by these people to Dutch society. Those people who watched several parts of the series would have come away with a very different impression of the Turkish residents in the Netherlands than the one based on prejudice and overgeneralization.

Migranten TV (Migrant TV or MTV)

This weekly series that repeats once during the week produced about fifty hours of television programs a year in 1995. Its purpose is to improve the knowledge about civic affairs and other topics and is directed to the Antilleans, Surinamers, Turks, and Moroccans who live in Amsterdam. Şeref Acer, head of programming for the station, is concerned that fewer and fewer people watch MTV. According to the data collected over the years, Acer says that about 85 percent of the Turks in Amsterdam used to watch the program. Once TRT-INT (the Turkish state-sponsored channel on the Dutch cable system) came to Holland in 1991, the audience for MTV began to drop to about 60 percent of the potential audience. In 1994, the satellite dishes first became popular, he said. Before that time they were too expensive to be in common use. Now the viewers of the program are about 40 percent of the possible audience. Acer believes that MTV has a regular viewing audience of about 25 percent of the Turks in Amsterdam, with an additional 25 percent who view occasionally. This bothers him as a producer who is interested in attracting the widest audience, but it bothers him more because he says the community's attention is now turned away from the Netherlands and toward Turkey. In his view, the Turkish people who live in Amsterdam have regressed since the adoption of Turkish satellite television. "They have moved back toward being Turks and not being integrated into Dutch society. All they talk about in the coffeehouses, the mosques, and their homes is Turkey. They used to talk about what was going on in Holland and in Amsterdam, but no more," he said.

Acer thinks that MTV offers great value to the viewers. As the only program on television that has Dutch subtitles when the interviews are conducted in Turkish, and Turkish subtitles when the spoken language is Dutch, the producers think of these programs as a bridge between what is Dutch and what is foreign. Dutch people could watch these programs and learn about Turkish or other ethnic groups' language and culture and interests. However, there is not likely a very large Dutch audience for MTV.

Of all the local media Turkish participants in this study talked about, MTV was most frequently mentioned as a channel they knew about and one that they occasionally viewed. They said they found useful information on the channel and watched when they could—but that happened less often now than when they didn't have satellite television available.

Acer believes there will be a need for an MTV-type program for a long time, since many of the second-generation Turkish people here return to Turkey to find a spouse when they decide to marry. So there is a constant flow of new migrants into the country, all in need of information about living in the Netherlands.

> The children of these marriages are always a second generation. And if at home the family is only speaking Turkish, the cycle continues. The children who speak Turkish at home start school not knowing any Dutch or very little. This puts them behind in school. And it takes a long time for the spouse who comes from Turkey to get adjusted to life here and learn enough Dutch.

Doomernik et al., report on a study from the Central Bureau for Statistics that supports Acer's view. In 1991, it estimated that 27 percent of the migration of Turks to Holland was for family reunion, while 29 percent was for family formation. For all migrant groups, between 1987 and 1991, the migration for family reunion declined from 22 to 16 percent, while the migration for family formation increased from 19 to 23 percent.[11] As long as the Netherlands permits migration from Turkey for either reason, it means that Acer's assessment is accurate that problems related to the first generation will not disappear, despite the fact that one or more members of a family may be from the second generation.

Acer's position likely derives from his personal history. Born in a village in Turkey, he came to Holland after elementary school and received the rest of his education there. He left school before finishing university and has been working at MTV for fourteen years.

He views the advent of the satellite dishes critically and wishes people would focus more on the events of the place in which they live. Otherwise they cannot be a real part of that culture.

> You need to be active in the social life of the country to call yourself a citizen of that country. A government can't force you to be a citizen; it is a matter of your caring about what's happening in that country and being involved. If there is no difference between the person who lives in Ankara and the one who lives here, then you can't call that person who lives here a Dutch-Turk.

Acer believes his job is to keep providing the information for the people who are not Dutch-Turks needed to achieve that status. The bottom line for him is that research isn't necessary to tell him what kinds of programs to produce. "Even if they don't like it, it is usually good for them," he says.

I analyzed the content of three MTV programs aimed at the Turkish audience. All three were in Turkish with Dutch subtitles. Where Dutch people were speaking, the subtitles were in Turkish. The magazine-formatted program was announced by two different women in the three different programs. For each one, the day's topics would be announced before beginning the segments. Each program contained a mix of cultural, educational and informative, and feature material. Though some might view the informational topics as didactic, they did contain useful information for living and working in Amsterdam.

Of the three programs analyzed, two aired in January and one in March 1999. Each program lasts about one-half hour and is organized in magazine format with a female host who introduces the segments and ties them together. The three programs could be broken down in the following categories:

1. Educational Information: In these segments, a single speaker is usually explaining some feature of the Dutch educational system to Turkish parents who may not understand procedures. The Dutch system is very complicated and provides a number of choices for students after elementary school. Since in the Netherlands parents can also choose the particular elementary school they want their children to attend, they need to deliberate on that choice. Three educational topics were aired, one in each of the programs. The first discussed how parents should choose a school and the procedure for doing that. The second explained the nature and purpose of an exam administered at the end of primary school. It also advised parents on how to help students prepare for the exam. The last program described a preschool program designed for children who speak no Dutch at home. It stressed the importance of exposing children to Dutch through this program, rather than waiting until they enter primary school where they will be held back because of their lack of language facility.

2. Culture: Two features that fall into this category were aired. The first was an excerpt from a public performance by the Whirling Dervishes in Amsterdam. The group came from Konya and demonstrated the music, dance, and text of the Sufi religious form. The second feature was presented on the first day of Ramazan [Turkish spelling of the religious observance] and contained video recorded in several Amsterdam mosques as Muslims broke their fast when the sun went down. The video showed people eating and interviewed leaders in the mosques as well as their Dutch guests for the special İftar meal [or meal where the fast is broken].

3. Expert Interviews: One of these was with a lawyer about a small change in the law governing immigrants and their application for permanent residence status. He provided detailed information about the changes and advised applicants on the procedure for application. The

second was an interview with an Amsterdam representative to the municipal council. He described the election process, spoke of the successes and failures of municipal government as it related to minorities, and detailed his vision for the future.

4. News: These were timely news segments that were relevant to the Turkish community. The first came under the category of "Social News," and included announcements about programs for the poor, or for youth and senior citizens. A short explanation of the newly introduced Euro was also given. A second news item reported on a human rights event that honored a Turkish prisoner of conscience, Akın Bırdal. The last item covered a hunger strike by women at a Turkish organization to bring attention of city government to a women's issue.

5. Individual Profiles: These were perhaps the most interesting and attention holding. One focused on a homeless man who played music on the street and sold newspapers for homeless people. A second featured a homosexual Imam whose goal was to have a place of worship for other homosexual Muslims who had been rejected by orthodox Islamic groups. The last of the features focused on a woman who had written her first novel. The story described the problems of a married Turkish woman who left her husband because of cultural conflict in the marriage and who sought love elsewhere in Amsterdam.

At the end of the programs, several public service announcements of programs relevant to immigrants were announced, along with telephone numbers and addresses.

Islamic Broadcasting

Broadcasting by Islamic organizations in Amsterdam is all on the local radio and television stations on A2. This is also the home for other religious broadcasting in Amsterdam. Three Islamic organizations supervise the three different types of Turkish-language Islamic programs. The larger supervising body is the Netherlands Muslim Council, which set up the Netherlands Muslim Network. It has been operating under that organization since 1993. But Islamic broadcasting began in 1986, operating with a government subsidy and approval.

Turkse Omroep Stichting (The Turkish Broadcasting Authority or TOS TV), TTA, and *Feyza*: these organizations are given time to broadcast locally in Amsterdam. The content is religious messages by various Islamic groups—the *Ülkücüs* (the ultranationalist political group), the *Milli Görüş*, and the Fethullah Gülen followers. Operating both radio and television production, the groups have been running programs for about four years, according to Abdullah Sarı, chief editor of TOS. Unlike the subtitled MTV, Turkish is the only language of TOS broadcasts that air religious messages for ten hours a week on radio and four hours on television. Many of those programs also carry political messages. Because the presenters speak only in Turkish, it is likely that more things get by than would on MTV. Sarı says that there is no bias in TOS's messages, however.

> Our doors are open to all people. We do not distinguish among people. We never had and never will. . . .Yes, and when I first broadcasted I emphasized the point that we are not prejudiced against any idea.

While he claims that his programs are the only ones that lack an ideology in Amsterdam, others might say that TOS carries a heavy ideological bias.

TOS television programs are aired from 3:00 to 5:00 P.M. Tuesdays and repeat on Sundays from 7:00 to 9:00 P.M. The radio program is on the air five days a week from 1:00 to 3:00 P.M. When I asked people what they watched on Dutch television, TOS was most often mentioned by the people who expressed strong religious affiliations and beliefs. Abdullah Sari reported that a magazine published in the Netherlands presented the results of a survey in 1998 that found that most Turks in Amsterdam believe that TOS was the station they found to be "honest, objective and addressing everyone." I believe that would be the response of all people who practiced Islam in their daily lives. Others would likely not accept that view. And still others don't watch for the same reason they don't watch MTV. Özlem, a woman who has lived in Amsterdam for twelve years, regrets the change of habit.

> Before we had the dish, there was only the half hour of news that TOS brought. And we would await that news with four eyes [a Turkish expression meaning with great anticipation]. Now we comfortably watch whatever we want from Turkey. Since the dish came, we don't watch TOS or MTV—and that is bad. No matter how little it was, it kept us in touch with Holland and helped us speak a little Dutch, she said. Now we never watch those programs.

TOS is supported by members, as most Dutch national broadcast programs are. Programs are allocated time based on the number of paying members who support the programs. Sari said that between 60,000 and 70,000 Turks support the religious programs. It should also be noted that TOS television and radio leadership has a connection to the National Action Party (right-wing nationalists or *Ülkücüs* in Europe) in Turkey. TTA (*Turkse Televisie Amsterdam*) is a second program that is more tied to the *Milli Görüş* (the European wing of the Virtue Party in Turkey) and Feza is a third program tied to the Fethullah Gülen supporters in Turkey (considered a more politically moderate group by the current administration in Turkey, but Gülen has reportedly made videotaped statements that refer to infiltrating key positions in Turkish state offices).[12] All of these groups operate on the same basis as TOS—with government subsidy and membership fees. They all broadcast on the Amsterdam channel, A2. And all of them operate out of Amsterdam mosques as their headquarters. Ratings in 1998 as reported by Mehmet Akıf Çelik, the man responsible for TTA television, indicated that Feza was most watched, TTA was second, and TOS was third. But Çelik said that there is often confusion over which channel is which. He said that people call TTA representatives "TOS" when they see camera operators shooting in the streets, despite the TTA logo on the cameras. When asked about what they watched on Dutch television, all participants who said they watched any of the religious programs on A2 referred to them as "TOS."

Turks Jongerencentrum Alternatif (Alternative Turkish Youth Center)

As noted above, this organization has multiple media outlets and activities, but the central purpose is to engage Turkish and other minority youth in activities that develop their "social education," according to Yilmaz Yilmaz, coordinator of the center, who used to work in theatre and in musical groups in the Netherlands. Nearly forty young people, mostly Turkish, work at *Alternatif* in the hours after school and on weekends. Yilmaz believes the organization helps migrant youth find an identity. They work on creative projects, learn responsibility, and make good friends. But some of the youth are at the margins, according to Yilmaz. One young man, with whom I talked a year after the interview with Yilmaz, is typical of those who are less responsible. "They don't come on time, say they can't do things because they 'have no time.' We try to get them involved and aren't interested if they decide not to work," said Yilmaz.

> Kids like Kerem can't do it because they have a laziness of spirit. He wants money and to have a store but he can't get his act together. There's a lot of work to do, but these kids can't realize their dreams. The parents don't want them to leave home, but they want to have their own place and don't have the money. The parents live in fear here that their kids will get involved in activities they [the parents] don't want—like religion or drugs or politics.
>
> We take the place of these kids' psychiatrists. We put them to work and get them going on their lives. Then they don't need psychiatrists.

Lengthy discussions with several of the teenagers who work at *Alternatif* confirmed Yilmaz's view. Many of them were troubled kids who thrived in this environment where they had a job to do and could become expert at doing it if they worked hard. Or as Yilmaz put it, *Alternatif* allows the youth to become empowered by completing projects.

Gül is one who really fits Yilmaz's description. Born and raised in the Netherlands, Gül, eighteen, has lived most of her life without her father. At the time I talked with her, she said her father was about to be released from jail. She didn't even know what he was convicted of because her mother didn't want to tell her. Her parents have been divorced for several years, and her mother has raised her mostly alone. Gül first went to a Friday entertainment night at *Alter-*

natif when she was thirteen. Her mother was fearful of her going because she was so young and it was a great distance from her home (more than an hour by public transportation). But Gül was hooked from the first evening.

> I really had fun that night, but because I was so young, my mother was worried about my going. I started going more regularly to work when I was fifteen. At that time I had a part-time job at a shoe store. Then I started to go with a friend. I found it a warm place to be. Everyone welcomed me. I began to make friends with everyone. Everyone was friendly. There were no arguments among the people who came to *Alternatif.* I kept going and I liked it there. After I felt comfortable, Yilmaz asked why I wasn't involved with the television and radio programs. I decided there was no harm in getting involved. And it started like that. The first videotaping I was involved in was of a group of Japanese who came to *Alternatif.* But I mostly watched others do it. The second time it was at a disco where we interviewed people about why boys have more rights than girls—in going out from home on their own, for example. That's the way it started and I want to continue, because as you work, you are able to advance.
>
> It is a center for youth, and rather than hang out on the streets or get into trouble, you have something to contribute—as a presenter in a video, as a camera operator. You start out taking small steps, and then advance. You can work at the entertainment nights operating the equipment or selling drinks.

Gül saw her involvement in *Alternatif* as incredibly positive. "Before I started going there, I was headed in a bad direction, had bad habits. My Turkish was terrible. After I went there, I stopped swearing, I improved my Turkish." Variations on Gül's story were told by several other youths at the center.

Fatih's parents are also separated. And he is at the end of one phase of his schooling, wondering whether to quit or continue. He is nineteen and has lived in Amsterdam for seven years. He works at designing publications at *Alternatif.* And he is good at computer graphics. Despite the fact that he sees no connection between what happens at the center and his life outside the place, it has helped him to adjust to the Netherlands.

> I see my life as a Turk here from both positive and negative perspectives. The good side is the economic one. The bad part is that you miss your country. You are always wishing you were there. It was much worse when I first came, though. Nothing is familiar; you have no friends; you don't know the language. It's hard. But as time passes you get used to it. But now, when I look ahead, I see good possibilities for jobs and earning money.

Alternatif's television programs have been broadcast once a week since the beginning of 1998—on Tuesdays from 7:00 to 9:00 P.M. But recent program guides for A2 indicate that the programs are on Tuesdays and Thursdays for one hour at 10:00 P.M. They deal with health issues, like AIDS; political topics of interest to youths; and social issues, like personal security and disabled people. The radio program is about four years old. It is broadcast on cable three days a week from 3:00 to 5:00 P.M. And the publication *Duvar* printed its twenty-fourth issue in May 1999.

An analysis of three programs aired in May 1999 indicates that the youths who participate do much of the technical and in front of camera work. That means that the quality of the program varies with the quality of the technicians and the interviewers. Some are excellent; others need more training. But they learn on the job in the programs they produce for A2, called the "open channel," where many amateur programs appear. Most of *Alternatif*'s programs consist of interviews or tapes of Turkish performers who appear at the *Alternatif* studio or interviews with young people who show up for performances. One program included several interviews with young people who work at *Alternatif*. It could probably be considered a recruiting tool, as all of the people interviewed talked about how the work had enriched their lives, kept them from hanging out on the streets, and given them a purpose. It helped them improve their speaking skills—particularly in Turkish—and gave them ideas about what they might want to do in the future. The programs alternate between Dutch and Turkish.

Those young men and women who speak Dutch are very comfortable in the language. Frequently the ones who speak Turkish have lived in the Netherlands a shorter time and likely find speaking Dutch more difficult. In the three programs examined, interviews were conducted with visiting comedians and musicians performing in the Netherlands, and a doctor about the importance of maintaining good health in a section called "Health Corner" of the magazine program. On a May 1999 program, one segment alternates between shots of young people dancing at an *Alternatif* disco night and interviews with the people who came to dance about why they like coming there. These interviews are conducted in Dutch. Some of the young people come from other countries—Chile and Yugoslavia, for example. Others are Dutch. They also comment about senseless violence in the Netherlands and its causes and what can be done about it. They make reference to the Turks who have been involved in a recent shooting and whether they should have been identified by their ethnicity in the media. One young man comments that "It is about character, not about ethnic groups."

Because *Duvar* is also attached to the center, it is appropriate to describe it here. Together with the adults who run *Alternatif*, the teenage participants produce the monthly magazine—and even print it themselves. It is full of a variety of articles, poems, interviews, cartoons, and stories—whatever creative work will fit.

Two issues of *Duvar* were analyzed, one for May 1998 and another for May 1999. Both issues have original cartoon drawings on the cover. One of them is particularly characteristic of a difficulty Turks have when living in the European climate. It is a drawing of a man holding a large sign with a picture of a sun drawn on it. And all around him the raindrops are falling. Both issues contain a mix of Dutch- and Turkish-language contributions. The individual contributor writes in whichever language comes easiest. The publication could best be characterized as a literary magazine, although it also contains announcements, reviews of theatrical and musical productions, as well as summaries of conferences and programs for youths. Youths who write for the publication are often dealing with issues of identity or maturity, like self-confidence or personal feelings. Essays run the gamut of topics interesting to the community—the situation for Turkish youth in Dutch schools, people who create fear for others, problems for struggling theater groups in Turkey, human rights, and the interest in Turkish elections in Holland. Cartoons and poems often examine the situation for migrant youths.

Yeni Express (New Express) and *İkibinbir* (2001)

From time to time, journalists in Amsterdam decide it is important to produce a newspaper to serve the Turkish community. Unfortunately such ventures are usually underfunded and the journalists spend money from their own pockets and take time away from their families to produce these labors of love. One such paper, *Yeni Express*, a weekly, appeared and disappeared in the time I was in the Netherlands. *İkibinbir*, a monthly, survives. They likely serve a valuable role now that so many Turks have decided not to watch Dutch television much anymore. If they do not tune into MTV or NPS radio, Turks get no public affairs information relevant to their lives in Amsterdam. These newspapers have been circulating without charge. I found copies of them at Turkish organizations and in stores catering to Turkish consumers. Some of the journalists who work for other organizations with whom I talked have also invested time in these publications on a freelance basis.

I analyzed the content of *İkibinbir* for April and May 1999. An ambitious undertaking, the color offset newspaper contained forty-eight pages of features, political and other cartoons, poems, interviews with prominent Turks in the Netherlands, and advertising. Mostly written in Turkish, the content appears to be directed to a fairly educated audience. Each issue is in tabloid format, features a woman's picture on the front page—a classy photo of an attractive young woman. A second picture of a woman that could be characterized as a "cheesecake photo" is included in each issue (perhaps to attract more attention to the publication). The first page also contains teasers and headlines for the stories. The newspaper began in September 1998, with Mehmet Okur as editor. It is directed at Turks who live all over the Netherlands, but mostly draws on events and personalities from Amsterdam, Rotterdam, and Utrecht. It is distributed by a large Turkish daily, *Hürriyet*, from its Frankfort location, and the editorial offices are located in Utrecht. Though issues of the paper were available without cost, subscriptions at a rate of thirty guilders a year are possible. The newspaper also circulates in Belgium. A summary of the content of the two issues follows:

Culture: This is a major category of content. It includes interviews with an actor, a Turkish consulate about his work as a photographer, a cartoonist who works for Turkish and Dutch publications, an author and translator of books, and an artist and sculptor. One issue included pictures of the winning art in a children's art contest. Reviews of performances of a comedian, a pop music star's performance, and the events of a theatrical festival were included. Other stories were on a group staging a play for the Rotterdam Theater Festival; another group involved in a children's theater production; and a historical figure in Turkish music, "Deniz kızı Eftalya." Ahmet Azdural wrote a column on the twelve-part television series on the Dutch-Turks. And several of the cartoons could be considered as cultural rather than political. Another column tried to persuade readers of the value of travel to places other than Turkey to enrich their life experience.

Politics: It would not be a Turkish newspaper without a heavy dose of political content. Several different people had regular columns, where they treated political topics—both in Turkey and in Holland. Topics of columns included a persuasive argument for voting for the Turkish representative to the European Council, the role of women in the political future of the Turks, commentary on the outcome of elections in Turkey, and an appraisal of the small percentage of minorities in the Dutch mass media and how it reflects on the state of democracy in the Netherlands. A two-page spread treated a column written for the Dutch paper *Volkskraant*. The column, called "Crime against Humanity," raises the whole issue of the so-called genocide against the Armenians. It was critical of the French for not passing a resolution to condemn the Turks for the acts of 1915 and 1916. The reprint of the column was followed by a response by the Turkish columnist on its racist approach to Turks and a full-page letter to the editor of *Volkskraant* on the unbalanced nature of the column and the alleged lack of accurate historical detail. Many political cartoons focused on political attitudes of migrants in the Netherlands. One article was based on several interviews with experts on whether ethnicity should be mentioned in connection with a crime in the Dutch press. Finally a short history of Kosovo that included a time line appeared.

Social/legal/educational: A variety of topics relevant to the Turkish migrants was included. A forum treated the future of education for minorities in the "black" schools by focusing on the small number of students from ethnic minorities who are studying to be teachers. An interview featured two of the directors of the *Alternatif* program on the value to Turkish youth for participating in the organization's activities. Another feature with a high-ranking police officer in the Dutch force treated the history of Turks in the police force (from a handful to 465 today) and the problems of discrimination that have existed in the field over the years. Another interview was with a man in charge of the Intellectual and Social Development Institute that has projects aiming at advanced education for gifted youth, and another one for older students who want to be writers. A Turkish teacher was interviewed about his ideas related to the teaching of Turkish to children in the public schools. And a journalist who has worked in the Netherlands for more than thirty years reflected on the history of migrants in the Netherlands. He said he believes that satellite television has improved the Turkish-language competence of second- and third-generation migrants, allowing the Turkish press to retain strong circulation across Europe. Another feature detailed the changes in social rights for residents of the European Union. Finally, there was a feature on high blood pressure, its causes and treatments.

Children: This section contained a lot of items contributed by children. There were poems, short stories, artwork, and cartoons mostly contributed by children.

Literary: Two stories in Dutch appeared. These were written by a Dutch man who lived for sixteen years in a village in southwest Turkey about his experiences and his observations of the people who live there. Only one poem appeared in the two issues, and it was called "Anatolia," and written in Dutch.

Proposed (and Failed) Media Venture

Though he was unsuccessful in raising enough signatures on a petition to begin a new program to be broadcast to all the viewers of Dutch television, Rıza Şeref may decide to continue to pursue his dream sometime again. Şeref, a former director of continuity for VARA, a public, member-based channel that shares time on Nederland 3, Şeref quit his job in July 1999 to devote his complete time to securing enough members for one hour of television time on a public channel.

Şeref was one of the first second-generation Turkish minorities. Born in Barneveldt in the Netherlands in 1969, Şeref grew up away from all other Turks and that likely that affected his outlook. "When I was growing up it was all Dutch—the books and music. I didn't have one Turkish friend. My whole family was unusual, my brother and my two sisters. We were unusual because we didn't have any Turkish friends." At some point, Şeref decided that he needed to do his part to help integrate the Turks in the Netherlands so that they could contribute their culture to the Dutch and also receive Dutch culture the way he had.

> I think the Turkish minority, based on a survey of about 3,000 Turks, want to have something for themselves—a voice here. I want to integrate the Turkish people here. I want to make the process of integration work better than it is right now. I can feel that a second and a third generation have a lot of difficulties here. They don't talk with their mothers and their fathers. There is a gap between the generations. And to help them bring some quality into their lives, I want to do this thing and make a voice for the Turkish people here in Holland.

Şeref also wanted to bring the Dutch closer to the Turkish residents. He believes that this is not a one-sided affair with the Turkish people doing all the work to change and adapt.

> But I'm here to make the gap between the two groups of people disappear. Eventually I want to see as many Dutch viewers as Turkish viewers. Dutch viewers can also be members of the organization and they can work there [at the station]. I think Dutch people don't really care here. In general, it's Turkish. It's OK, don't bother. And what you don't know, you don't hear or feel.

Getting the Dutch to "bother" can be achieved if they gain respect for Turkish culture, just as they expect the Turkish minority to respect their culture, Şeref thinks. The types of programming he sees that might accomplish this include the following:

- We want a talk show between Turkish viewers and Dutch viewers—young people, on all kinds of topics. On abortion or euthanasia or Tarkan's [a pop singer who was raised in Germany] new album. But let them talk together—the Turkish and the Dutch.
- Also we want a language program that will help the first generation get more into the society here. We would use books and magazines and newspapers and would hope to help them speak Dutch a little better than they do now.
- We would like to present to the Dutch people Turkish classical music events. I think they won't like it, but I also thought that Tarkan would not be a great success here. But he is very popular here. So as they listen to more Turkish music, they get used to it.

Şeref has other program plans. He would include discussions surrounding Dutch topics and music based on performers who come to Holland. He would also present Turkish artists here—poets, painters, and writers.

At thirty-one years of age, Şeref is both young and idealistic about what such a station could accomplish in the Netherlands. But he seems to have analyzed the problem accurately—to attract and hold Turkish viewers and at the same time bring them some great benefit on a national television channel.

Unfortunately Şeref did not succeed in his attempt to get the signatures or the membership fees. He may not decide to continue his efforts immediately, as he has taken a job as program director for a children's television channel in Holland, Kindernet 5.[13] But he sees what many others don't see. The attraction of television from Turkey is in the cultural appeal to its audiences living so far away from the culture they may have grown up in or were taught by their parents. All the other types of programs described in this chapter miss the mark in that regard. They provide information and not much entertainment. They may even be pedantic and are likely boring in their attempt to present that information. The one exception is the youth-produced programs. Those speak to the interests of other second- and third-generation children of migrant families.

Producers and Identity

There are several problems in producing content for the Turkish audience in Amsterdam, especially in producing content that can successfully compete with the television, and even the print media, that come from Turkey. The first is the language. Naturally the audiences will seek media that are easier to consume. And reading or listening to one's native language is easier than one's adopted language. Many of the second- or third-generation migrants still communicate in

Turkish at least as much as they do in Dutch. But those people grew up in a bilingual world. The first generation did not have that opportunity.

The second is the cultural appeal. Some media content doesn't travel very well to other countries and to other cultures. As with language, the first-generation migrants are more comfortable with the culture they grew up in and the media content retains features of that culture, even though the culture of the home country has changed in the years since the migrants left.

The third problem is the control placed on the content. Most of the media described in this chapter are funded or subsidized by the Dutch government under certain guidelines for the content. The purpose for creating most of these programs is to further the policy of integration as outlined by the Dutch government. To do that means to provide news and public affairs programs on topics related to the adaptation of the migrants to the host culture. Acer said the other programs aimed at the Turkish community were dropped when the government adopted a policy of integration.

> Our main purpose is to inform the public. About a new law, about the school system, etc. That is the reason we were founded. For example, somewhere something happens, and it has an effect on something. Our job is to show that effect.

It would not serve their purpose to continue to support and promote a variety of programs that sustained the group's difference and strengthened their ties to Turkey.

But perhaps an even bigger obstacle to creating programs to attract and sustain the Turkish audience lies in the producers of that content themselves. Most of the producers are fluent in Dutch and may be even more comfortable in Amsterdam than they would be in Istanbul. Most of them have lived all of their adult lives in the Netherlands, and others were born there. Many of them were at least partially educated in the Netherlands. More importantly, most of them have been socialized by the Dutch institutions for which they are employed. And they believe that for their fellow Turks to be successful in Dutch society, they too must adapt. But Acer doesn't think that has happened.

> For someone to say they are a Dutch-Turk, they have to be immersed in the social fabric of the Dutch. It isn't enough for them to go to work and come home. You don't even have to have Dutch friends; you have to know what's going on in the political and social life of the country. There may be a small portion of the population who could call themselves Dutch-Turks, but at least 70 percent are Turks only. It's not a matter of where they live—in a neighborhood in Ankara or Amsterdam. It is where their heads are.

Though at least two of the journalists complained of discrimination in the workplace and said they were compartmentalized as "minority journalists" capable only of covering the Turkish community, most did not express such feelings. Haluk Bakır of NPS was the most articulate about that discrimination.

> The undersecretary for media affairs says beautiful things about increasing the number of minority journalists working in the media, like for NPS (*Nederlandse Programma Stichting*, the Netherlands Program Foundation), and so on. So but when you look at the practice, of the way we are treated in the NPS. [I say, You mean you are not a real journalist?] That's right. It's not true. We have enough experience. I mean I speak five languages. What is a minority? I work for the BBC and *Cumhuriyet* (a respected national daily) and I interview their prime ministers. They don't know that maybe. And they think we are just doing some programs in our corner. And nobody ever comes to ask what we think. They have their own opinion. They always pick the persons who tell things the way they want to hear them. And that makes you frustrated.

With the exception of Yilmaz and his colleagues at *Alternatif*, these journalists believe it is important for them to bring about some change in their Turkish viewers or listeners or readers. Ahmet Azdural characterizes that change as getting people to think about the Netherlands being their reference point, rather than Turkey.

> They have to see themselves and their interests on television, or they won't watch or won't listen to radio. How will we do that? Now their reference point is Turkey—for example, people who are unemployed here get 2,900 guilders a month and feel that they are rich. That's not bad, but not a lot of money. Why do they feel this way? Because they compare themselves to how it would be in Turkey.
>
> So he sits in the coffeehouse. But if he thinks of his unemployment in terms of Holland, he'll say to himself, "I'm sitting around here all day. Will I never find a job?" And his anxiety level will rise. We'll talk about this on the radio programs, but we need to find a solution.

And Azdural believes the comparison with Turkey is made more often since the satellite dishes became available. He sees the mission of his radio program as reaching people where they are—as providing information that will help them make Amsterdam and the Netherlands their reference point.

My conversations with these men lead me to believe that they are not now, if they ever were, able to put themselves in the position of the majority of their listeners. Sure, they may also watch a little of the entertainment or even the news programs on Turkish television, but it is not their main media source. They prefer the primary Dutch channels or the international media—like the BBC or CNN. So it is really hard for them to understand the audience interest in Turkish entertainment and political affairs. NPS tries to add a little flavor of this by inserting pop, folk, or arabesque songs from Turkey. But mostly these only seem to be inserted to break the program into segments when a change of topic occurs or when they are interviewing the performer of that music.

The men who work at *Alternatif* are different. And they are different because they have daily personal contact with the young people of the second generation whose lives are conflicted in the Netherlands. They see the difficulties these young men and women have communicating with their parents, staying in school, finding a direction for their lives. And the content they help produce or guide the youths to produce allows them to express the difficulties and frustrations that surround their lives in the Netherlands. Their jobs are not to create content for the Turkish community to consume. This is a participative effort, where the young people who are the audience become the producers as well as the audience for the content they produce. Yilmaz sees his own role as using the media projects to help the teenagers work through their own problems.

Kerem, for example, wants to be a filmmaker. His father would prefer he stay and work in the family business. His father and mother sew and sell inexpensive clothing in their own and other stores, and go out on the weekends to sell them in open-air markets. Yilmaz tries to encourage Kerem to work in the store to help earn his way now that he no longer attends school. Ahmet, another of the *Alternatif* directors, says Yilmaz should lighten up with Kerem. It doesn't happen quickly at this age. They both give Kerem projects to work on, but he frequently doesn't come through, says Yilmaz.

Since *Alternatif*'s mandate is to help the youths more than it is to produce media, more freedom is allowed to Yilmaz and the other directors. That helps in creating media content that is of great interest to both the youth who produce it and other Turkish youth in Amsterdam. The programs are produced primarily in Dutch, so those with poor language skills might have a problem, but the target audience for the programs is immigrant youth, so the program reaches them. It also reaches their families who may gain respect for the work their children do.

Kerem sees more value in what is produced at *Alternatif* than on other programs aimed at Turks. He's never watched *Migranten Television.* He thinks that some programs that he watches in Holland are against Turks. "It is their point of view, the way they see it. But I think they look at it wrong," Kerem says. So when he is not involved with *Alternatif* productions, he watches satellite television from Turkey.

Rıza Şeref is different from the rest here described. Though all of the previously described producers are more or less limited by the guidelines which structure their organizations, Şeref wants to set out on a new mission and wants to beat Turkish television at its own game. This comes from his own background—growing up in the only Turkish family in a Dutch town where he was not exposed to any Turkish media. His dream is to create television programs that speak to people like him. He points out that there are no Turkish journalists in Dutch media and there are no Turkish producers of entertainment in Dutch media. His programs would change that. His failure may have deterred him, but perhaps that is only a temporary distraction on the way to his goal.

So as we can see here, it is a combination of factors in the Dutch media that turn off many people in the Turkish audience in Amsterdam. They look for more than news about ways to conduct their lives here. And they are tired of seeing their fellow Turks being portrayed as criminals or poverty-stricken welfare recipients. They want to be shown having fun, participating in mainstream society, contributing some of the culture they brought from Turkey here to Europe and not just receiving the Western European culture they encountered here. They have changed of course too. They are not the same people who left the villages in Turkey to take jobs in factories. But they haven't entirely lost what they were either. They would like to see this reflected in the television programs, in the magazines, in the newspapers, and on the radio they have access to here. As Şeref says in reflecting on the Turkish channels he has watched,

> I didn't care about the satellite channels. It's not made for me. It's Turkish but not made for me. Because I think that you see programs that you can't learn anything from watching the programs. It is entertainment and news that doesn't relate to me.

And it likely isn't suited to the rest of the Turkish community here either. But based on this analysis of the existing media targeted to them, satellite channels from Turkey come closer than most of the programs in Dutch media.

This could be a problem for any Dutch opinion leaders who wish to use the mass media to reach all the residents of Amsterdam or of the Netherlands. It will be impossible to form any kind of public sphere that includes all minority groups as long as they don't attend to the messages of the national media. Mendelsohn and Nadeau, in a study of audiences for Canadian media, examined the views of the audience based on their ethnic makeup. They found that when audiences attended to a common message, increased exposure to the mass media minimized "preexisting sociodemographic cleavages and encouraged opinion convergence across groups."[14] But when a media outlet was directing messages to a particular ethnic group, French-speaking residents of Quebec, the mainstreaming did not occur. Mendelsohn and Nadeau conclude that, "In our Quebec experiment, where the segmented audience had a distinct point of view and the creators of the media messages were aware of this point of view, opinion polarization was the result."[15] When applied to the environment in the Netherlands, the findings of this study should make broadcast authorities reconsider the de facto pillarization of the stations and programs directed to ethnic and linguistic minorities. If integration is the policy goal, it would seem that separating groups out for specific messages will maintain and even exacerbate existing differences in Dutch society and make integration even more difficult.

Integration may not even be an appropriate policy goal for the migrant communities. True integration will come because people feel they want to grow closer to the Dutch majority. If by integration we mean the mastering of the Dutch language, then that is a good goal. The migrants who don't speak Dutch will always be at a disadvantage if they can't communicate in the language of the government, the policy makers, and the employers in the country. But that isn't the definition of integration in my mind; that is just adding a linguistic skill to other skills you already have. But it certainly is the first step toward integration. By learning a language, individuals are also becoming free to learn more about a culture and to make decisions about the extent to which they wish to be a part of that culture. On the other end of things, the Dutch need to decide whether they will embrace these people who wish to become integrated as true Dutch citizens, not as the "black other."

Notes

1. Gerd Baumann, *The Multicultural Riddle* (London: Routledge, 1999), 12.

2. Jerome Bourdon, "Foreigners on Prime Time or Is Television Xenophobic?" in *European Television: Immigrants and Ethnic Minorities* (London: John Libbey, 1995), 27.

3. Bourdon, "Foreigners on Prime Time," 27.

4. Ayşe Çağlar, "Hyphenated Identities and Limits of 'Culture,'" in *The Politics of Multiculturalism in the New Europe,* Tariq Modood and Pnina Werbner, eds. (London: Zed Books, 1997), 175.

5. Claire Frachon and Marion Vargaftig, "The Netherlands," in *European Television: Immigrants and Ethnic Minorities,* Claire Frachon and Marion Vargaftig, eds. (London: John Libbey, 1995), 204.

6. Frachon and Vargaftig, "The Netherlands," 204.

7. Arrien Kruyt and Jan Niessen, "Integration," in *Immigrant Policy for a Multicultural Society*, Hans Vermeulen, ed. (Brussels: Migration Policy Group, May 1997), 48.

8. Kruyt and Niessen, "Integration," 45-46.

9. Yolanda Schothorst, Dick Verzijden, and Ingmar Doeven, *Mediagebruik Etnische Publieksgroepen 1998* (Amsterdam: Veldkamp Marktonderzoek bv, June 1999), 48.

10. Frachon and Vargaftig, "The Netherlands," 204.

11. Jeroen Doomernik, Rinus Penninx, and Hans van Amersfoort, *A Migration Policy for the Future: Possibilities and Limitations (*Brussels: Migation Policy Group, n.d.), 29.

12. "Islamic Evangelists," *Economist* (8 July 2000), 52.

13. "From Turks to Kids," *Haagsche Courant* (13 July 2000), B10.

14. Matthew Mendelsohn and Richard Nadeau, "The Magnification and Minimization of Social Cleavages by the Broadcast and Narrowcast Media," *International Journal of Public Opinion Research* 8, no. 4 (1996): 383.

15. Mendelsohn and Nadeau, "Magnification," 383.

Chapter 5

Consuming Media from Home

Some views on watching television from Turkey:

Ayfer, a mother of two teenage girls, on getting a satellite dish six months previously.

“I was afraid to get one, afraid that I might become a slave to watching television from Turkey. But it didn’t turn out that way,” she says, laughing. “My daughters watch too, especially music programs.”

Mehmet, a boy of twelve, about the impact television from Turkey has had on the family since they got their satellite dish about a year ago.

“We watch it all the time. And it means that we don’t pay attention to the events going on in Holland. The government fell and at school I asked, when did that happen? There was a huge train crash in Germany and I didn’t know about it. So at school I am not quite in step with what is going on.”

Fatih, nineteen, who came from Turkey after elementary school, doesn’t watch more than a half hour of Turkish television a day and some days not at all. He prefers programs on Dutch television.

“Usually I watch when my older sister has it on, and I sit down with her to watch. I don’t really like Turkish television because it seems so phony or unreal. There are also too many commercials and you get fed up with it. I’ve seen most of the programs in Dutch anyway.”

fiule came to Holland with her husband in 1970. Now she speaks good Dutch and watches soaps and news on Dutch television, but she believes Turkish television has made an enormous difference in her life.

"When I first came to Holland, I watched Turkish news on a German channel—and later the Dutch channel carried a half hour of Turkish news from Germany in the morning from 8 to 8:30. There was no other news from home. Having all those Turkish television channels made life better. The newspapers weren't enough. Once television came, we could really understand what was happening in Turkey and other places in the world."

Turkish Media in Amsterdam

Though Turks are not the only diasporic community to receive media directly from their homeland, they probably receive more of it than most migrant populations in the world. Appadurai believes that when "moving images meet deterritorialized viewers, diasporic public spheres, phenomena that confound theories that depend on the continued salience of the nation-state as the key arbiter of important social changes" are created. He is concerned that the combination of a mass migration with mass-mediated images from the homelands creates a "new order of instability in the production of modern subjectives."[1] If that is true, it is important to know something about the content of those images that reach the Turks in Amsterdam and throughout Europe.

Though the number of channels increases periodically, at the time of this study at least eleven channels were available to Amsterdam residents who owned satellite dishes. These channels included nine privately owned, one publicly owned and one pay cinema and sports channel. The 1995 Veldkamp survey of migrants in the Netherlands found that 43 percent of Turks owned a satellite dish and 52 percent subscribed to cable. An additional 34 percent had a master antenna.[2] That percentage has increased significantly in the intervening years. It takes two dishes to receive the range of channels, but switching between them and from those channels to the cable channels has been made seamless through updated technology. Early on the cost of the dishes was more prohibitive and diffusion was therefore slowed. But as the price dropped, the penetration of dishes in Turkish households increased. Şeref Acer, program director for *Migranten Television*, said that a dish cost about $125 in 1997. If you add a motor to the dish, it might go as high as $300. And of course, if you want to receive all the available channels, two dishes are required.

In this study, only more educated and affluent Turkish families chose not to purchase a dish. But even many educated families owned a dish. Only eight participants said they did not own a dish. And several of those said they would purchase one soon. Those families or individuals without a dish had decided that buying one was not in their best interests. In 1999, satellite penetration estimates were about 60 percent, but judging from the people I interviewed, I believe it may be as high as 80 percent.

My conclusion is also based on responses to another survey conducted for NPS (*Nederlandse Programma Stichting*) in 1998. When respondents (including

Islamic women waving flags at the Milli Görüş rally in Amsterdam.

Muslim women leaving Arena, the Dutch Ajax Soccer stadium.

Ottoman-style band performing at the Milli Görüş rally.

Turkish and Dutch women shopping in Amsterdam street market.

Turkish grocery on Kinkerstraat.

Kinkerstraat pastry shop and grocery store.

A view of Kinkerstraat through the Turkish pastry shop.

Pastry shop owner on Kinkerstraat.

Video shop owner standing behind the flags of Turkey and the Netherlands.

Video and CD shop in Amsterdam called Hasret (Longing).

145 Turks) were asked about television stations they watched (a range of Dutch stations and channels from their home country), 68 percent said they watched Turkish channels almost every day. In another question, respondents were asked if they watched television from their home country, and 89 percent said they did.[3] Of course, channels from home could include TRT-INT carried on cable, but it is more likely that most of the respondents were referring to the channels they receive by satellite. All of the participants in this study did have access to TRT-INT via cable. It was not a prerequisite for selection of participants that the household have a dish.

Though I have no direct knowledge of media use among Turkish migrants in Europe prior to the advent of satellite television, I am told that widespread video viewing was popular. Video rental shop owners, of which few remain today, explain that they once did a booming business in the rental of cassettes of Turkish films, television programs, and music concerts. Now those are no longer popular, as people can watch television without cost after they pay for the dishes.

In the 1980s video rental shops could be found in abundance in Turkey. Many of the films made available in these shops were pirated from the United States and dubbed in Turkish. Turkish films also were pirated. Since that time new laws and enforcement of old laws, together with pressure from the Motion Picture Association of America, have worked to reduce the amount of piracy in Turkey somewhat. The advent of private television also has made video rental less popular among consumers. It is likely that the Turks in Europe followed the same pattern in their media use, and over time pirated products also became less available in European markets.[4]

Because no specific data are available that describe Turkish migrants' use of video before 1990, it is hard to know whether people watched imported videos in place of Dutch media. The participants in this study did report a greater amount of viewing of Dutch media prior to the advent of Turkish television, however. Given the dramatic drop off in radio listening to Radio 5 (the Amsterdam station that carries the daily news program in Turkish) from 52 percent in 1992 to 23 percent in 1995 to 2 percent in 1998, it is likely that a shift from Dutch-based media to Turkish-based media has occurred in the years since satellite-delivered media have been received.

Other Turkish media are available in Amsterdam. Several European editions of Turkish newspapers and magazines are distributed. Those newspapers can be found in central Amsterdam newsstands and in all neighborhoods where Turks live. However, most of the people I talked with often read the paper away from home (at mosques, centers for organizations they belong to, in coffee shops, or at work). Others shared papers with friends and relatives. Four or five people reported reading those papers on the Internet. All major national newspapers have a Web site and provide a daily version of the newspaper there.

Privately owned channels began in Turkey in the summer of 1990 and have been broadcasting to Europe for much of the decade. There have been great increases in the number of both national and municipal channels in that time. Since many of them are delivered by satellite, it is easy to reach the European Turks at the same time. With the exception of TRT-INT, the Turkish public channel, programming is overwhelmingly directed to Turks living in Turkey, however. Analysis of these channels along with TRT-INT was conducted to determine whether the content might be so appealing to Turks living abroad that they maintained or developed greater attachments to Turkey than they had to the Netherlands.

Great variety exists in the content of these channels. With so many channels available in this country of about sixty-five million people and several million living in Europe, there is great competition for audience. Stations are constantly advertising their position in the commercial ratings for audience share. Programming also is related to the philosophy of the stations' owners. Even if insufficient advertising revenues are raised, channels stay on the air to disseminate particular religious or political views. Two of the channels received in Amsterdam (TGRT and Kanal 7) are owned by Islamic interests and claim to broadcast programs that promote Turkish cultural and moral values. Both channels' content includes daily religious programming and import a minimum amount of content, 18 percent for Kanal 7 and 25 percent for TGRT (see table 5.1). Kanal 7 is the more religiously conservative of the two. Some channels also have ties to political parties or points of view, leading to certain biases in reporting. The high cost of producing local programming leads to schedules that include a lot of imports of cheap content (old Hollywood films, cartoons, and soap operas) or the production of cheap domestic shows (game shows, live music, variety entertainment, and talk shows). Little time goes to local productions of drama or of documentaries. When a popular series is produced, as much as twenty-five minutes an hour can be taken up by advertising, while less popular content aired in other than prime-time slots may have only five minutes of advertising in an hour.

The content analysis, which was based on viewing each channel for a different two-hour period on each of seven days in the designated week, was qualitative in nature. Coders, who were members of an international communication class at Middle East Technical University in Ankara, Turkey, were guided by a set of questions regarding programs that might include content that would depict Turkish culture. They also examined daily news programs for content that would show their native country in a positive or a negative light and for news stories about Turkish citizens in Europe.

Table 5.1

Origin of Programs on Privately Owned Television Channels*

Television Channel	Percent Domestic Content	Percent Imported Content
Kanal D	52	48
HBB	76	24
TGRT	75	25
InterStar	69	31
Kanal 7	82	18
Show	60	40
ATV	74	26

*All channels broadcast between twenty and twenty-four hours a day, but several repeat daytime broadcasts in early morning hours to stay on the air.

Though a detailed summary of the analysis would be interesting, it is sufficient here to say that receiving entertainment, news, and sports programs in Turkish is enough to attract and hold the attention of viewers in the Netherlands. Despite the lack of domestically produced entertainment programs, there was certainly enough news and public affairs programming and a sufficient number of soccer matches to say that the European-Turks would have lots of reminders of their homeland. The information about the tumultuous political situation in Turkey during this time period would have been interesting to Turks living in Holland, but did not portray the country in a very positive light. Bickering and charges of immoral and illegal conduct being made from all parties was particularly disconcerting. A couple of the channels also began broadcasting tabloid-style journalistic programs with political and religious topics and scandals. And uncertainty about the economy and political stability of the nation at that time would not likely have encouraged many migrants to return home. Very little news of Turks living in Europe, or indeed of Europeans in Europe, was broadcast during the time. Broadcast news was very focused on the domestic Turkish environment. Of the channels analyzed, a low of four minutes (InterStar) for a seven-day period and a high of 81.5 minutes (ATV) of news was reported from Europe or that included European actors (see table 5.2). The last week of April was the time of the election of Tony Blair in the U.K. and provided many opportunities for reports from Europe. Though TRT-INT was not analyzed for its European news content, it broadcasts an evening half-hour newscast to Europe. Most of the news on the government-owned channel is protocol news and takes the side of the government in power and avoids some controversial news, especially if it is critical of government action. Evening news was broadcast on all channels from 7 to 8 P.M. or from 8 to 9 P.M. News programs are the most popular of all television content, according to a survey of 1,000 people conducted in Ankara. An amazing 99 percent of the respondents reported watching news on a regular basis.[5]

Table 5.2

Amount of European News on Six Channels' Evening Newscast

April 28-May 4, 1997

Channel	Number Of Stories	Total Number of Minutes
TGRT	15	33.0
InterStar*	3	4.0
Show	7	21.0
ATV	17	81.5
HBB	28	20.0
Kanal D	23	67.0

*InterStar is now referred to as Star.

TRT-INT is different from the other privately owned channels received in Europe. Because public funds are used to finance the public channel, it can afford to produce more of its own content. Broadcasting 168 hours a week since 1990, the channel was set up to reach the Turkish population in Europe with cultural, educational, and public affairs information. More than 95 percent of TRT-INT's programming is domestically produced and about 60 percent of all programs include content directly related to Turkey. One-fourth of all the programming is domestic music. In the Netherlands, TRT-INT is carried on the cable received by about 90 percent of the households.

Though the content is created for the audience living abroad, most of the participants in this study said it was not relevant to their lives and carried an incorrect presumption about the nature of the Turkish audience in Europe. An interview with the program director for the station, Mustafa Kuzum, revealed that the lack of audience research may be at fault for the disconnect between audience and program content. Though the channel once had a contract with a German market research company to determine audience interests, the research was only conducted once. Kuzum said he felt he was able to determine what the audience needs were, and that the letters received from audience members indicated great satisfaction with the programs the channel produces. According to Kuzum, the goal of TRT-INT is to reach Turkish citizens. "We don't want them to forget Turkey or Turkish culture. We don't promote assimilation [into any European country's culture], but integration is our goal. And for those who want to return to Turkey, we try to make it easier."[6]

The content of the programs is not particularly appealing because it is not considered up to date in its approach. A content analysis of two weeks' programs was conducted in 1997—from March 24 to 30 and from May 5 to 11 by one of the students in the International Communications class at Middle East Technical University, Fareea Ma. Table 5.3 summarizes her findings.

Table 5.3

Program Content of TRT-INT
(Weeks of March 24-30 and May 5-11, 1997)

Type of Program	Percentage of Total Time	Hours per Week
Domestic Music	24.60	41.00
Foreign Music	.55	1.00
Informational Programs	14.30	24.08
News	10.02	17.00
Domestic Drama/Sitcoms	9.42	16.00
Foreign Drama/Sitcoms	.55	.50
Current Affairs	7.69	13.00
Game/Variety	7.64	13.00
Tourism Programs	4.31	7.00
Domestic Films	3.57	6.00
Foreign Films	2.48	4.00
Domestic Children's Entertainment	.70	1.00
Domestic Children's Educational Programs	2.33	4.00
Domestic Documentaries	2.73	4.00
Foreign Documentaries	.30	.50
Sports	2.53	4.00
Cultural Awareness	2.08	4.00
Religious Programs	.40	.50
Women's Educational Programs	.20	.50
TOTAL	**100.00**	**168 hours**

(figures are rounded)

While an examination of the content reveals a heavy emphasis on domestic content and a wide variety of types of programs, viewers complain about the films being too old, too many repeats of previously produced programs, and a lack of interesting content. News tends to carry a pro-government slant and much protocol news is included, so many viewers complain about the bias and an inability to trust what they hear. However, it is interesting that those people who said they preferred news on TRT-INT to that of the private channels said it was because of the lack of bias—that you could trust the station to deliver the truth. The people who complained about the government-owned channels also report that the station's portrayals of life in Europe are incorrect, and it is clear that the producers of programs don't have a very good grasp on what life is like in Europe. On the other hand, some parents and children told me that they improved their Turkish by watching TRT-INT. Since many of the migrants had little education and may have come from rural areas where a particular Turkish dialect was spoken, they found it useful to be exposed to educated Turkish on a regular basis. Drama and comedy series focus on neighborhood life in Turkey, which may be remote and unfamiliar to those now living in Dutch neighborhoods. Second-generation migrants may find even less common ground in these programs.

ATV News

The 1997 content analysis of the private channels revealed no specific content aimed at the European-based audience. Since that time, however, ATV has been producing a nearly nightly segment of the news that is designed primarily for the Turks living in Germany, but has some interest to all of the Turks in Europe. I analyzed a week of those programs in the summer of 1999. That week began on July 16 and ran to July 23. Each of the news programs lasts about fifteen minutes. It is often difficult to tell when it will be on, since it follows the main news program that begins at 8 P.M., and the length of that program can vary. On Thursdays the station also airs a longer program—about an hour, but the length can also vary—called *7 Gün Avrupada* (Seven Days in Europe). The program has a magazine format and tells stories and hosts discussions of issues related to the Turks in Europe. However, the focus of the programs I viewed was all German. That does not mean the migrants in other European countries don't encounter the same problems. But it does mean that many of the migrants I talked with noticed that both the news program and the magazine program did not tell them information that was directly relevant to their circumstances.

A typical program will contain five news items, usually about events, conferences, or research that took place in Europe. Not all of these will have direct relevance to migrants, but most of them will have some relation to their interests. For example, an update on the problem of mad cow disease and other contaminated food in Europe includes a warning about cooking meat long enough before eating it. A discussion of research about the effects of the sun is carried at the time when families are planning for their summer vacation in Turkey. An example of a directly related item would be the news of a German sociologist's research that finds that retired foreign workers in Germany get about half the amount that retired German workers get. Another example was an item about the change in the tax laws in Germany that results in benefit for workers if they know what the new law says.

Two other types of news are included in this newscast. The first is a roundup of news from the United States. These are very brief—usually less than thirty seconds—and they often announce research results in at least one of the items. Some of the research is useful to the viewers but other items are clearly fillers. For example, one research result related to the increase in the number of young girls in the United States who have had silicone breast implants. Many of these items relate to the economy—inflation figures, e-business increases. Others are political news that might be interesting to those living in Turkey or the Middle East. Some are entertainment news—a feature on the price of scalper tickets to the Ricky Martin concert in New York. A second set of roundup stories is called the *Haber Turu* (News Tour) which provides some interesting international news—Bastille Day celebrations in France, bombs being set in Australia, and Japan's unemployment rate. The items from the *Haber Turu* and the U.S. news and about half the content of the other news is not all that useful to the Turks who live in Europe (Mick Jagger's divorce, Elton John's heart operation, the marriage of a Greek princess). The news show seems to be designed more as a vehicle for advertising directed to European viewers than for any serious interest in the audience's need for information.

There were exceptions to that conclusion, however. In at least three news items during the week, information that could be construed as being provided as a public service were included. The first example of this kind of news was one based on interviews conducted at the Turkish borders of Kapıkule and İpsala. Because of the war in Yugoslavia, the people coming via that route into Romania, then entering Turkey through Bulgaria have not found it easy to go that way. Those migrants (the reporter uses that term) who enter through that route report having to pay bribes along the way in excess of 1,200 deutsche marks. He shows us the border checkpoint and announces that usually this entry would be crammed with cars waiting to clear customs and passport control, but on that day there is no line. Then the reporter interviews people in İpsala. If vacationers take this route, they enter Turkey through Greece and Italy. Most of the travelers interviewed at that entrance said it was safe and they had no problems. Two of them reported thefts of wallets and handbags. Maps of the alternate routes were shown. The news feature should have provided good information to those planning their trip to Turkey.

The second important news item related to an incident that occurred in Germany where two women broke down the door of an apartment. They sought entry to rob the residents. Inside were four children, left alone while their parents went out. Acting together, they were able to alert people on the street to their situation, and the thieves fled the scene. The report used the opportunity to try to teach people not to leave their children home alone, and to educate them about what to do should such a situation ever occur.

The third item was a story about a man who has lived in Germany for twenty-six years and cannot return because he didn't make his last payment on his military service debt and therefore cannot return to Turkey or have his Turkish passport renewed. Turkey has a policy of reducing mandatory military service for its male citizens who live abroad and cannot return for the complete time. It can be reduced to as little as one month if the individual pays a sum of money to the Turkish government in place of serving the entire time. This story served as a warning to all of the young men living abroad who wish to retain their rights of citizenship of the law regarding military service.

Although the news content of these few stories would be both relevant and useful to Turks who live in Europe, the main purpose of the newscast seemed to be a commercial one. Any of the general news items, the News Tour, or the U.S. news could be included in international news clips for anyone. Very little attempt was made at selecting news to be targeted to this particular audience. And when it was, it often carried the message that Turkey was a good place to be, and Europe was not so good.

A look at the advertising content might support the argument that despite messages to the contrary, the greatest concern was to deliver consumers to advertisers. Most of the ads are for banks or businesses that have branches in European cities (Jetpa, Etibank, Demirbank, *Sabah*, and ATV were all owned by Dinc Bilgin at the time. Many ads for *Sabah*, a Turkish daily newspaper with a European edition, were carried before, during, and after this newscast.

The advertising messages promote the idea of longing (*hasret*) for the home country, saying to the viewer, "If you value your ties to home, you will use our bank (or other company)." The ad for Etibank is a particularly good example of this ploy. It features a man sitting in his living room in what we presume is a European location. He is looking at a photograph album and drinking tea from a glass in the Turkish style. A voice-over (presumably that of the man looking at the album) tells us that there are many ways he is tied to Turkey. There is the tie of friendship, the warmth of the people and family. Then he tells us that the pictures we are looking at are those of his mother, father, nieces and nephews, and a family he met at the beach on last year's vacation. Then he wipes a tear from his eye. Then he says that he also has a little investment in Turkey—a winter home in Istanbul and a summer home on the beach. Of course the bank helps him keep up all these ties he has to the homeland.

A second ad for Yaşar Bank carries the same message. This time a man of about sixty to sixty-five is waiting in the Istanbul Airport. Soon a plane's arrival is announced. The plane comes from Frankfurt. Then he goes to the gate to meet his son, daughter-in-law, and grandson. They are, of course, overjoyed to see him. The next scene is of the son driving home. His father tells him that his mother has been cooking his favorite foods and getting ready for this visit for a week. Then the son says he has to stop at the bank, where he has had money transferred from Europe ahead of his visit. The next scene is in the bank where the son gets the money and hands over a bankbook to his father. We are led to believe that the son has established an account for his parents to help take care of them. Again, the message is one of the happy return to the home country and how the bank helps make the family secure, despite the absence of the son.

The voice-over tells us, “We don’t leave you alone in Germany.” These ads, and many of the news stories, tell us that though they understand that people have to live in Europe for a number of reasons, those Turks would rather be in Turkey. And if they can’t be in Turkey, they do what they can to visit regularly, invest in the country, and make contact with their families who live there.

ATV’s magazine program has the same underlying theme. The assumption of many of the news items in the July 15th program (and in others I watched but did not analyze in detail) was that European governments, and specifically the German government, were trying to exploit the Turks who lived in their midst. The government didn’t keep its promises to its Turkish residents, discriminated against them in a variety of ways, and left them poor and helpless when they were most vulnerable. The program created this impression by failing to provide any balance to the news features. They usually only interviewed the individual or family who was negatively impacted by the event or policy, and did not seek to get a response from any German official or other individual responsible for the situation. The July 15, 1999 program contained the following stories:

1. The first feature is called *Outside the Border*, or *Sınır Dışı*. It is a story about immigration and marriages of convenience to avoid deportation. It focuses on a Turkish woman, her German husband (who is not interviewed), and their four-year-old son. The woman claims that the government is accusing her of marrying this much older man so she could stay in the country legally, and not because she really loved him. We only hear her perspective on the story. An attempt to gain sympathy for her case is heightened because we hear that the son has a serious illness for which he must get constant medical care.

2. The second story is about a widow in Munich who is being told to sell her house in order to get complete welfare and retirement benefits. She said she has lived in Germany for thirty-four years and her husband worked for thirty years. She couldn’t get by on her husband’s pension, so applied for additional aid. The government gave her an additional supplement for one year. Later she was told to return the money and sell her apartment. She had three grown children, but one of them is sick and cannot work. The story doesn’t provide complete details concerning the law, and no official from social services is interviewed. The story leaves viewers up in the air and feeling the government has been exploiting this poor old woman.

3. The third story surrounds the citizenship application of a family with several children. All of them are given German citizenship except one son, who was attending school in Turkey. The father tells us that they brought the child back and reenrolled him in his German school, but the government told them they would have to reapply after some waiting time. The father said, "They are trying to separate families. He was born and raised here and we are all Germans now." Again, no official is interviewed to provide the German perspective on this case.

4. The next story, *İzin Yolu* (Vacation, or literally "leave time," Road) repeats the story about vacationers choosing between the two ways to return to Turkey from Europe and the problems that have ensued on both roads. Additional interviews are included in this version of the story. All of the returnees are asked about their reasons for returning. All of them speak of getting back to Turkey as quickly as possible when leave time comes. The word *hasret,* or longing, is used often. One man tells of his feelings for Turkey in poetic form. The gist of his message is that this is his home, his life. This is a special place. Another person says that the pain of being away from his homeland is unbearable.

These stories are followed by a series of clips that last no more than fifteen to twenty seconds each featuring a variety of parties and celebrations in various German cities. At all of these there is Turkish music and food, and people are dancing. These short items are followed by a series of ads. Most of them have been previously aired. Advertising for *Sabah* is repeated several times.

The final part of the program is a discussion of a particular court case that features a young couple who live in Germany. It is presented in a panel discussion with three members of *Sabah*'s news staff. One of the men, Fatih Güllapoğlu, also has a column in *Sabah* by the same name as the program, *Seven Days in Europe*. The case is introduced by one of the men who asks the young woman if such a thing could ever have happened to anyone who came from any other European country but Turkey. She says that it could not have, and that she and her husband were singled out for this treatment by the Germans because they were Turkish. The story told by the young couple has to do with benefits they did not receive from the German government, benefits that could be received by all other EU residents living in Germany. The young man came to Germany as a student. He was only permitted to work sixteen hours a week in that capacity. His wife had a child while they lived there, and they were given a financial supplement for this child. They were told they were not entitled to a supplement for the mother—one received by all other mothers living in Germany. After a year, they were cut off from the child's supplement. The wife took the case to court, based on an agreement between the German and Turkish governments regarding mutual benefits given to citizens living in either country (said to have been signed in 1993). Eventually the case went to the EU court and the couple won the right to receive these benefits. The rest of the program focused on discrimination against Turkey by the Germans, the relevance of this case for Turkey in the EU, and the need to tell other Turks living in Germany of their rights under the law. Many disparaging remarks were also made about Turkish officials, who expressed little interest in the case and expressed no thanks to the couple for pressing it. They also talked long distance with a legal expert from Ankara about the significance of the matter.

This story certainly had direct relevance for the Turks who live in Europe and provided important information. But it also contained a lot of inflammatory remarks regarding the EU and Germany and Turkish officials that were unnecessary and did not add any new information to the story. Instead, these remarks only added to the message that Turks in Europe were getting a bad deal and this shouldn't have to happen to them.

It is important to say here that no matter how little ATV's news and magazine program created for the Turkish audience in Europe is doing to speak to the needs of that audience, no other private television channel is making any effort at all. It is likely that ATV has very few reporters assigned to producing the newscast and the weekly magazine program, so it is understandable that these reports do not contain the balance in reporting they should. However, to simply reinforce the feeling that Turkish migrants are Turks first and foremost, and that they are constantly having to fight discrimination in the European environment, is probably not the best message to send. This may be happening because ATV officials have little understanding of the migrants in their role as citizens or permanent residents of Holland, Germany, France, or Belgium. Instead, they view the migrants much like many Europeans do, as Turks who have taken up temporary residence in a foreign land and are not being treated fairly. And if the station continues to broadcast content like this, it encourages more alienation from the local cultures where the migrants live, rather than assisting them to find ways to fit into their adopted homelands. On the other hand, it is good to help find solutions to the incidents of discrimination wherever they exist.

Media Effects

It is now generally accepted that a powerful media effects model is largely inappropriate for understanding the impact media might have on individuals in society. Instead, communication scholars tend to accept a more limited effects model, one that says that the media can influence attitudes and behaviors under certain conditions and with certain kinds of people and at certain times. Denis McQuail has reviewed the range of media effects studies over the years. In general, he argues that media can induce several types of change. Those include intended, unintended, and minor change. The media can also facilitate change (intended or not), reinforce what exists (no change), or prevent change. McQuail also formed a typology of the theory and research in the effects literature. That typology places the studies on two axes—planned effects versus unplanned effects on the vertical axis and short-term versus long-term effects on the horizontal axis.[7]

Some of the programs aired on TRT-INT may have some broad-based plan for effect (i.e., have intended change) on the audience in Europe, but without any organized feedback on how well it is working, it is difficult to say that the producers are reaching their goal to bring Turkish culture and educate Turkish viewers in particular ways. And given that the only people in this study who reported much exposure to this channel are those who didn't own a satellite dish (and therefore couldn't receive any of the private channels from Turkey), it is likely that TRT-INT programs have very little impact on the audience.

With the exception of ATV's evening news magazine program, the content for the private channels is made for Turks in Turkey, not Turks in Europe. So there is no "intended" effect on the Turkish population in Amsterdam or any other European city.

I would argue that of the types of change McQuail describes, the Turkish television channels (and to a lesser extent the print media from Turkey) may be facilitating change, reinforcing change, and possibly preventing change. I will later explain how those conflicting results can be taking place with the people in this study. With reference to specific effects, I suggest that for those people who make regular use of the Turkish media, the television program and newspaper contents operate to define reality and construct meaning for the audience. McQuail defines that process as "similar to social control, but different in having more to do with broad structures of cognitions and frames of interpretation than with behavior. This [very extensive] kind of effect is also different in requiring the more or less active participation of the receivers in the process of constructing their own meaning."[8] I believe that happens when viewers tune out most or all of Dutch television and print media and only attend to messages on Turkish television or in the Turkish press. When audiences make that choice, they are deciding to define reality and construct meaning from messages that originate in the Turkish culture and not in the Dutch culture. And if we accept that Herbert Gans's enduring values, described in chapter 3, are carried in televised and print messages of a particular culture, then the audience is exposed to those values exclusively.

A second type of effect that may have taken place is that of cultural change. McQuail defines this as "shifts in the overall pattern of values, behaviors and symbolic forms characterizing a sector of society [such as youth], a whole society or a set of societies. . . . The possible strengthening or weakening of cultural identity may also be an example of effect."[9]

In this study, cultural identity with the home culture (Turkish) strengthens as the audience tunes out Dutch media messages, and cultural identity with the Dutch culture weakens. Conversely, if audience members choose to select most messages from Dutch media, the cultural identity with the Dutch culture strengthens and that with the Turkish culture weakens.

According to McQuail's typology, both the reality defining and cultural change types of effects fall in the quadrant where long-term change and unplanned effects intersect. From his review of the research, McQuail concludes that it is difficult, perhaps impossible, to prove that media have been a direct or indirect cause of cultural change, defined reality, or constructed social meaning. He makes that argument because of the interactive and open-ended nature of the process. I agree with that position, but believe that evidence from this research will help support the theory that says that media can influence cultural change and construct social meaning and define reality—especially when combined with other factors. I would also agree with McQuail and others that any effects of watching great amounts of television from Turkey and reading of the Turkish press, particularly to the exclusion of consuming any Dutch media, would be both long term and unplanned. I will return to this theoretical frame after describing the media consumption process of the study participants.

Media Imperialism: A Type of Cultural Change

Media imperialism can be understood as cultural change that comes about as a result of consuming a lot of media content produced in the West. In the view of scholars who have espoused this process, the consumption of large amounts of imported media content causes people to change attitudes and behavior, and the society importing this content becomes culturally and economically dominated. The so-called victims of this process begin to adopt the values and behavior of the producers of the content. A powerful media effects model is assumed in the writing on this subject.

Though the economic aspects of media imperialism have been well documented,[10] cultural domination is more difficult to prove. John Tomlinson, who wrote an excellent theoretical explication of cultural imperialism, said:

> Because of the constant tendency to revert to an economic account, where cultural "effects" of media imperialism are posited, they are invariably problematic. Either they are simply assumed and allowed to function in the discourse as a self-evident concomitant of the sheer presence of alien cultural goods, or else they are inferred using fairly crude interpretative assumptions.[11]

The discussion of media imperialism is important to this study because it confounds the issue of media content selection by the Turkish migrants. If in fact what they are watching on their televisions via satellite from Turkey is mostly content that has been imported from the United States and then dubbed in Turkish, we have to ask whether this is a Turkish product or a U.S. product. The same question with regard to Dutch content on Dutch channels must also be asked. Many of the same soap operas, game shows, and talk shows appear on the Dutch and the Turkish channels. However, the policy of the Dutch channels is to subtitle programs that originate in English rather than dub them. Many Dutch people say this practice helps viewers improve their English language skills. Up to this point we have been concerned with the migrants' proficiency in Dutch, not in English. But many of the second and third generation of migrants also will be fluent in English since they all study it in school. For example, in one of the interviews I conducted with a second-generation Turk who was born and raised in the Netherlands, we spoke English. His Turkish was not good enough to respond to my questions, and I do not speak Dutch.

Though I originally thought this research could contribute to our understanding of how audiences approach foreign content on their television screens, it turns out that Tomlinson is right about those crude assumptions. If I conclude that Turkish people in Amsterdam prefer Turkish television over Dutch television, that may say nothing about a rejection of the Dutch media as a force for imperialism, since the people may be selecting American programs in their native language instead of Dutch programs—or instead of some of the same American programs aired on Dutch television. It might tell us something about the overall cultural orientation of this audience, however. Since the content analysis indicates that the majority of the content on Turkish channels is domestic, it is likely that many of the programs watched will be of Turkish origin. Later in this chapter when I discuss viewing choices of the participants, the notion of media imperialism will be reintroduced. Here, it is important to point out that when content is chosen based at least partially on the language of delivery, another layer of complexity is added to our understanding of media effects.

Satellite Television Content and Opportunities for Diversity

Private television channels from Turkey have been only received in Europe since 1990, when they also began broadcasting to Turkey. Up to that time the Turkish Radio and Television Corporation held a monopoly for broadcasting within Turkey. That monopoly was tested when one company, InterStar, set up shop in Europe, rented space on an Eutelsat transponder and began broadcasting to the Republic of Turkey. Several other companies followed with their own channels. The Turkish government claimed that this broadcasting was illegal, while the companies that had been founded in various spots in Europe argued that they were not Turkish companies, and that if Turks could receive them in Turkey, it did not constitute an illegal act. It took four years for private radio and television broadcasting in Turkey to become legal. Private domestic radio and television operations sprung up all over Turkey, emboldened by the acts of the companies operating from outside the country in the years following the first station, Magic Box. The broadcasting scene became chaotic, as no station was operating on a frequency authorized by the government, and great numbers of stations were competing with one another. In a measure to take control of the situation, Parliament declared all the stations illegal in April 1993. Aksoy and Robins say that a variety of reasons were given for the government action. Included in those reasons was the expression of concern about the popularity of religious channels, the massive violation of copyright by music radio stations, and then prime minister Süleyman Demirel's statement that the closure was necessary to create a climate of order so that broadcasting regulation could be introduced.[12] The government also was eager to ensure that the large amount of revenue earned from advertising was taxed.[13] Legalization, and therefore regulation, of private radio and television broadcasting finally occurred with a new broadcasting law in April 1994.

As Aksoy and Robins describe it, the introduction of private broadcasting channels opened up the opportunity for a public shift from official culture to real culture. Prior to the introduction of private broadcasting, the Turkish Radio and Television Corporation, through geographic, political, and cultural centralization, was able to control all public messages that reached the people.

> The explicit intention was to establish a cultural industry that would work to create a Turkish cultural identity in conformity with the elite's modern and now "official" image. TRT's output was directed to an ideal, and idealized people who were unified in their shared citizenship and national attachment. The broadcasting monopoly assumed a highly censorious attitude—which gave rise to practices of exclusion and open censorship—towards whatever it regarded as deviant in cultural tone or attitude. This stance has amounted to a purification of the cultural space: TRT has sought to rid the cultural environment of what it perceived as its peripheral, rural, sentimental, unruly, or disorderly elements. The "real" Turkey, with all the complexities and diversity of its civil society and cultural identities, has been denied, or more correctly, disavowed, in the name of the "official" cultural ideal.[14]

The ideal espoused by TRT was one derived from Kemalism, an ideology based on the philosophy of Mustafa Kemal Ataturk, father of the Turkish Republic. Ataturk created the republic in 1923, socially, politically, militarily, to conform to his own image of a modern Western nation. He advocated a secular government, separated from religious influence, among many radical changes that included banning the fez and the veil, and changing the alphabet from Arabic to Latin. Over the years, what constitutes Kemalism has become a matter of major discussion. And many groups have come to challenge the right of political leaders to use Kemalism as a rationale for a whole range of decisions. Nicole Pope and Hugh Pope, authors of a well-documented history of modern Turkey, quote newspaper editor Şahin Alpay for his definition of a 1990s Kemalist. "He is above all secular, he wants to banish religion, he believes in progress, he worships reason. But he cannot accept rational criticism."[15] Alpay's views are likely based on several actions of the Turkish government and the military over the years related to censorship, military coups, and repressive laws.

To this day, journalists and ordinary citizens complain of laws that restrict free speech, but the government defends its position out of a concern for national security.

The challenge to Kemalism also came from the private stations. That challenge took place on several fronts. It was religious, in that a number of radio and television stations were owned or backed by Islamic groups. These stations opposed the perceived immorality of the Western programming that dominated the air waves. Two of these stations, Kanal 7 and TGRT, are received on most satellite dishes in Europe. The goal of Kanal 7, with main holdings by Yimpaş—a major Islamic business in Turkey—is to present Turkish culture and information about Islam. It opens its broadcasting day with a reading from the Koran, expresses its opposition to Western culture, and contains many programs about Islamic traditions and rules. Music programs are based on Turkish folk or classical forms. TGRT, owned by İhlas holding and affiliated with *Türkiye*, a daily newspaper with pro-Islamic content, follows a similar philosophy to Kanal 7. It airs old Turkish films (about one-fourth of the total content), religious programs, news and public affairs, etc. TGRT includes no lovemaking scenes and avoids other forms of perceived Western immorality. *Samanyolu*, another channel controlled by the Fethullah Gülen supporters, can be received in Europe, but was not mentioned by the participants in this study. That may have to do with the positioning of satellite dishes.

The challenge to Kemalism also has been political. The political arena was also opened by private channels. Since TRT was government owned, it frequently limited messages to those supporting the government's perspective, and opposing political views were not allowed—particularly if they deviated from acceptable positions. Ayşe Öncü writes of the ways in which politics was addressed in this new environment, and particularly of how politicians crossed what would have been a hard-and-fast barrier in the TRT era, where they became television personalities. "For the first time, the world of politics began to intermingle with the world of commodities and entertainment, blurring the boundaries bracketing off the ceremonial-public realm."[16]

Aksoy and Robins talk of another example of peripheral culture penetrating the center with private broadcasting. Music, particularly Arabesk music, always popular among the urban poor, became a legitimate form on radio and television. They define Arabesk as a "synthesis of Turkish classical music, rural folk genres, western pop, and belly-dancing music, with strong 'oriental' associations, and heavily laden with emotion and sentiment."[17] TRT had banned Arabesk, and because the private stations were competing for audiences, all audiences were targeted with programs that would attract and hold their interest. No longer was a monopoly allowed to dictate what was an acceptable cultural form.

Once private broadcasting began to compete with TRT in Turkey, it was also appealing to the audiences in Europe, particularly the first generation. These were Turkish citizens who left Turkey because they constituted the economic and geographic periphery, the very audience now privileged by the new channels. Never particularly interested in high culture, the guest workers were eager to obtain dishes to receive the range of programs that spoke to their taste and values. And now it was possible to pick and choose among the offerings to locate specific programs of interest and channels that adopted philosophical positions consistent with their own belief systems.

Şeref Acer, program director of *Migranten Television* in Amsterdam, understands the appeal of the new programs. He believes that the Turks in Europe were never very interested in public affairs programs, and the new channels that bring game shows, reality-based magazine shows, and variety shows are enjoyable. "But when they watch these programs and the news and political programs from Turkey, they get disattached from Holland."

Acer believes this means that integration into Dutch society will take much longer as a consequence. In June 1999 he said in reference to satellite viewing that "what is different is that this is no longer a novelty, but just part of life in the community now. A big part of their lives. They just don't associate with the Dutch life and culture anymore. And for people to say, 'I'm Dutch,' will take a very long time."

Of course, not everyone is so worried about the effect that viewing these channels is having on the people. Some see this as more liberating. The audience is mostly made up of people with limited resources to explore entertainment options. And Amsterdam is an expensive city. So for the cost of a couple dishes attached to the balcony, the whole family can receive a range of programs that entertains and informs, presented in a familiar cultural context, and delivered in a language that may be much easier to understand than the local alternatives.

Diversity in this new set of television alternatives needs to be understood in the Turkish media context. First of all, Turkish media ownership is characterized by intense concentration by a limited number of players. And most all of the owners are also involved in banking. Four television channels—ATV, Kanal D, Show, and InterStar (or Star)—account for 80 percent of the advertising money spent in television.[18]

Kemal Balci wrote in a 1998 account of media ownership that none of the television channels are profitable. "The TV channels, whose sole source of income is advertisement, can continue their costly broadcasts only with the open support of the holding companies they are affiliated with. Those who have a TV channel, newspaper or magazine, gain an edge in the business world because they can have a say in the finance sector too."[19] Television station owners usually own several newspapers as well. Despite the large number of dailies circulating in Turkey, not one of them has a circulation as high as one million (though *Hürriyet* claims to have 1.7 million) in Turkey, where the population is about sixty-five million.

Table 5.4
Turkish Media Owners and Their Other Financial Holdings[20]
As of November 1998

Media Owner	Television Holdings	Newspaper Holdings	Other Business (partial listing)
Doğan Group (Aydin Doğan)	Kanal D CNN-Turk (part owner)	*Hürriyet* *Milliyet* (64%) *Milliyet* News Agency (20%) Other printing and publishing interests	Dışbank Alternatif Bank 3 radio stations Doğan Media International (42%)—in Germany Marketing Company Insurance Company Auto Parts Company Automotive Company (and several others)
Erol Aksoy	Show TV	*Hürriyet* (20%)	İktisat Bank Avrupa-Amerika Holding
Uzan family	InterStar TV Kral TV	Star	
Dinc Bilgin[21]	ATV	*Sabah*	Etibank partner
Enver Ören	TGRT TV	*Türkiye*	İmar Bank Ada Bank Turkcell (part owner) İhlas Holding Company
Cavit Çağlar	NTV Olay TV		Etibank partner Nergis Holding
Recai Kutan (Chairman of Virtue Party) Yimpaş Holding	Kanal 7 shareholder (Major shareholder of Kanal 7)	*Milli Gazete* (Said to be owned by Virtue Party)	Yimpaş Holding
Gülen Collective	Samanyolu TV	*Zaman*	Asya Finans "activity"
Bilge Has family	HBB		Former owner of Istanbul Bank
Korkmaz Yiğit	Kanal 6 Kanal E	Former owner of *Milliyet* and *Yeniyuzyil*	Bought Türkbank but government suspended sale

As table 5.4 shows, ownership of television and newspaper outlets also may relate to political interests of the owners. Though profits may be of concern to those owners, the size of the audience may have more political than financial interest. However, ratings still drive the selection of programs. Intense ratings wars have led to the production of several lottery-type programs where valuable gifts are given away. Aslaneli reported in February 1999 that Türk Telekom officials warned stations that the nearly ten million calls that were made to stations in an attempt to win the prizes were crippling the national telephone system. Prizes included household appliances, large sums of money, and even apartments.[22]

The ratings wars have also allowed for extremes in program content. Aslaneli describes one program on ATV that has been considered particularly outrageous.

> During a recent program that was broadcast live, he [Güner Ümit] fell just short of making love to a television hostess. Leaning heavily on the woman and lying on her for an unnaturally long period of time, Ümit later explained that this was "all for ratings." The next day, Ümit appeared on television dressed as a transsexual, claiming to have a special message for the Turkish people. This was the last straw. The first reaction came from the transsexuals. They said that they did not deserve this contempt, that Ümit was distorting the truth and that they would file a case against him. Every evening, eight people have to suffer through Ümit's show. But it is also reported, sadly enough, that the eight so-called artists who appear in each program, four on each team, are even willing to pay bribes to appear on this program.[23]

Ratings also have been known to drive the news magazine-type shows, where so-called investigative reporting has led to the invasion of people's privacy and other acts of dubious ethical nature.

Curiously, the over-the-top behavior of the private broadcasters may have returned viewers to TRT programs. TRT's ratings had tripled in the three-month period at the end of 1998 and beginning of 1999.[24]

Role of Television in Home Life

The interviews for this study were conducted in the homes of the participants. The Turks in Amsterdam tend to live near other Turks, but those neighborhoods are in several parts of the city—in the east, the west, and the north. Participants in this study lived in all those neighborhoods. You can usually tell you are in a neighborhood where many Turks live by the display of satellite dishes on the balconies. Serap, a young woman who recently moved to Amsterdam because she married a second-generation Turk there, characterizes the Turkish neighborhoods as one where antennas are "displayed like flowers on the balconies." In reaching the homes of participants, sometimes I rode on a tram or a bus for forty-five minutes or more. But more often, I could reach the homes from the city center by tram in about twenty minutes. All of the participants lived in apartments. Depending on the residents' economic circumstances, the apartments were of varying quality and size. Since housing in the Netherlands is so scarce, the government intervenes in all parts of the housing industry, including rental price and selection of the individuals who rent the space.[25] So the size of the family and its economic circumstances have some bearing on its quality, but it often was hard to determine how well-off a family might be by observation of the living space. Almost all of the participants rented their homes, though a few did own property. Several of the participants also owned property in Turkey—usually summer homes by the seaside, or homes in the villages of their birth, where they would spend their summer holidays of five to six weeks.

More often than not, the homes were decorated in traditional Turkish style, and contained vases of plastic flowers, Turkish rugs or kilims on the floor, a rack by the door where shoes were placed when removed at the entrance, lace doilies on the tops of tables, and Turkish mementos decorating walls and furniture. Middle-class homes were more modern in style but still had Turkish features, particularly carpets. Homes where the residents were more religious contained framed quotations from the Koran on the walls. Most all of the apartments had only one living-dining room area and the television set was prominently placed with furniture arranged to obtain a good view.

It was clear that television, and specifically television from Turkey, was central to the lives of the participants in this study. I say that because in all but about ten of the homes I visited, the television was on and was tuned to a Turkish station when I entered. Some of the residents kept the television on during the interview, making it difficult to hear responses and to record them on tape. Occasionally, the conversation would drift toward something that was happening on the screen—a bit of news or discussion. At other times, participants became distracted by the television programs.

It was apparent to me from the beginning of this study that no matter what any person said about the importance of receiving television programs from Turkey, the fact that the television was on and those programs were being viewed indicated the residents of those households considered it very important. Even if the television served as no more than background noise, it was on and could attract a viewer who happened to be passing by or who was working in the next room. If the act of viewing television can be considered a media effect, then in my view, Turkish satellite television has a great effect on the Turks who live in Amsterdam.

In a 1998 migrant media use study in the Netherlands, Turks reported watching more television and video than any other minority group. In a typical week, they said they watched television an average of 32.1 hours. That was up from the reported figure from a similar study in 1992, where Turks said they watched about 22.7 hours of television and 3.2 hours of video per week. In the same survey, respondents were asked whether they watched particular channels. One of the options was "channels from the motherland." Though only 18 percent of the Turks reported watching any of the Dutch channels (that figure applied only to SBS6 and Veronica, two private channels), 68 percent of the Turks said they watched television from Turkey.[26]

In this study the participants reported watching Dutch television an average of one to two hours a day. The median was between less than one hour and one to two hours a day. They watched much more television from Turkey. The mean number of hours of reported viewing was between three and four hours, while the median was between three to four hours and five to six hours. Only one family said they watched no television from Turkey, while 5 percent of the participants said they watched more than eight hours a day, and 15 percent reported watching more than seven hours a day. But let's examine television viewing in this study in a more qualitative way.

What Television from Home Means to Migrants

From observing the many families in this study, I could conclude that being able to tune into programs from the home country changed many lives. Probably the group that was most affected consisted of women in their forties, fifties, or early sixties (nobody in the study was older than that) who had lived in Holland for fifteen to thirty years, and who had never been able to learn Dutch. That was about a third of the women I talked with. The women in this group who were illiterate especially depended on Turkish television to fill their days. Although they had family and friends to talk with, they told me they turned on the television in the morning and left it on all day. Some women talked of the television functioning as a companion, a companion that speaks their language in a foreign land.

Tülin, who is educated and speaks Dutch but cannot read it, said the Turkish channels "help our lives a little. They reduce the longing we have to go back there." Though she has an active life, heading a women's group at the mosque, and taking correspondence courses from a university in Turkey, Tülin would prefer to live in Turkey. She feels a moral separation from the Dutch, one that leads her to oppose integration. She wants to live in a separate space and respect the Dutch ways of doing things, but not mix with them. So she thinks Turkish television fills the void that is left because her geographic surroundings are not what she would prefer.

Ömer agrees with Tülin, though he isn't interested in returning to Turkey. He also is educated, with a university degree, and is a professional musician. Though he has learned very little Dutch, he gets by on his English skills. He sees Turkish television as a wonderful thing for the Turks who live in Europe.

> It improved their lives one thousand percent. These were people who lived in the closed box. Their world was their home and the mosque, and they had nothing else. The children who were born and raised here had no knowledge of their native culture and their parents had forgotten their culture. Through television they learned or relearned their own language and culture.

Niyazi and Raziye didn't even know how much it might mean to them when their children bought them a dish four years ago. They claim it hasn't changed their lives, but Raziye says she wouldn't know what to do without it now. They've lived in Amsterdam for thirty years, and so have had lots of time to become adjusted. They learned enough Dutch to get along, and they raised four children in the Netherlands. Now retired, Niyazi learned his Dutch while working in the post office, and though he says he is not 100 percent adjusted to life here, he admits to a 50 percent adjustment. He looks upon the recent arrivals from Turkey as ones who are unwilling to adapt at all. He views it as the visitors' obligation to a country to adapt. And yet, since they have had the satellite dish, they both admit to speaking less Dutch, spending time only with family and close Turkish friends, and not watching Dutch television anymore. They have pulled back to a life where the Turkish media, language, and culture predominate.

Perhaps it is understandable for people who are of retirement age to slip into old habits and the comfort of their home culture, but it also happens with younger people. Nazlı, a thirty-four-year-old woman with a young baby, came to Amsterdam after elementary school. She only got two more years of education in the Netherlands and learned Dutch in a special course. But before her family installed a dish, she watched only Dutch television. Now she watches only Turkish television. She said Dutch television is occasionally on for a soccer match or the news, but otherwise the television is constantly tuned to a Turkish channel. Having become used to the Dutch programs and news style, she is critical of the content of Turkish television. She doesn't like the many bloody traffic accidents depicted on the news. And she thinks that many programs exaggerate the real situations and sensationalize people's tragedies. She doesn't know why she continues to watch those programs. Maybe it is habit, she says. Now she doesn't know anything about public affairs in Holland. She can't even answer a question about the biggest problem facing Dutch society today since she doesn't watch the news. "I used to read the subtitles in Dutch on imported programs on television and my Dutch was good. Now my Dutch has deteriorated. And I haven't gone to school to keep up my language skills in two years. It's like I've really forgotten everything."

Rıza Şeref, the young man who wanted to start his own national Turkish television programs, thinks he understands what satellite television means to people like his parents.

> When I go home, I see them watching Turkish television all the time. Before they watched Dutch television. I think they do this because they understand the language and because it is amusement. And what do you do when you go home at night after work and you are tired and you want to be entertained. And also it is identification. It's Turkish and that's the first thing you have to look at. I'm here. They're there. But they are like me. It's Turkish. There are no programs for us here in Holland.

Sadık Yemni, an author who has written several novels about the diasporic experience of Turks in Europe, also understands this feeling. But he sees a mix of good and bad in the influence satellite television has had.

> It is violent and powerful. I don't necessarily mean that in a negative way, however. People can live the events in Turkey here just as if they were there. It has lifted the borders between the countries. Of course, when you watch too much television, it makes you stupid. That's just an impact of television in general. When you watch television, you don't think. You can't be reading. And it is expensive. It is also hard to get information from television programs because the station owners and producers manipulate the information. The expense is on the production end, so it ends up limiting the kind of information and the amount that can be sent.

But when asked about the impact television from Turkey might have on people who watched all day, he responded, "You have to ask what they were doing with their time before the entry of satellite television. They went to visit one another if they were women, and they went to the coffeehouse if they were men." But Yemni is most concerned with the impact on youth. "Those who grew up with Turkish television in their homes speak better Turkish, know what today's Turkey is about and see it as an alternative to Holland as a country to live in." Yemni also thought that women got ideas about the possibilities for their lives, too. The ones who lived in conservative families could see that women are able to work outside the home.

I have mentioned the religious or political orientation of some of the Turkish channels. The participants in this study often talked about why they watched certain channels and not others. Those who were less religious and who didn't have a specific political view they looked for usually mentioned *Kanal D, ATV*, Show, or Star TV as their choices. They moved around to select particular programs on each of these. Favorite sources for news of the people who chose more "secular" channels were *Kanal D* and *ATV*. *ATV* is the channel that includes the nightly European edition of the news. Several participants pointed to that newscast as important for them, but others were not even aware of any newscast that related to European-Turks. Since *ATV* tends to focus on Germany for its European news, some viewers might not have thought of the content as directed to them. One young man, in commenting about the European news on *ATV*, says the channel provides this service "just to say they did. They don't reflect the differences between the various groups of Turks living in Europe. And they don't show people who live on low levels or are having difficulties in their lives."

Kanal 7 and *TGRT* were chosen by those who said that the moral values of the broadcasts were important for them. A participant who also has an administrative role at a *Milli Görüfl* mosque in Amsterdam claimed that *Kanal 7* is the best program to come out of Turkey today. He said it was the only channel that brings people together and speaks for all of them. "It helps wipe out the inferiority complex that most Turks suffer from," he said. A group of women from another *Milli Görüfl*-affiliated family disagreed among themselves about whether the most accurate news out of Turkey is broadcast on *TGRT* or on *Kanal 7*.

Yusuf, a thirty-three-year-old father of two daughters, also chooses the more conservative channels, though only he watches *Kanal 7* for news. He believes that those channels that privilege political views on the right depict people who are more like him. For example, he said, "I sometimes see people like me on *Kanal 7*, but I never do on Show."

Since the private channels have been available in Europe for less than a decade—in reality only since 1993 or 1994—and TRT-INT has only been available for ten years, most of the Turks in Amsterdam did not have an opportunity when they lived in Turkey to choose television content they thought was consistent with their worldview. So the choice to adopt Turkish language television is not just a turn away from Dutch television, but also a selection of a point of view within the Turkish-language offerings.

Different Choices for Parent and Child

As might be expected, the first-generation migrants are more tied to the television from Turkey than are their children. In this study, I also found differences among the types of programs selected by the parents and the children. But choosing to view different content and actually being able to act on that choice are different things. In many households, only one television, the one placed in the main living space, was available. Agreements needed to be worked out in families where only one television was in the house.

Hayri, fifty-one, one of the early migrants, is now on disability because of an accident at work. So watching television has taken on increased importance in his daily life. His typical day is spent hanging out with friends at the coffeehouse or sitting around at home. He says the television is turned on in the early morning and goes off at midnight or later. He has motorized dishes and an automatic changer so he can get to any channel he wants at the flick of a button. He said that news programs were most important to him. The father of four children, Hayri explains to the family, "After I listen to the news, I tell the children, 'you can watch anything you want.'" Yeşim, the youngest, who is in elementary school, prefers cartoons and other children's programs. She and her older siblings go upstairs to watch Dutch television on the smaller set when Hayri won't relinquish the one in the living room.

Kıvılcım, thirty-four, mother of a son, sixteen, and a daughter, eleven, has worked out a plan where each member of the family gets to watch their programs. Before the dish came, they all watched only Dutch television. "Now it is all Turkish except for the children's programs, which they get to watch after school. In the evening it is my turn. When my husband is home, he watches what he wants." She doesn't think the children's preference for Dutch television should matter too much. "It is better for them if they read, do their homework, or get some exercise."

The Second Generation's View of Television Programs

Without any empirical knowledge of the situation, we might think that youth would automatically reject the television programs that come from Turkey. They would see these as something that belongs to their parents' generation, a group of people who can't speak the local language and who are neither as modern nor as integrated into Dutch society as they are. In fact, we might think they would be embarrassed by their parents' choice to live in the past, remembering a country they left long ago—a place in which the children would never want to live.

But when we consider what these imported channels mean to the second generation, some surprises emerge. Though the second generation may be selective about the programs they watch from Turkey, they still watch. And many of them spend a lot of time following sports, music, and dramatic series on a regular basis. Others are critical of the content of programs and the role of television in the lives of their parents.

I'll begin with an exchange in a group interview with several young men—all of university age or in their late twenties whose parents were first-generation migrants. These young men belong to a conservative Islamic organization and I interviewed them on a day when they were holding a meeting at the mosque. All of them were born in Turkey, but came to the Netherlands at a relatively young age. In the exchange below, the participants are discussing the power of Turkish television to hold an audience. Sema Razak, who worked with me on some of the interviews, is about the age of the young men. She came to Amsterdam to study for a graduate degree at the university. Engin, one of the participants in this exchange, is a teacher who came to Amsterdam more recently than the others. The rest of the group are students.

> *İbrahim*: At our school my friends all watch Turkish channels. . . . I mean when the train crash happened in Germany, nobody knew about it. They only heard about it four or five days later.
>
> *Sema*: It was even on TRT.
>
> *İbrahim*: They asked me, "There was a train crash?" They were watching music, entertainment—this and that instead. Of course they pay no attention to what is going on here. There is a train crash right under their noses, and they don't even know about it.
>
> *Christine*: After Turkish television came, didn't the people continue to watch Dutch television?
>
> *İbrahim*: No.
>
> *Sema*: They don't even know about the events here, as you say.
>
> *Cevdet*: If you asked who the prime minister is, they wouldn't know.

Erol: Yes, apart from the last generation [second or third] of Turks living here. Except for the latest generation, the rest all really took to Turkish television once it arrived. That first generation didn't speak Dutch, but only heard it or had children who watched television. They had one or two televisions, but only the kids watched the Dutch programs.
Christine: Now after you are connected to the dish, and you have an extra television at home, you can watch a different channel.
Erol: You can.
Christine: Can you have one on the cable and another on the dish?
İbrahim: Everything is possible.
Engin: Now I am going to a language course so I shouldn't be watching Turkish television, but whether I want to or not, it happens.
Cevdet: Really it is a terrible habit.
Engin: Yes, if you have it, you are destined to watch it.
İbrahim: But it is more important to follow what is going on here than what is happening in Turkey. We live here, not there. I can understand about those who came here when they were in their thirties, but how about the next generation? Why are they so interested in Turkey and not in the Netherlands?

In this conversation, Turkish television is criticized because it takes viewers out of their surroundings. At the same time, the programs coming from Turkey have a certain attraction for these young people or their friends who consider themselves more a part of Dutch society than of Turkish society. A little later in this conversation they discuss how Turks are portrayed on Dutch television, again noting that many people in the Turkish community never see these programs.

Engin: Really, they don't reflect our conditions ever.
İbrahim: It is the same for Europe. As if Europe is all rosy—but we have the world's problems here. Problems of pollution, youth gangs, and other things.
Sema: Are there really gangs on the street?
İbrahim: Of course. Two weeks ago, I went to see the school's director, asking how we would find a solution for this. The men don't do anything about this. And none of it comes out in public.
Sema: But doesn't it come out in the Dutch press?
İbrahim: Yes, but people here don't have any news of it. It's all about what's happening in Turkey. We follow what goes on in Turkey. Our biggest fault is that, I mean here laws are passed that relate to us. And they say, "Yass, how is that?" "Ya, it is like this?" "Ya, my dear father, when did you come? Thirty-five years ago?" [He says this, imitating the dialect of a father.] Then it was current or in effect. How many years have passed? Things like this, I mean these are the big deficiencies here.
Cevdet: And there is misinformation circulated. A lot of times this happens—for example I was watching *ATV* the other day. They were providing information about a road, and later when I researched the issue, I discovered they gave wrong information. They give incorrect information a lot.
Sema: That was on *ATV*?
Cevdet: It came out on *ATV*. They also said Turkish citizens don't need a visa to go to Bulgaria. "Good," I said. I believed it. I went to get a road map. My

> Dutch passport will be on me and I won't have to get a visa, I said. Then I learned that I need a visa. Finally, I went to the Bulgarian Embassy and learned that Turks do need visas to go.
> *Sema*: Don't you trust the Turkish press?
> *Cevdet*: No, I don't. I won't ever trust it again.
> *Erol*: They go after easy news, I think. I mean where is it easy to get news? Without relying on research they go for the easy news—for example, entertainment.

This discussion reflects a certain contempt for the ways of the Turkish press, and is also critical of the first generation for its lack of interest in the issues that surround them every day. At the same time, these young men are supportive of their parents' generation. They are also respectful to their elders and try to help them with difficulties they have with the Dutch government and Dutch officials. One of the young men in this group says he spends a lot of time volunteering his services to older men who come to the mosque with documents that they need to have translated, forms they need to fill out, or official letters they must write. He said he feels sorry for them, and understands their difficulties in dealing with life in the Netherlands. But at the same time, they would all like to see their parents think less about the events in Turkey and more about the life of Turkish citizens in the Netherlands. As İbrahim put it, "What do I care about news of a Turkish politician? I didn't vote for him. What does he have to do with me?" Yet he feels his parents or others in their generation can have extensive discussions about that politician. It is also interesting that while İbrahim is critical of his parents' generation and their interest in Turkish politics, the group of young men in this interview spent a lot of time discussing Turkey's entry to the European Union and why there were problems, whether the country would ever get full membership and so forth. They also spent a long time discussing what they perceived to be the deteriorating political situation in Turkey. So they are split in their feelings about their own identity. And their discussion about the good and bad in television programs from Turkey reflected that same split in their personal attachment to Turkey or to the Netherlands.

If Rıza Şeref's plan for a new television station in the Netherlands had worked, he might have addressed the need to deal with problems that Turks face in the Netherlands. A major goal he had regarding a new television service was to bring public awareness to some of those issues.

> They say that Turks live in the past. I want to do something with their minds. We have to express ourselves. We live in Holland, one of the richest countries in the world. Last night I saw a newspaper article about how Turkish and Moroccan students were failing their exams at a higher rate than Dutch students. There has to be a problem. And there has to be a problem when Turks don't work in public organizations. There has to be a problem when they don't work in the higher levels of businesses here. I want to know what the reasons are and how we can get around them.

Şeref's idealism is shared by the young men at the mosque. They all see television as a vehicle for addressing the problems in their community. They identify themselves as Turks and want the image and the reality of the life of their minority group to improve. And they would all like the media to play a bigger role in that process. At the same time, they believe the media from Turkey are not making a positive contribution in that regard.

Narin also would not place any faith in Turkish media to help bring about change. At twenty-seven, she is about the same age as the young men, and has lived in the Netherlands her whole life. She speaks excellent Turkish, but chooses to write professionally in Dutch. She and her husband do not own a dish, and she has little use for the programs on TRT either.

> TRT is really bad. You can't imagine a broadcast this bad. On Saturday night, a time when you are looking to be entertained. On that night there is the *Diyanet Saat*. [Religious Hour from the government-supported Islamic organization]. And before that there is a *Nur Zamandan* program [from the time of Said Nursi, an Islamic leader].

Narin laughs as she thinks of how inappropriate such programming is. She says she has also noticed a difference between the way Turkish and Dutch television programs are presented. About Turkish programs, she says:

> The voices are too loud. The lights are too bright. Everything is excessive on the private television programs. That makes much excitement in presenting everything at one pitch—loud—and it turns viewers off. It is like they are beating up on you. It makes you tired just watching it. The newspapers are the same, with so much color and huge headlines. It attacks you. *Hürriyet* and *Milliyet* are like that. Dutch television isn't like that—in the voices and in the music.

Narin's husband and most of her friends are Turkish. She is involved with an organization for Turkish youth. Yet she looks at the culture, as it is presented on Turkish television, more as an outsider might.

Meryem, another educated woman in her twenties who is involved in organizing a group of young second-generation Turks to improve the image of migrants and their families, also doesn't have a dish and sees satellite television as a phenomenon that only applies to her parents' generation and others who don't have a social life outside their family.

> Because they cannot satisfy their need for communication with other Turks and with friends here, they watch these shows from Turkey to meet that need. They are focused on Turkey and tied there because of the need to be connected to Turkish culture. They are not interested in Dutch politics. They would rather watch any entertainment program from Turkey because of this need. They are estranged from Dutch public affairs.

Meryem satisfies her own need with TRT-INT on the cable. She says she doesn't have time to bother with Turkish news on a daily basis. But she does have a special love for old Turkish films. And TRT-INT airs a lot of those films made in the 1970s. Otherwise, she can visit her parents to watch *Kanal D* or *ATV*, the only channels in which she has any interest.

Younger people may not be so critical of the content, the tone, or the approach of Turkish television. When they watch it, it is for their enjoyment. Few of the people younger than twenty-one with whom I talked had any comments about the meaning television from Turkey had for them. Most of them watched it. Some said that was a very small amount of the time; others said they watched it exclusively. Because the dishes have been in most of their homes for four or five years, they couldn't remember a time when it wasn't there. Instead, they chose to talk about specific programs they watched on either Dutch or Turkish television.

Youth and Music Programs

It is difficult to interpret what it means when so many young people say they prefer Turkish music to Dutch music, and so they enjoy watching music videos and other music entertainment programs on Turkish television. Many of these young people were either born and raised in the Netherlands or they arrived before they were ten or eleven years old. Of course most of their families return to Turkey every summer for five or six weeks on holiday. So these are times when they would be most exposed to Turkish music and Turkish media. Fond memories of summers may be related to musical favorites. Here is the way some of the participants described it.

Ayfer's teenaged daughters love Turkish music, but it wasn't always so.

> My daughters watch Turkish television since we got the dish about six months ago. Until they were fifteen or so, they only listened to music in English. They went to concerts given by Western singers. Then when they became sixteen, they started listening to Turkish music. I found it very interesting. We go to Turkey and they buy cassettes and CDs to bring back here. I think they will want to return to Turkey after finishing their studies. They want to work there. They go to Turkey for vacation and have a good time. So they are filled with thoughts of Turkey as it is during vacations. They think it is always like that. They have never lived real life in Turkey.

Kerem, the young man who spends much of his free time at *Alternatif*, says he never watches TRT-INT. "They don't make programs for me. I like music clips and TRT doesn't do many of those. They play more Turkish folk music and I don't like that much." Kerem didn't enthusiastically respond to many of my questions until we got to the subject of music, and then he said to me that I had finally come to a subject that interested him. "I can tell you what I think about that. I listen only to Tarkan. He recorded only three albums and I also have concert tapes. I went to a Tarkan concert once. He sang in April—on the twelfth. And I watch his clips on TV."

Tarkan is an exception in Turkish pop music. He is popular with Turks in Turkey, Turkish migrants in Europe, and also with other European youths. He is one of the very few Turkish musicians who has been able to cross over into the European pop market. For the young people in my study, he is also a success story. Tarkan, born twenty-eight years ago near Frankfurt, Germany, is the son of migrant workers. His parents came to work in a factory in Germany, but later his father established a successful business as an interior decorator.[27]

His family returned to Turkey when he was fourteen, and he began to study music—first at a music high school in Karamürsel, and then in İstanbul. His second album, released in 1994, sold two million in Turkey and 700,000 in Europe. He followed a 1995 Turkish tour with several concerts in Europe. His third album release was followed with a second tour of Europe to sold-out stadiums that included London, Paris and Berlin. And his single, "Şimarık" (Spoiled), went to number three on the French charts, number one in Belgium, and to high positions in Germany and the Netherlands.[28]

But Tarkan may well be a unique case of a Turkish singer able to crossover to other cultures. Though he has not had a new release for more than three years, one of his singles and at least one of his CDs has caught on in the U.S. Latin market, being played regularly on Latin Radio stations and rising to the top of Billboard's World Chart.[29]

No doubt Tarkan's European popularity has attracted more interest among migrant youth to pop music on Turkish television. And a certain pride accompanies discussions of Tarkan's success, since he comes from the same background as the other second-generation migrants in the Netherlands.

While I was in Amsterdam in the summer of 1999, I had an opportunity to attend a concert of a group of pop singers who had come from Istanbul at the Arena, a small theater on the east side of the city. Though they had recorded a CD, they were not all that well known in musical circles. Of the 100 or so concertgoers, almost all were men and women under the age of thirty. I noticed that none of the young women had their heads covered (so this was not an occasion preferred by youth who were religious), and most of them were dressed in drab colors—lots of black leather jackets and black pants. Many of the group appeared to be acquainted with one another, all of them speaking Turkish with one another. No Dutch people appeared to be among those who attended, but to my knowledge, the concert only was advertised in Turkish circles—local businesses, etc. The group played to a very enthusiastic crowd. If I hadn't known otherwise, I would have thought I was in Turkey, not the center of Amsterdam, on that evening. The pull of the music, popular with all of the concertgoers, is another force to bind these mostly second-generation migrants more to each other than to the social networks in the rest of Amsterdam. The solidarity I observed among these young people at the event indicated that this is a group of friends who spend a lot of time socializing with one another.

Other Program Choices among Young People

Youth who are religious. The heterogeneous nature of the second generation of Turkish migrants is also reflected in their selection of favorite programs. The split in types of programs they mentioned watching broke along lines related to religious affiliation. Here, I should say that young women who also told me they were particularly religious, belonged to a specific Islamic group, attended Islamic summer or weekend camps, and expressed interest in the problems related to religious freedom in Turkey, also wore head scarves and covered their arms and legs—usually in long skirts and long-sleeved blouses. Young men who expressed those beliefs and affiliations, of course, dressed no differently than anyone else. This group of people often said they watched *Kanal 7* or *TGRT* as their channel of choice.

In one household of quite religious people, I arrived to be greeted by a mother, Gülay, two of her middle-aged friends, a neighbor woman with a small child, and two adult daughters. One of the daughters, Betül, is a midwife. The second oldest, Ela, is still studying. Both the daughters, the mother, and the other women visitors were covered with scarves and long dresses. When asked about their television viewing, they were quick to point out that it is mostly restricted to *Kanal 7* and *TGRT*. They believe that those channels are more on track with their moral stance and provide news that is politically unbiased. I talk with them the day after the big *Milli Görüş* international rally was held in Amsterdam's Ajax stadium. *Kanal 7* had broadcast the day's events live, so this family was particularly pleased that the station's moral position and theirs were in sync. Betül says that her mother and the rest of the family always watch the religious programs on the local Amsterdam channel, but they also watch religious programs on *TGRT* and *Kanal 7*. Gülay said they also try to watch a historical program about the Islamic prophets. They select *Kanal 7* for news because of its accuracy, and not *TRT-INT* because they say it doesn't tell the whole story. The daughters say they never watch soap operas (Turkish or imported) nor do they watch the popular comedy series. Gülay said that many Dutch programs and also some on the other Turkish channels are not appropriate for them to watch. "They are too open," she said, referring to the sexual content on these programs.

The news and public affairs programs they watch from Turkey have upset them. They are greatly disturbed by the crackdown on head scarves in the universities. It offends them that women cannot wear head scarves and men cannot have beards if they are students in the university, because they see this as an important part of their religion and culture. Without satellite television, these women might not be so well informed about this situation in Turkey. They have an opportunity to see the Turkish political point of view on this matter. It serves as a comparison for these young women who are free to dress as they like at work or in school in the Netherlands. And watching coverage of this issue psychologically transports them to the scene of this political battle.

The youngest sibling in this family, Sevda, is not particularly interested in the religious programs or the political content on television. She prefers the Cartoon Network, which she watches in English with Dutch subtitles. She also likes a Turkish comedy.

Youth who are not religious. It would take many months, and probably years, to be able to determine how the various groups of youth are differentiated in Amsterdam. Discussing the difference between those who are religious and those who are not is a clear-cut way to distinguish one group from another. In describing program choices among the youth who are not particularly religious, I don't mean to imply that the young people who generally align with the secular group are all alike. But they are certainly different in attitudes and behavior from those who align themselves with particular religious beliefs.

Overall, the young men in their teens or early twenties differ in their viewing habits from the young women in that age group. In general, it breaks down the way it might in most societies. The males prefer sports—and lots of it—music videos and news and political information. The latter choice—of news programs—may seem unusual, but almost everyone in this study expressed an interest in the news, whether in Dutch or in Turkish. I believe the interest in political affairs has to do with the often volatile political situation in Turkey. In the United States, where the economy is more or less stable, young people tend not to be so interested in politics. That is especially true as the two major parties come closer together in their positions. But in Turkey, where double-digit inflation is common, where military coups have taken place three times in the last forty years, and where political parties can be banned for trying to mix religion with state affairs, politics can be rather exciting. It is the frequent subject of conversation, both in the Netherlands and in Turkey. More popular with young men, politics is also discussed among young women, but less so.

Young women in this study also tend to choose television programs similar to those selected by young women around the world—soaps, music programs, and entertainment programs were most often selected. But many said they also watched the news and political programs. Selma, the young woman who spent a lot of time working with media at *Alternatif*, described her viewing and compared it with that of her mother.

> I watch television about two hours a day, at most. I have more time to relax on Sunday, so then I watch more, about seven hours. But not my mother. When she is home, we watch television from Turkey. She doesn't like Dutch television. Mostly she watches TGRT. The television in the living room is attached to the satellite, so if she has that TV on, I have to watch the Turkish programs. But if I go to my room or my brother's room, I'll watch RTL4 and 5, SBS, or Veronica. I watch Star and TGRT on the other television. My favorite programs are *Goede Tijden, Slechte Tijden,* (Good Times, Bad Times), *Beverly Hills 90210*, *Melrose Place*, and *Baywatch* on Dutch television. I watch other series on *TGRT*, and also *Hülya Avşar* and *Kara Melek*. I don't like to watch

> the news. It is depressing, particularly the news from Turkey. But because my mother always watches the news, sometimes I watch with her.

Of her selections for viewing on Dutch television, all but one are programs that originate in the United States. *Good Times, Bad Times*, is a Dutch soap that was first presented in Australia but adapted for the Dutch audience. I will discuss that program in more detail later. Both Turkish programs Selma mentions originate in Turkey. Hülya Avşar is a singer who hosts her own variety show. And *Kara Melek* (Dark Angel) is a Turkish soap opera. Watching the soap operas on Dutch television means hearing them in English with Dutch subtitles. So when youth watch these programs—and *Beverly Hills*, *Melrose Place*, and *Baywatch* were popular with many young people in this study—it is more exposure to U.S. culture than to Dutch culture. Other soaps popular among Turkish young (and older) women are *The Bold and the Beautiful* and *The Young and the Restless*. These programs are dubbed on Turkish television, so if they are watched in Turkish, viewers receive a product that has been culturally altered to a degree.

For young men, soccer—or football as it is called in Europe—is extremely popular. And that goes for both Dutch men and Turkish men. But allegiances to particular teams are revealing. In many homes I visited, young boys (and sometimes young girls) would be wearing hats or shirts with logos of Fenerbahçe or Galata Saray (the champions of the European Football Association in 2000). These are both Turkish teams, and it seems odd that kids would be fans of teams in Turkey when Ajax, the Amsterdam team is located right in their city. Other young men said they supported Ajax and one twelve-year-old said he wanted to play for that team when he grew up. Another young boy, who plays soccer for a youth team now, said his dream was to be a player for Galata Saray. What makes the difference? Ahmet Azdural, the journalist from NPS, said he believes that the television from Turkey makes fans out of the kids. "Say, you live near the Ajax stadium and every week there is a game in the stadium and you know about this. But you don't go; instead you watch Galata Saray on television and root for that team. I find this very interesting." Another person said he believed that young boys follow what their fathers watch. And if the father is supporting a Turkish team, the son will too.

Several of the young men and women reported that *The Jerry Springer Show* was one of their favorites. They said they liked the disagreements, and even the fighting, on the show. One woman in her early thirties said that she likes this program so much, she hates it when the weekend comes and she cannot watch.

Goede Tijden, Slechte Tijden

Goede Tidjen, Slechte Tijden (Good Times, Bad Times) is a special case on which I will focus more attention here. Though the soap began as a translated version of the Australian soap, *The Restless Years*, it is now written for the Dutch audience. Joost DeBruin writes that it has been culturally characterized as being very Dutch because of its serious and somber nature.[30] DeBruin cites research that found that in 1999, one-half of all youths (aged thirteen to nineteen) watching television on an average evening were tuned to the daily soap. When only girls were selected, two-thirds of that group were tuned into *Good Times, Bad Times*. And older people watch it as well. Ayfer said she watches with her teenaged daughters.

> That's the only reason. I tell them not to bring those troubles [of the characters on the soap] into our home. The relationships in the soap are very disjointed. They finish and start romantic liaisons at the drop of a hat. Just like in *Dallas*, the relationships are opposite what they should be, we think. Their lifestyle is very comfortable. We don't accept the morals of the Dutch.

I had been told of a Turkish girl who played a role on the soap a couple of years previous to the study. So I wondered if her presence might have increased interest among the Turkish community. I asked participants whether they watched it or not, and their opinions of the program. Often sensitive topics will be treated, like extramarital affairs or incest—topics that would clearly not be acceptable to religiously conservative families. Ahmet, a man who serves as a spokesman for the *Milli Görüş*, said his family didn't watch because the program didn't reflect real life. "And the morals on this channel were troublesome. We shut off such channels," he said.

Tülin, the woman who heads a women's organization for *Milli Görüş*, agrees with that assessment. Since she also believes the Turks and Dutch should live separate lives because of their separate value bases, it is not surprising that she said that *Good Times, Bad Times* can destroy a family's morals. She goes even further to say that watching these programs can actually break up families. So she doesn't permit her children to watch it or any other soap operas. Hediye, thirty-six, a mother of two sons, stopped watching the program following her pilgrimage to Mecca. Before that event, she watched it and other soaps from the United States on Dutch television. Now she believes these programs are not good to watch. While she and her husband were away on the pilgrimage, her father-in-law, who stayed in their apartment, installed the dish to get Turkish television. It was not clear how much of the decision to switch viewing habits was due to the addition of the Turkish channels.

Other participants who were faithful watchers of *Good Times, Bad Times*, also had problems with the content. Meral, a young woman in her early thirties who watches two or three times a week, and also watches several U.S. soaps, was bothered by the episodes that addressed incest. It wasn't just that the program dealt with the subject, but it was the nonchalant attitude, "like well, what has happened, forgive and forget," that bothered her. Leyla, a married woman in her twenties with a young son, is a faithful viewer of the program. She began watching when the Turkish girl joined the program. But she also believed that the program went over the edge when they introduced the topic of incest. She not only found it "disgusting," but believes that it is not a good example to set for children who may watch. She is also concerned that young people who see such things may be confused about what is real life and what is fiction.

Though DeBruin cites research that claims that serials like *Good Times, Bad Times* can provide ethnic youth with a frame of reference for real life as it might be lived in the Netherlands, nobody who said they watched the program commented on it in that way. The people in this study who watched this program at any time referred to it more in terms of its entertainment value or its negative influence on children. The people who didn't watch it themselves, or didn't want their children to watch it because of its immoral content, feared that they or their children might actually evaluate real-life situations in terms of the soap. Perhaps that is what happened for them when they watched. In Marie Gillespie's research of Punjabi youth in London and their use of television, she finds that watching soaps helps guide young girls' lives. "Especially for girls who have little direct access to people outside their kinship and peer networks, soaps are seen to provide an extension to their immediate social experience."[31]

It is of greater concern here that those who interact little with Dutch people should think that the characters on this soap reflect the way Dutch families really live. If that is the case, the program will never contribute to bringing ethnic minorities in Holland closer to the Dutch people. Those viewers who were less religious, and who watched as much Dutch television as they did Turkish television in this study, were less concerned with the morality of the content of *Good Times, Bad Times*.

Yasemin, the single young woman in her early thirties who works for a Turkish organization, thinks this is part of a larger problem that will prevent real integration of the Turks in Dutch society.

> You know, people who go back to Turkey from here are not necessarily happy. But staying here, they cannot become completely integrated into this society. And the society doesn't change here. You would think that each group would be affected by the existence of the other and both groups would make a change to evolve to something new. But that doesn't happen here. They don't come closer to one another because neither side is open to the other's culture. There is little attempt to get to know one another's culture because neither side has real interest in learning about the other.

If that is true of a large number of the Turks who live in Amsterdam, it can only change as subsequent generations are born and make their lives in the Netherlands. And no television program can do a lot to impact that. But programs like *Good Times, Bad Times* might not be helping that come about either.

Other Content Choices

Adult viewers certainly make program choices, and they talked about those. But for a lot of the participants, it is more about choosing a channel or two or three and watching whatever is presented on those channels than it is about selecting particular programs. As discussed earlier, if the people expressed particular interest in the moral stance of the channel, they watched whatever was on *Kanal 7* or *TGRT*. If they did not make their choices on that basis, they generally selected *ATV, Kanal D*, or Show TV. These channels are also the ones with high ratings in Turkey. News was a top priority for all of the adult participants. And the most popular news show was on *ATV* with anchor Ali Kırca. *ATV* also carries the European news, and it follows the hour-long domestic news each evening. Political discussion shows were also mentioned frequently—particularly *Siyaset Meydanı* (Politics Arena) and *A Takımı* (A Team).

Variety programs are mentioned by nearly everyone and the most popular of these are the Hülya Avşar show and the İbo show. Both are popular singers who present entertainment of all kinds.

The soaps and the drama or comedy series are also mentioned frequently. One very popular series, *Super Baba* (Super Father), that concerns a single father and his family's adventures, carries so many ads that it is sometimes difficult to sustain interest. One man commented that there are far too many ads on television. "Are you watching programs or advertising? You are never certain," he said. Other series (or *dizi* as they are called) were also mentioned. Such programs often come and go as they do in the United States.

Quiz programs are popular with families, as kids are often interested in them as well, so the family can watch together. And of course football games and other sports attract the attention of many Turkish people—especially the boys and men.

As the television serves as backdrop for most other activity in the household, the families tend to half-watch a number of programs. And many people admitted to turning on the television early in the morning for the news and just leaving it on until bedtime.

Print Media Consumption

The Dutch press circulates on six days of the week. There are no Sunday papers. Every household in Amsterdam (and in most cities) receives a free newspaper on Wednesdays. The paper contains local news and is mostly a vehicle for advertising. But for many of the families in this study, it is the only Dutch print medium they ever see. Even the women who say they don't read Dutch are able to make out the advertising to know where the sales are.

The print press is also expensive, no matter whether it is a Dutch or Turkish paper. A Dutch daily paper costs about the same as a Turkish paper—about $1 for each one. The Turkish papers are not usually circulated by subscription, although that is possible. *Milli Gazete*, the newspaper of the Virtue Party and therefore supported by the *Milli Görüş*, circulates only by subscription. Most Dutch papers are sold by subscription, however.

The Turkish press and the Dutch press are very different from one another. In general, the Dutch press is considered a "serious" press, with little use of color or other attention-getting layout or design. The largest circulating national newspapers all originate in Amsterdam—*De Telegraaf, Het Parool*, and *De Volkskraant.* The top circulating Turkish newspapers (and all have European editions) are *Hürriyet, Sabah*, and *Milliyet.* Left of center *Cumhuriyet*, considered the best quality paper, circulates only a weekly edition in Europe. The Turkish press tends to emphasize color, large headlines, and many stories on the front page that jump to the inside. In general, the Dutch press is well trusted, while the Turkish press is not so well respected among its readers.

The lack of respect for the accuracy of the press was reflected in the statements made by many of the participants. Mustafa, who works for Dutch social services and is religiously conservative, was able to tick off five or six columnists he reads in the Turkish press that he accesses on the Internet from work. But he says he reads no news in the Turkish papers. "There are no lies in the Dutch press as there are in the Turkish newspapers," he said, noting that he subscribes to *Volkskraant* and reads *Het Parool* on-line. "The Dutch press is at a more established level than the Turkish press. The Turkish newspapers can write about things that never happened. Sometimes they get advance notice of things and write about things that they say have happened when they haven't yet occurred."

The group of young men at the mosque who are critical of Turkish television have a low opinion of the Turkish press as well.

> *Cevdet*: All of us have satellite dishes at our homes. Because of that we don't need to read the Turkish newspapers. Not at all.
> *İbrahim*: I read the papers on the Internet. At school, in the recreation room, there are Turkish papers—*Sabah*, *Hürriyet*, *Milliyet*. It is enough to read the front page.
> *Erol*: A little nonsense is in these papers, not much to put faith in. A lot of nonsense, really.

Author Sadık Yemni reads only the Dutch press, though he said he stopped subscribing to *Volkskraant* because he had too many things to read. "I don't read the Turkish press because it is reactionary and exaggerates everything. The newspapers pump up the news."

The criticisms of the Turkish press come from more educated people in the study. But that doesn't mean that all the less educated participants think highly of the print medium. Fatih, who has a lower level secondary education, says he reads Turkish papers once in a while, but it doesn't matter which paper it is. "In fact, I don't really even like newspapers. I'd rather watch television. The newspapers repeat the news every day and in each paper. So if I read once a week, I can get the news."

No matter how critical the first generation might be of the Turkish press, they continue to read it. In a study by Fennema and Tillie of political participation and trust among ethnic groups in Amsterdam, 51 percent of the Turkish respondents reported regular readership of the Turkish press.[32] Ayfer says the reason migrants continue to prefer the Turkish press to the Dutch press is based on language difficulties. Though she subscribes to *Volkskraant*, she prefers reading Turkish papers.

> When it is your second language, you always prefer your native language newspaper. You don't get the esprit or the jokes. And you don't get the proverbs and idioms. Even when I have lived here for thirty years—it is still a foreign place. Everything is foreign—the lifestyle, the methodology—customs. I get tired in school meetings. You have to process the Dutch, translate to Turkish, and then prepare a response. I have just never been able to process Dutch firsthand. It means that the language has just not set with me.

Several patterns of reading emerged from the study. The professionals, who are both interested in Dutch public affairs and need to know about what goes on in the Netherlands, say they read at least one Dutch paper every day. Often those people will read the Turkish papers on the Internet, or wherever they may come across them.

The second group of people are those who read a Dutch paper only occasionally—once or twice a week or less—and read the Turkish press more regularly. These are usually people whose Dutch isn't reported to be very good. Some of these people will buy a Turkish newspaper every day, but more often they will read them in coffee shops, at their organization's headquarters, or at the mosque. The young people who come to *Alternatif* are in this group too, because the Turkish newspapers are available there. I visited the organization several times and always observed young men and women reading the newspapers. Sometimes they were discussing a news story that appeared that day. Some of the older men who are unemployed or retired go to the coffee shop, their favorite organization's meeting place, or the mosque to meet friends and read the Turkish newspapers as part of their daily ritual.

But women don't have the habit of reading the papers or visiting a particular place where newspapers are located as much. If the husband or one of the children brings a paper home, then the mother gets a chance to read it, too. But very few of the women reported making a trip out to pick up a paper. If the family subscribes to *Milli Gazete* (and very few did), then the mother would have the opportunity to see a newspaper every day.

The last group of people include those who don't read any newspapers of any kind. Some of these people said they used to read a Turkish paper regularly, but stopped doing that once television from Turkey allowed them to watch the news. Others were illiterate and couldn't read the newspaper. For these people, mostly women, the advent of television meant they didn't have to depend on literate members of the household to tell them what was going on in the world. Before television from Turkey, the world outside their neighborhoods was relatively closed off to them.

Effects of Turkish Television on Migrant Families

The imperialism thesis: Though I did not conduct focus groups in which audience members watch a particular program and talk about their interpretations of the content of that program to determine the extent to which the audience might be influenced by the core values of U.S. programs, I can still make some conclusions about the context for media imperialism here. While I don't dismiss the possibility of its existence, it wasn't the most powerful force at work here. The language base of the program was the most powerful force.

If the group of people I interviewed were to be split according to their language facility in Dutch, their viewing habits regarding Dutch television would match up well. In other words, the higher the migrants' literacy in Dutch, the more they viewed Dutch television. And the less literate they are in Dutch, the more Turkish television they watch. Those participants who are not literate in Dutch or Turkish are the most dependent on Turkish television for all of their news, information, and entertainment.

In an earlier chapter, I presented views of Turkish people who work in Dutch media who believe that it is a bad thing for Turks to watch all this television from Turkey. And they claimed that before satellite television came to Holland, this audience tuned into more programs presented by Dutch television. But the only measures they have from an earlier time are the results of surveys that focus on particular programs created for migrants on Dutch television in Turkish or with Turkish subtitles. It is likely that people who spoke no Dutch simply didn't watch television, or they just watched programs for which little language skill was required (entertainment variety programs and some game shows). Perhaps those people were early adopters of VCRs and made trips to the neighborhood video shop for Turkish films to satisfy their need for entertainment.

If this is the case, the coming of satellite television from Turkey did not signal a great loss of viewers from one country's television programs to another. Rather, it was only a loss from the few informational programs designed to reach the migrants. And the introduction of Turkish television created an audience that had not been watching much of anything before. The only data available on use of video over time comes from the media use studies conducted for NPS radio. The Turkish respondents in that survey reported watching 3.2 hours per week of video in 1992, .9 hours in 1995, and 1.8 hours in 1998. Unfortunately, no data are available from the time before satellite television began. But most of the people who were adopting satellite dishes probably had them by 1995. So by that time video viewing was at its lowest point. Wicker has said, based on his own research and that of Pierre Bourdieu, that habits of first-generation migrants are difficult to change.

> However, since dispositions are inert—*hysteresis* is the term Bourdieu uses in this context—and the dynamics of adaptation are thus reduced, the change from one field to another—from lower to higher social stratum, from country to city, from one country to another—is characteristically slow. It is not cultural persistence, therefore, that is responsible for the typical formation of field-related or field-ethnic enclaves—particularly among first-generation immigrants—but the dialectic of existing barriers of integration and the staying power of habits.[33]

The habit of consuming information in Turkish—from friends, through official channels, or from the media—persisted because it was easier to continue processing information in the only language they knew than to learn to communicate in Dutch.

The origin of those programs—whether from Turkey or from the United States—mattered little in this study. Many of the people in this study who were totally illiterate, or could only read and write and understand Turkish, were so thrilled to be receiving some entertainment in their homes that they could understand, that they were relatively unconcerned about the substance of that entertainment. So I conclude that even if the middle-aged women were watching daily doses of *The Bold and the Beautiful* in Turkish, the women saw this more as a *Turkish* experience within their cultural framework than an experience that exposed them to alien values. And if they did notice that these values were inconsistent with their own, they simply selected other programs whose content was more acceptable. Aside from one or two U.S. soap operas, all the programs the participants said they watched were made in Turkey. The only exceptions to this would be U.S. films. The conservative channels do show Hollywood films—but those films are often musicals and dramatic productions made in the 1930s to the 1950s, in an era when less sex and violence appeared on the screen. Other channels broadcast recent Hollywood films, but since I did not ask for film titles in questions about their favorite television programs, I don't know which films they have watched.

Effect of viewing and cultural orientation: Second-generation Turks and others who had varying amounts of literacy in Dutch were the people who moved back and forth between Dutch and Turkish television with greater ease. While it is true that a number of these people reported watching a lot more television in Dutch prior to the entry of satellite television from Turkey, this viewing had more to do with their facility in Dutch than in their newfound interest in Turkish television. The most educated and the most literate in Dutch watched the least amount of Turkish television. There is some kind of continuum here, where language is still the most important variable determining viewing habits. After that, it comes down to program choice, taste, and also cultural attachment.

Earlier, I said it was surprising that so many of the younger people, the second generation, who lived in Amsterdam, watched so much television from Turkey. Kerem, the young man who was an avid follower of Tarkan, was typical of that group. He said he could spend eight-hour stretches watching Turkish channels when he had nothing else to do. Though Kerem is the son of migrants, he has lived only in Amsterdam for seven years. He left Turkey after finishing elementary school. So his formative years were spent in Turkey, not in the Netherlands. In this study, those participants who were born and spent their early years there and then migrated, or left as teenagers and were now in their twenties, or who returned to Turkey for some years during their early life, were the ones who also spent more time watching Turkish television. They were also the people who had less education, having dropped out of school before getting a diploma (about half of all Turkish youth in Amsterdam, according to Atilla Arda, the city council representative) or who were unable to find a job because they didn't have the right credentials. As Yilmaz Yilmaz, one of the *Alternatif* directors said about Kerem, "He doesn't want to work hard at school or at *Alternatif*." Kerem's interest in Tarkan and in Turkish television isn't really so hard to understand. He and the others who spent about an equal amount of time in Turkey and in the Netherlands don't know where they belong. When he talked with me about his plans for his future, Kerem said he thought he might drop out of school and go back to Turkey to live and work. When I say that in Turkey he will also need a diploma and skills to find a job, he shrugs it off. He responds that he has friends there who can find him a job.

Several other young people like Kerem talked of returning to Turkey. Whether they have sufficient education to make it there or not, they think Turkey is the ideal place—the place where they will finally fit in. And the television programs they watch support that view. They finally see on the television screen the people who look like them, who like the same music, who speak the language they are most comfortable with, and who share the same cultural traditions. Several people in their twenties with whom I talked actually had gone back to Turkey to live a while, and then returned to Amsterdam, finding it was not all they hoped it would be. Some realized there were major cultural differences between themselves and the Turks in Turkey. Lale is a good example. She is the young woman who did her apprenticeship in a Turkish business and decided that she was more at home with the Dutch in Amsterdam than with the people from the country of her birth. Other young people have experienced Turkey only during their summer vacations by the sea, and thought that being in Turkey meant late nights out with friends, days spent in the sun, and pleasant visits with relatives. These young people never experienced the workaday world in Turkey, never spent a winter trudging through snow or mud, never saw the smog-filled skies of the cities in January. Once they returned to Turkey to work, they realized that it was not the way they remembered.

In chapter 3, I argued that cultural orientation—a multidimensional concept that was based on educational level, socioeconomic level, facility in foreign languages, amount of travel and length of stay in other places, and religious point of view—was related to the types of media people consume. The results of this study confirm that this is so. The easiest of these variables to measure in this study were language, educational background, and religious point of view. Perhaps that is why they carry the most weight in the findings. And it is true also that the more educated, the more languages spoken, and the higher socio-economic level achieved, the more likely a person is to have traveled. In other words, these variables often cluster together, such that people who are poor are also often uneducated and therefore don't speak several languages and haven't had the opportunity to travel.

But examining the concept of cultural orientation related to these migrants is different. Almost everyone in the first generation—except those who might have come for political reasons or advanced education—arrived in this foreign location as poor and uneducated. Many were even illiterate or semiliterate in their mother tongue, and certainly had no skills in foreign languages. What caused them to decide to work in Europe had little or nothing to do with a cultural orientation that was receptive to things foreign. They went to improve their economic status in life, to earn enough money to support their families. Though many of them likely had some spirit of adventure, they were motivated more by a lack of options in their Turkish environment than out of any curiosity about life in foreign countries, i.e., more by push than pull factors.

So why did some of those people decide to get more education for themselves and learn to speak Dutch while others did not? Why did some of them decide that life would be different for their children? Rıza Şeref said he grew up in a town where no other Turks lived. Why did his parents make that decision? And why did Banu, the woman who married as a teenager and whose husband helped her adjust to the Dutch environment, decide that it was important to spend vacation time traveling in Holland as well as to Turkey in the free time the family had? How was it that in some of the families of the first generation the children all grew up to get university degrees and in other families the children all dropped out of school before getting a diploma? Unfortunately, this study doesn't provide answers for those questions. A much more in-depth study that would examine social psychological variables and study individuals and families over time would be needed to determine that. But it is true that when people learned more Dutch, tried to educate themselves and their children, and looked upon Europe as a place to travel around and not just to drive through on the way to Turkey, that they also developed a wider cultural orientation—and were less tied to their home culture. They also consumed a mix of media from Turkey and from the Netherlands.

When it became possible to add the television channels from Turkey to the channels people were already receiving in the Netherlands (and those included other foreign channels, like the BBC, CNN International, Eurosport, etc.), it enriched and expanded the worldview of the Turkish residents of Amsterdam. And to make the choice to add the Turkish channels to the ones they already received on cable would mean that the households would add some news and entertainment from their home country to what they were already watching. That did happen for those people in this study who were bilingual or trilingual, who were better educated overall, and who were of a higher socioecomic level. It even happened for some people who had conservative religious beliefs—if they also valued education and were literate in Dutch.

Television as companion: Those people who spent little time outside their households or their neighborhoods—and in this study that group consists of women in their forties or older—look to television as a source of comfort. The story of the following woman illustrates this use of television.

Because Sevil now lives alone, she is not typical of this group, but her story is like that of many others who came here. And her use of television is more typical. Her husband came to Amsterdam as a guest worker in the early 1970s. She was reluctant to follow, because she thought her children would be better off going to school in their own culture. But he insisted. So she left her family and friends and settled in Amsterdam with him. There they raised their children, who became so comfortable with Dutch life and customs that one of her sons now lives with a Dutch woman, another unmarried son lives away from home with several friends (not a common Turkish practice), and her daughter is married and visits her infrequently. Unlike most wives of guest workers, she worked in factories and cleaned in a hospital at night. She worked about twelve years in all, but had to quit because of illness. Sevil is now middle-aged and quite ill. She has lived alone in the nine years since her husband died. She has had two cancer operations and has limited energy and economic resources. She can no longer visit Turkey as often as she would like because of her illness. When she was well, she would go for several months at a time.

What she treasures most is her television contact with Turkey. Though she speaks Dutch, she says she no longer has the energy to keep it up. And she also pays less attention to Dutch media. She turns on the satellite television when she wakes up in the morning, and it is on throughout the day. "I get up in the morning, wash my face, and put on the tea kettle. Then I sit down and drink my tea and watch the news." When I ask how much television she watches from Turkey, she says, "So there will be sound in the house and the loneliness will go away, sometimes I keep it on all day." She knows more about the details of Turkish political and social life than many Turks who live in Turkey do. The television allows her to transport herself psychologically to a place where she was once happy and had a better sense of belonging. She imagines that she would be happier if she were there today. She believes her children would have been more devoted and more *Turkish*, had she raised them there. The stories on television allow her to continuously live a vicarious existence. To a great extent, she has removed herself from Dutch daily life and culture.

Facilitating change, reinforcing change, preventing change: It may at first be hard to imagine that media can accomplish all three of these things simultaneously. But that actually happened with different people in this study, depending on what media they consumed, what approach they took to the media content, and what effect the media intended.

The media that intended certain effects—TRT-INT programs, Dutch television programs aimed at migrants, ATV's European news and magazine program, and other media in Turkish targeting the migrants in the Netherlands—could have no impact at all when the audience didn't attend to the messages. We know from the low percentages in the various studies of NPS radio and *Migranten TV* that very few people listen to or watch these programs. Very few participants said they watched the European news program for Turks. And an overwhelming number of participants disparaged the program content on TRT-INT.

The people who did attend to those messages that intended change were affected, however. In those homes where the parents said they exposed their children to TRT-INT so their children would learn better Turkish the children actually did speak a more standard urban Turkish than did their parents, who spoke village dialects. How much they learned at school and from their friends as opposed to how much they learned from television is difficult to determine. In homes where parents said they wanted their children to be more in touch with the Turkish culture, many of the children reported liking certain television programs from Turkey and learning from the content. It is also hard to separate out the influence of the family from the influence of television. Ayfer's teenaged daughter Elif attributes most of her feeling about her cultural identity to her mother.

> No, I don't think I feel like I am caught between two cultures. I take the positive things from Dutch culture. But I'm not pleased with the Dutch culture, in general. My mother raised me from the perspective of the Turkish culture, so many things the Dutch do are opposite the way they ought to be. Like the concept of family relations. I think about returning to Turkey, but recently things have been very bad—the economy and the educational system. For those reasons I am distancing myself from the decision to return permanently. It might happen, it might not. Really, the best is for me to spend six months there and six months here every year.

Media that had no particular intended impact could still have facilitated change, reinforced change, or prevented change. If the participants consumed Turkish media exclusively, they were not attending to any messages aimed at integrating Turkish people into the Dutch culture. So the Turkish media have in this case prevented change. What we don't know is whether people would have received those messages had Turkish media not been available, and if they did receive the messages, whether they might have acted on them. The religious messages that were carried on both Dutch and Turkish media may have been aimed at both believers and nonbelievers. But in this study, none of the participants who said they were not practicing Muslims reported watching religious programs. So those media were reinforcing in their impact. The devout found guidance and support in the religious messages. Those who were not religious rejected those messages.

The second generation may be more impressionable when it comes to the messages carried on Turkish television. Since the only frame of reference for Turkey many of them have is that of Turkey in the summer holiday time, many young people saw it as the ideal place to live. Ayfer worried about that. "They make me think, they make me think," she said about the tumultuous political events described on television news at the time. "I say that because I have lived in Turkey. Whatever happens there, I can contend with it, I can adapt to it. But I don't think the same about my children. They want to live there, and I think they will have a lot of trouble," she said.

Didim, a seventeen-year-old girl whose parents wouldn't consider a permanent return to Turkey, thinks she might have a better life in that country. "I think from time to time of going to live in Turkey. I'd like to escape the feeling of being different here, of the problems for Turks here—and there the people are warmer, more friendly. Life has more meaning," she said. Of course it is hard to know whether that idea came to her from her experiences in the Netherlands, her trips to Turkey, or the programs she watched on television. But television supported the message that life in Turkey carried more meaning and that in Turkey people are warm and friendly.

Music programs on television also have a special impact on youths. Earlier, I discussed the popularity of Tarkan and the attendance at the concert given by the Istanbul group. Television, with its many music videos, reinforces the interest in Turkish popular music. With some youths, those who developed a liking for Turkish popular music after their exposure to those programs, television facilitated change.

Identity, Media Use, and the Participants

To this point identity has been mentioned a lot, but has not been treated as a separate topic. Marie Gillespie's book on Punjabi youth in Southall, London, focuses on the relationship between media and identity, but says in the conclusion of her study:

> Though much of this book may be read as an affirmation of media consumers' resourcefulness in constructing their own identities, we should not lose sight of the very real constraints upon their freedom to do so: the nation state continues to define its ethnic minorities as internal others; and class, gender, religion, locality, generation and other factors, which are not freely chosen, continue to set limits on self-invention.[34]

Her study was set in a different country with a different ethnic minority from this one, but what she says applies to this group of migrants, too. Certainly the Turks in Amsterdam are free to move back and forth between Dutch and Turkish media, selecting content that reinforces who they are or that helps them discover who they will be. But I agree that many other factors are involved. A few extended examples here might illustrate the diversity of identity, but also the ways the environment in Amsterdam helps people become something different than they might have been had they stayed in Turkey, whether they spend lots of time consuming Turkish media or not. The examples I have chosen are all women, because for them, being in Amsterdam may have made more difference to their lives than it has for the men in the study. Though they come from quite different backgrounds, they all value the freedom allowed them in Amsterdam, freedom they believe they would not have had if their lives had been spent in Turkey.

Keriman owns a wholesale and retail clothing business with her husband Ayhan. She is the only seamstress, and produces racks full of simply made and inexpensive blouses, skirts, and dresses. She and her husband come to the shop around nine in the morning and work from then until midnight. The day I came to the store for an interview, they arrived about 9:30, saying they were late because they had been working until 2 A.M. Ayhan claims they could not survive if they worked only eight hours a day. On weekends, they travel to Utrecht, where they sell in an open market. He goes alone on Saturday and she joins him on Sunday. Their one bit of fun together is the picnic they have on the weekend. They have no time off except for the occasional Turkish holiday. And twice they have closed down for a month to go back to Turkey.

They have two children, a daughter and a son. Kerem, who has been introduced earlier in this study, is their son—and has no interest in the business. Their daughter is unemployed, but she too does not help them in the business. Both children have at least high school educations.[35] Neither Keriman nor Ayhan have much time for media. Since Keriman sews all day, she listens to the radio a lot. She says she finds it comforting. They are one of the few families who listen to the news in Turkish on Dutch public radio. Ayhan says he reads the headlines of the Dutch newspapers, but doesn't have language skills that allow him to read in depth. The only time he reads Turkish newspapers is when he goes to the coffeehouse or to another Turkish store where he might find it. At home they watch some news on the Turkish channels—NTV, ATV, or Star. They have no time for entertainment programs.

As I talk with Keriman, her husband and his brother, who also works in the store, leave. Then she begins to tell me more about herself and her life in Amsterdam. Since she works all day, she has little time for socializing with friends. And as she spends more time in Amsterdam, she wants less to do with Turks. They chose the neighborhood they live in because it had few Turks. Though her husband is quite nationalistic and says he would like to return home, she would not. "Women have a much better life here. They are free to do what they want. If I were in Turkey, I would have to get permission from my husband to go out and to do things." Here she doesn't consult with him on such issues. "Nobody knows me here," she says. That is a comment on her memory of Turkey, where all the people in a neighborhood might know a person's business, and where privacy is difficult to achieve.

She is critical of many of her countrymen here in Amsterdam because they live off welfare, then work illegally. She says that many businesses like theirs employ illegal workers, then lock them up in a basement where they work full time. She tells me that she has reported some of these people to the police. Though she has limited skill in Dutch, she has gone to the police to turn them in, because she believes such activity is immoral. "More than half of the Turks who live here collect unemployment and work illegally," she said. She does not back this up with any official data, but it is true that the unemployment rate among Turks in the Netherlands is quite high. How many of those people work illegally is unknown.

When her husband was gone, she also complained about how hard she has to work. She said they could not afford to hire someone to help them, when salary plus benefits were considered. But she said her husband is often away buying and selling merchandise, while she is the sole producer of goods. She said she even sews all day with the door locked on Dutch holidays. But she would never give this up to go on welfare. She has very strong feelings about her independence and ability to support herself and her family.

She would very much like to take a language course, but she has no time away from the shop. She also has no time for religion. She is critical of those women who cover themselves completely, though she herself wears a head scarf—but more in village tradition than with any religious significance.

In Keriman's life, her identity is driven by her work and her family. She has little life outside that. Yet, she says she would never choose to live in Turkey. The Netherlands has allowed her a sense of freedom, though it doesn't appear that way to an outside observer. She likes that she is able to decide her own fate—no matter how limited that ability might be. However it is, she believes it would be worse for her in Turkey. In Keriman's life, the media only make it a little bit more bearable. The radio becomes her companion as she works, and the television is only used to give her information about what's going on in the world. Otherwise, no media from either country make a lot of difference.

Tülin, the young woman who heads the women's organization at the mosque, has created her identity within this environment in a way that also might not have been possible back in Turkey. She has chosen a more religious life for herself, and chooses her media according to her beliefs, rather than being influenced by the range of content available on the private channels. Though she has three small children, she spends much of her time volunteering for the women's organization. Like Keriman, Tülin believes she would be restricted from living that kind of life in Turkey—as a woman who covers herself. Here it is not so out of the ordinary to dress as she does, but she says she would be forbidden to work or practice her Islamic lifestyle in Turkey. "Many women talk about democracy and freedom, but they mean very different things by it," she says. She may have concluded that she would not be allowed freedom in Turkey from what she sees on television about the politics of Islam.

I sense that what she feels about the repression of Islam in Turkey is rage, but she is very controlled in her speech. She says she dislikes immoral television programs, whether in Dutch or Turkish, and turns them off. She is angry that children get messages and a point of view that is inappropriate when they mix in Dutch society. Her organization, the Dutch Muslim Women's Platform, has several goals. One is to convince youth to avoid drugs. Another is to turn passive women into activists in the cause of improving their lives and those of their families—within an Islamic context. She is free to spend so much time with this group because day care is provided for the women who attend.

She and Keriman are both strong women who have taken different paths and have different ideas about what's important in their lives. But media don't play a large role in either of their lives. The fact that they live in Amsterdam in this social and political environment is of much greater importance in carving out their identities than any media content. Though Tülin claims that she lives in a country that is hostile to her values, instead of leaving that environment, she works to change it. She sees the media as opposing her beliefs—even working against what she believes in, but she doesn't give up in the face of their power. She constructs her life within the media messages that she thinks are acceptable and rejects all others. And when she sees on Turkish television that women are not permitted to attend the university with a head covering and praying in some public places is not allowed, it makes her angry. And it makes her appreciate the place where she lives, where she is free to work to bring about change, not just accept what is there.

Şenol is different from the other women in several ways. First she is educated—with a master's degree. Second, she is married to a Dutch man. Third, she is fluent in Dutch. And she has a work life that is even more independent than the others. She is an artist who has her own studio and has exhibits in the Netherlands and in Turkey. She takes her identity even more from the Dutch culture that surrounds her than she does from Turkey. She confronted her difference when she exhibited her art in Turkey. Her art is driven by her protest against consumer culture by using only waste materials or recycled items in her sculptures. In Turkey it has not been appreciated, she said. Consumerism is embraced rather than rejected by most Turks, and people are often searching for the latest fad or fashion to come out of the United States or Europe. So the people who came to see her art didn't understand her mockery of consumerism. In a book of collages that portrayed her view of the consumerist culture in Turkey, she included all kinds of advertising messages. "Excess is the key in Turkey," she said. When she displayed her sculptures in Turkey, they didn't know how to appreciate a sculpture made out of milk cartons, for example. With a single-minded definition of what constitutes sculpture, Şenol said they expected her work to be of imposing size.

She doesn't want to be too immersed in Turkish culture, since she makes her life in Dutch culture. And that includes her choice not to get a satellite dish. Yet she spends about three months every year in Turkey, and moves freely between educated and artistic circles in Amsterdam and in Turkey. As much as the other two women, Şenol values the freedom she has in the Netherlands. "As a woman, I live a free life here. I go out whenever I want, whatever time of the day I want, wherever I want. It is not that way in Turkey. I can't go out after a certain time at night."

Though she is like the other women, she also is different. And what most separates her from them is her ability to communicate in Dutch. That makes her feel different about herself and her place here.

> I am completely integrated here. Sometimes when I am speaking Dutch, I think of it as my native language. I have really found myself here. Of course, my husband is Dutch and that makes it easier. Many of my friends are Dutch. When I first came here I spoke English and it was difficult to be a part of this society. It took me at least two years to learn Dutch and after I did, communication became easier. I had learned English in school, and in college. The Dutch are not like us—they are colder, not sincere and warm like us. But you get used to it. You get used to everything.

"Getting used to it" in Amsterdam is something all three women have done. Though Şenol sees herself as changed by the culture—through her professional life and Dutch husband, she, too, is trying to change that environment as much as Tülin wants to make it a more "moral" place in which to live and to encourage other Muslim women to help her, and as much as Keriman wants to make Turkish people obey the Dutch laws and stop double-dipping in the Dutch economy. Media play some role in their lives. And they use it to support their identity, not change it.

Notes

1. Arjun Appadurai, *Modernity at Large* (Minneapolis: University of Minnesota Press, 1996), 4.

2. Veldkamp Marktondeerzoek bv, *Invloed Schotelantennes op Kijkgedrag Turken en Marokkanen* (Amsterdam: Veldkamp, 1996).

3. Veldkamp Marktonderzoek bv, *Mediagebruik Etnische Publieksgroepen 1998* (Amsterdam: Veldkamp, June 1999).

4. See Christine Ogan, "Developing Policy for Eliminating International Video Piracy," *Journal of Broadcasting and Electronic Media* 32, no. 2 (spring 1998): 163-182.

5. "TV Watchers Vote News as Favorite Program," *Turkish Daily News,* Domestic News (Ankara, 24 September 1997) http://www.turkishdailynews.com (25 September 1997).

6. Mustafa Kuzum, personal interview, Ankara, Turkey (1 May 1997).

7. Denis McQuail, *McQuail's Mass Communication Theory,* 4th ed. (London: Sage, 2000), 426.

8. McQuail, *McQuai's Mass,* 427, 428.

9. McQuail, *McQuail's Mass,* 428.

10. See, for example, Herbert Schiller, *Mass Communication and the American Empire* (Boulder, Colo.: Westview, 1992).

11. John Tomlinson, *Cultural Imperialism: A Critical Introduction* (Baltimore: Johns Hopkins University Press, 1991), 34.

12. Asu Aksoy and Kevin Robins, "Peripheral Vision: Cultural Industries and Cultural Identities in Turkey," *Environment and Planning* 29, no. 11 (1997): 1951.

13. For a discussion of the events surrounding the introduction of satellite broadcasting, see Christine Ogan, "Communications Policy Options in an Era of Rapid Technological Change," *Telecommunications Policy* 16, no. 7 (September-October 1992): 565-575.

14. Aksoy and Robins, "Peripheral Vision," 1942.

15. Nicole Pope and Hugh Pope, *Turkey Unveiled: A History of Modern Turkey* (Woodstock, N.Y.: Overlook, 1998), 67.

16. Ayşe Öncü, "Packaging Islam: Cultural Politics on the Landscape of Turkish Commercial Television," *Public Culture* 8, no. 1 (1995): 59.

17. Aksoy and Robins, "Peripheral Vision," 1944.

18. Mark Tungate, "Battle of the Big Four," *Media International* (September 1998): 40.

19. Kemal Balci, "Anatomy of the Media Bosses," *Turkish Probe* 303 (1 November 1998), electronic edition, <http://38.242.79.170/past_probe/11_01_98/contents.htm>.

20. Balci, "Anatomy of the Media."

21. Dinc Bilgin owned Sabah and ATV up until December 2000. While it has been common practice for media barons to finance their media properties from their banking holdings, in November 2000 the state took control of Bilgin's Etibank as part of a clean-up operation in the corrupt banking industry. Bilgin then sold off his media properties to Mehmet Emin Karamehmet (Çukurova Holding), who already has ownership in other media and in banking. Karamehmet also now owns Kanal 6 and *Yenibinyil*, the newspaper formerly called *Yeniyuzil*.

22. Hakan Aslaneli, "The Ratings War Corrupts Turkey's Entertainment World," *Turkish Probe* 317 (7 February 1999), http://38.242.79.170/past_probe/02_07_99/dom2.htm#d20 (1 May 2000).

23. Aslaneli, "The Ratings War."

24. Aslaneli, "The Ratings War."

25. Rinus Penninx, Jeannette Schoorl, and Carlo van Praag, *The Impact of International Migration on Receiving Countries: The Case of the Netherlands* (The Hague: Netherlands Interdisciplinary Demographic Institute, 1994), 141.

26. Veldkamp Marktonderzoek bv, *Mediagebruik Etnische Publieksgroepen 1998* (Amsterdam: Veldkamp, June 1999), 61, 62, 65.

27. Emrah Güler, "Tarkan: From the Stage to the Barracks," *Turkish Daily News* (16 January 2000), on-line edition. Feature section. http://www.turkishdailynews.com.

28. Güler, "From the Stage."

29. Alisa Valdez-Rodriguez, "Pop Beat: Turkish Singer's Latin Success Sealed with a Kiss or Two," *Los Angeles Times* (22 July 2000), F1.

30. Joost DeBruin, "'We Just Couldn't Behave Like That': Dutch Soap Opera, Adolescence, and Ethnicity." Paper presented at the Crossroads in Cultural Studies Conference, Birmingham, U.K., June 2000.

31. Marie Gillespie, *Television, Ethnicity, and Cultural Change* (London: Routledge, 1995), 148.

32. Meidert Fennema and Jean Tillie, "Political Participation and Political Trust in a Multicultural Democracy," unpublished paper (Amsterdam: Institute for Migration and Ethnic Studies and Department of Political Science, University of Amsterdam, July 1999), 19.

33. Hans-Rudolf Wicker, "From Complex Culture to Cultural Complexity," in *Debating Cultural Hybridity*, Pnina Werbner and Tariq Modood, eds. (London: Zed Books, 1997), 41.

34. Gillespie, *Television, Ethnicity, and Cultural Change*, 208.

35. The Dutch educational system is very difficult to explain in a short space. Several kinds of post-middle school educational options are available.

Chapter 6

Media, Identity, and the "Spiritual" Lives of Migrants

I detected an urban legend surrounding the religious community as I interviewed people who were not practicing Muslims. The story went like this. The devout religious community raises money from others and also from their own groups to support a political effort to overthrow the government in Ankara. These people see the government as oppressive and intolerant of the practice of Islam. Often, when the groups gather at the mosques they are asked to give of their resources. At these times, the women, who wear many gold bracelets, hold out their arms and shuck off the bracelets one by one, placing them in a central offering.

I believe this story to be an urban legend, though it may well have happened on one or more occasions. Because the people telling this story have not witnessed any such event, it is difficult to know how much truth may be in it. But the fact that such a story circulates is indicative of the lack of communication and the resulting misunderstanding among the Turkish migrants in Amsterdam. In some ways, one group of Turks in Amsterdam may be as ignorant of the lifestyle and habits of another group as the Dutch are about the migrants.

Affiliations and Identity

In previous chapters I have broken down the participants into two groups, those who are religious and have some affiliation with an Islamic organization and its mosque, and those who are not practicing Muslims. But there are many more distinctions to be made here. This chapter will discuss the "spiritual" identity of the migrants, where spiritual is used in the broadest sense of the term. The term is *ruhsal* in Turkish and it means the same—of the spirit or the soul. In Turkish it may also refer to something that is of the psyche. Though religious affiliations may fulfill a spiritual need of the migrants, other organizations fulfill the same function.

Earlier I noted that more than 100 organizations (some political, some social, some religious) exist for the Turks who live in Amsterdam. Specifically, that number is 156. In all of the Netherlands, 1,125 organizations serve Turks. Many of these organizations are branches of the same organization located in several cities. And even a single organization in Amsterdam may be made up of different groups that meet in several parts of the city.

The organizations serve several interests. Various Islamic groups, women's groups, sports organizations, youth, cultural, and political groups are the main categories found among the 156 in the list. Aside from all the mainstream Turkish organizations, several are listed that serve Kurdish and Armenian peoples. It is not known how many people belong to any particular organization nor how many organizations to which any individual may have membership.

Tillie, Fennema, and Kraal analyzed 106 of these organizations for their interrelationships. Of the eighty-nine for which they could trace the board of directors, they found that forty-one of them were not connected to any others. And the remaining forty-eight formed eight different groups.[1] They determined this based on interlocking directorates. In the study, they also interviewed thirteen representatives of various organizations, selected on the basis of their position in the network of interlocking directorates. Their study determined a number of things about the organizations. One is that religious organizations cooperate with other religious organizations. Second, politically leftist organizations also cooperate with others of the same political persuasion. Cultural organizations cooperate with other cultural organizations and also with left-wing organizations. And organizations on the political right cooperate with others of the same political persuasion and also with mosques. When organizations did not cooperate with others, political or ideological differences were cited.[2]

Most of the largest organizations have religious ties, as might be expected. What appeared to be missing was any significant presence of organizations based on the migrants' city or region of origin in Turkey. That is surprising because of the strong bond between people who come from the same region. A Turk who comes from the same region as another calls that person a *hemfleri,* compatriot or fellow citizen. In Turkey when people move from rural areas to the city, they often settle in the same neighborhoods and establish self-help organizations based on their place of origin. Perhaps the lack of regional organizations is indicative of a reconfiguration of the Turks who live in the Netherlands. As time has passed, allegiance to the region of one's birth may have declined as other affiliations become important.

There is some evidence to the contrary, however. In research conducted for the book and the television series on the Turks in the Netherlands, it was noted that around the big cities in the Netherlands where Turks live, many coffeehouses exist that are only frequented by men who came from the same region in Turkey.

One of the important affiliations is the Islamic group, as has been noted in several places in this book. A second is the organization based on political affiliation or age group. And a third may be based on educational and professional achievement. In this chapter, I will discuss these affiliations by describing several groups I observed during this research. Communication—interpersonal, small group, and mass—is important to sustaining all of these organizations. Tillie, Fennema, and Kraal claim that reading or viewing news programs from the mass media is part of life in the civic community. Their indicators of civic engagement included watching *Migranten* television and reading Turkish newspapers. I will also examine the broader issue of migrant identity.

The Religious Organization

Though specific information is not easy to obtain, I was able to learn some things about the functioning of some of the mosques. I visited four or five of them in different parts of the city. The Fatih mosque was the first to be established in Amsterdam by the *Diyanet* in Turkey. A second major mosque I visited was the Aya Sofia mosque (named after the mosque in Istanbul that was at various times in history a Byzantine church and a mosque, and now is a museum). In both places, I found the mosque to function as a cultural center as well as a place of worship. Some kind of restaurant is set up in both of them, serving lunch and short-order items to be eaten with tea as a snack. Tea and coffee are served all day in both mosques. I only saw men in these places. Though they wondered what a woman might want in the place, they welcomed me. Some of the men even shook my hand, though that is often not allowed in more orthodox Muslim groups. Several of the men also were happy to talk with me there or in their homes at a later time. In Aya Sofia, the grocery, television room, and restaurant are all on the same level. The grocery looked exactly as it might have in any Turkish town, and was well stocked with Turkish canned goods, nuts, coffee, and even fresh vegetables.

On the different times I visited the mosques, ten to twenty men would be congregated in various groups, talking or playing backgammon. More men would appear on Fridays, the Islamic Sabbath. Although this is a good place for men to socialize, they talked to me of establishing spaces in the mosque for their children to play sports and hang out. One man, who also counsels Turkish youth in the Dutch prisons, said many of the young people get in trouble because they have no cultural base. He believes that religion is what will keep children from participating in illegal activities. So there are martial arts classes and a soccer team based at Aya Sofia. But even if youths are not having problems, they believe the mosque helps maintain ties to Turkey and to their culture. In other rooms in the building, which is about 10,000 square meters and consists of several converted garages, women and youths have space for meetings. The young men described in an earlier chapter created their own organization there. Aya Sofia is affiliated with the *Milli Görüş*. The men told me their youth organization, SUN (*Studenten Unie Nederland* [Student Union Netherlands]), was not directly affiliated with either the mosque or the *Milli Görüş*, but the mosque officials allowed them to use the space for their meetings.

Aya Sofia serves as more than a location for meetings of these various groups; it is a place where identity can be formed (in the case of the children), nurtured (in the case of the young adults and women), or reinforced (in the case of the men who socialize as they might have in the coffeehouse in the village or small town). Because the space where they meet is tied up with a particular religious identity, those who go there get a heavy dose of religious ideology (Islam) and political ideology (*Milli Görüş* and *Fazilet* Party).

Yalçın-Heckmann studied issues of identity in two associations, one in France, the other in Germany. One of the organizations was tied to the *Milli Görüş* through the mosque where it met and where the head of the association was a member. Yalçın-Heckmann found there were difficulties in forming a local identity for this organization because of the link to *Milli Görüş*—an international single-interest organization with seventeen Amsterdam locations. Some members of the organization were therefore suspicious of a hidden agenda for the leader of the organization. This led to a certain fragmentation of the organization. But even when a person accepts the agenda of the organization, as Yalçın-Heckmann says in her analysis, it is often difficult to determine why people take part in certain acts in certain locations, such as praying at the mosque. It is impossible to say that identity with the mosque or with the act of praying is the same for all. But praying with others on a given day at a mosque does function "as a way of expressing a public identity and with it a set of values and attitudes."[3]

That public identity is expressed every time İbrahim and his friends meet to discuss their business for SUN, or when Tülin meets with her women's group, or when the youths gather for a karate lesson at Aya Sofia. Privately, however, it is more difficult to know how bound up with the mosque any individual's identity is.

Another expression of public identity was made when the *Milli Görüş* held its annual international meeting on June 14, 1998, in Arena, the new stadium for the Ajax football team. As mentioned in an earlier chapter, the *Avrupa Milli Görüş Teşkilatları* (European National View Organization) became an official organization in 1985 after several reorganizations. Its headquarters is in Cologne, Germany, and its Dutch headquarters is in Schiedam, a suburb of Rotterdam. It was considered the cultural and religious wing of the Turkish *Refah Partisi* (Welfare Party) until its banning in August 1997. Now it is affiliated with the party reorganized as *Fazilet* (Virtue) Party. According to Dassetto and Nonneman, this conservative religious party grew out of "efforts to merge three components: reference to Islam as a project of society; reference to the affirmation of Turco-Ottoman identity; and reference to technical and scientific modernity."[4] Talip Kuçükcan, participating in a 1997 discussion about identity issues and Islam in Europe, affirmed the presence of political Islam among migrants in Europe.

> There is no doubt that Islamic movements have a transnational nature. Their emergence in European countries over the last two decades lends support to the argument that there are connections between Islamic movements in the countries of origin and settlement. Reproduction and institutionalization of Islamic values in Europe did not take place in isolation from the politics of Islam in the countries of origin. The ideological positions and organizational structures of the current Islamic movements in various European countries reveal

> that they were predominantly established as branches and off-shoots of "model movements/groups" in the countries of origin. A religio-political movement, known as National Vision (*Milli Görüş*) among Turkish Muslims in several Western cities is an excellent example. It was established in Germany in 1985 as the European branch of the Welfare Party (*Refah Partisi*) [previously National Action Party—*Milli Selamet Partisi*]. National Vision has allied itself closely with the Welfare Party and more than 800 branches disseminate its Islamic ideology among Turkish immigrants. The transplantation of political Islam is facilitated by well-attended conferences.[5]

The day-long rally in Arena was one such conference. The first three meetings of the annual conference were held in Germany, but in 1998 that meeting was moved to Amsterdam. An estimated 40,000 people attended the event, which was broadcast live on *Kanal 7* and transmitted to Turkey and Europe simultaneously. Large television screens on the field also tracked the events of the day, which was unusually sunny and warm. Speakers and participants came from all over Europe, many of them sleeping on couches and floors of family and friends throughout the city. The women and most of the young boys and all of the girls sat in one half of the stadium, while the men and older boys were seated in the other half. The scene was a dramatic contrast to any other gathering ever held in this liberal Dutch city. Hundreds of large Turkish, *Milli Görüş*, and Islamic flags—of the size we see cheerleaders wave at American sports events—could be seen all over the stadium, being raised at every emotional high point during the day. It was an incredibly colorful sight—the red and white of the Turkish flags, white with a green map of Europe for the *Milli Görüş* flags, and the green with Arabic script on the Islamic flags. Banners with the conference logo and slogans of various kinds were hung around the stadium. Signs included messages like, "Honor to our coverings" (meaning head scarves and long dresses) and "The Principles of *Milli Görüş* are Love, Peace, and Tolerance." Advertising for Jetpa, a Turkish Islamic holding company, added to the scene. All around the hallways in the stadium, men and women (in their respective sections) spread out their prayer rugs and knelt on the floor at official prayer times. Friends greeted one another warmly—many of them having come from Germany, Belgium, and France. The feeling was one of a very large family reunion. When I left the celebration, I rode back to the city on the metro with some teen-age boys who were working at the event. They came from Germany, and were taking a break to check out the sights in downtown Amsterdam. I asked if they had ever been to one of these events before. One of them replied, "This is the fourth one of these. The last two were in Dortmund and the one before in Cologne. Every year it gets bigger. We wouldn't miss going."

Such an event offers an opportunity to reaffirm identity with Muslim brothers and sisters. The program was also structured to accomplish that goal. Many comparisons could be made to an athletic event in the sense that athletic events stir up loyalty to the home team. Here, there was a marching band, too—but not of the usual sort. Instead it was the *Mehter takımı* from Istanbul—a group of musicians who simulate, in dress and style, the old Janissary bands that thrived under the Ottomans until disbanded in the early 1800s. As they marched around the field, the crowd stood and waved their flags and cheered, identifying themselves with the days of Ottoman glory when the state and religion were not separated. The media joined in the celebration of identity, as a singer from *Kanal 7* sang a familiar song, causing the crowd to wave their flags to the music. The Turkish national anthem reinforced the identity with the homeland. The deposed leader and former prime minister, Necmettin Erbakan, had been forbidden to give political speeches by the courts after he was banned from politics, but he entered in a BMW and greeted the crowd from the podium. He embodies the *Milli Görüş* identity and is considered the group's spiritual leader.

The mass media were particularly important in this event, tying together the Islamic and political identity with that of *Kanal 7,* the television channel that represents both interests. On the field of the stadium, the large screens carried the action of the day—much like they would for a soccer game—and the same coverage was going out over *Kanal 7*. It reaffirmed for the people in the stadium and those at home watching on television that this channel was the one they should turn to if they wanted information and programming consistent with their values and beliefs. And indeed, it was the first channel of choice among the Muslim families in the study. Repeated references to *Kanal 7*'s involvement in the event were made, and several representatives from the station made presentations.

Nilufer Göle, who has written a book about veiling in Islam, believes that Islamic identity may have little to do with individual choices made by those who are believers, but is rather imposed from above by its leaders.

> The more one reinforces the relationship between "pure" self and "total" community, the more Islamic politics becomes an imposed lifestyle, veiling a compulsory emblem, and women the moral guardians of Islamic identity and community. This would entail the control of the public sphere by means of canceling out individual choices in determining lifestyles, monopolizing the cultural code, and instituting an Islamist form of the colonization of the self.
>
> In other words, the totalitarian dimension emerges from the utopian ideal of a single identity for the collectivity. The pairing of a fixed identity and a utopian community presupposes a harmonious, a historical nondifferentiated social order that avoids all subversive conflict. Women are the touchstones of this Islamic order in that they become, in their bodies and sexuality, a *trait d'union* between identity and community. This implies that the integrity of the Islamic community will be measured and reassured by women's politically regulated and confined modesty and identity (such as compulsory veiling, restricted public visibility, and the restrained encounter between the sexes). Traditional gender identities and roles underlie Islamic authoritarianism.[6]

There are other ways that identity with *Milli Görüş* is reinforced or perhaps controlled. The organization runs weekend and summer camps for children. The organization's Web site states that 13,801 children attended these camps in

Europe in 1998. The site also declares that one of its responsibilities is to maintain identity with the *Milli Görüş* community. "As a minority community we have to have consciousness of being a member of Muslim community." Organizing people to travel in groups on the annual pilgrimage to Mecca and collecting money to send to the poor in other countries during the time of the Islamic Sacrifice holiday are other ways they bind members of the community together. On the Web site for the group, it claims that enough money was donated in 1999 on that holiday to slaughter nearly 28,000 sheep and distribute the meat to the poor in Turkey and elsewhere.[7]

This Islamic group has a goal for Turkey, but most of the members I talked to have greater goals for their group in the Netherlands. They fight for their religious rights within the Dutch context. And though some of them talk of a return to Turkey, and actually do still vote in Turkish elections, they appear to be more interested in improving their religious position in the various European cities where they live. This may be especially true now that the party of their affiliation in Turkey is less influential.

The *Milli Görüş* may be the best organized Islamic group in the Netherlands, and the one that demands most from its members, but many other Muslim organizations exist that have been mentioned in earlier chapters. All of them have similar methods for establishing community and maintaining identity. Some of these groups were difficult to access because they are less open. Others were less focused in their plans and in activities for their members.

Secular Groups

Time spent at two other organizations, HTIB (Turkish Workers Association in the Netherlands) and ATKB (Foundation of Women of Turkey in Amsterdam) revealed that the organization headquarters fulfilled many of the same purposes for the individuals involved. Both are secular organizations that are left wing in their political orientation, according to analysis by Tillie, Fenneman, and Kraal.[8] And both provide educational, cultural, recreational, and social service activities and support. HTIB is an organization for both men and women, though my visits to the headquarters found mostly men in attendance. ATKB has only women members. Education programs in both organizations include instruction in Turkish and Dutch. ATKB tries to help women improve their position within their families and in Dutch society, while HTIB's role is more diffuse. Since most of the formal educational and social programs are shut down during the summer months when I visited, I was not able to observe these activities. The days I visited both organizations, people were socializing over coffee, backgammon, or cards. In fact, aside from the religious and political differences, it differed very little from the activity at the coffeehouse in the mosque complexes.

One day when I visited ATKB, only six women were there for morning coffee and conversation, so I spent time listening to them as they discussed their problems and their feelings about issues important to them. The women in attendance there do not cover themselves. All of them wore long pants and were dressed casually. Two of them were single mothers who used some of the services of the organization for support in their position. All of them appear to know one another well, and join in the conversation, voicing strong opinions. The discussion of welfare, for example, came up spontaneously. In general, they thought welfare led people, especially migrants, to be passive and without initiative. One woman, whose husband has been unemployed for more than a year, was very opposed to welfare. She said her husband would work if there was a bigger difference between what he earned on welfare and the salary in the jobs that have been offered. If he took one of those jobs, it would just be to pass the time. She said her husband was in her way at home, and she would prefer that he go out to work every day instead. She didn't like the idea that they would never be able to get ahead economically; they always stayed in the same place.

The topic shifted to religion and one woman talked about a novel she had been reading about a woman's struggle to make a choice between Islam and Christianity. Another woman, who prefaced her remarks with "I am a Muslim too," differentiating herself from the *Milli Görüş* or the *Süleymancis*, (described in chapter 3), thought out loud about her own beliefs, what Islam teaches, and what she thinks. They all appeared to be wanting to find a place for religion within their own identities, but not the way the women who chose to cover themselves did. They refused to participate in any religious group where they would be told what to wear, what to think, and how to act.

The three visits I made to ATKB went similarly. Each time the women discussed topics like welfare or religion or the position of Turkish women in Dutch society. Occasionally they talked about Turkish politics or what it might be like to go back to Turkey to live. For them and for the people who spent their days at HTIB, the organizations became places to find friends and acquaintances who shared a common background and from whom they could take sustenance—or maintain identity.

Earlier discussions in previous chapters of the youths who spent much time at the *Alternatif* organization came to the same conclusion about the function of that organization for the young people. In their case, identity formation, not maintenance, was a function of the organization.

All these organizations, whether religious or not, provide a space for people to gather and an anchor for them to carve out their identity as people with Turkish cultural roots who now live in a Dutch cultural environment. Without these spaces, many of the migrants, whether religious or not, would have a harder time defining who they are in this European city.

Television and Identity

Though *Kanal 7* has been able to exploit Islamic identity and identity with the Islamic political party, *Fazilet*, the opening of private channels allowed that process to occur for several different groups. As M. Hakan Yavuz, an Islamic scholar, has written, "media are spaces for cultural elites to articulate and redefine subcultures and to carve a space for themselves in the cultural arenas."[9] Yavuz's article about Turkish media as they relate to the Alevi Islamic group and the Kurds is about identity for these people in Turkey. But his work has as much importance for the Turks in Europe. As an earlier chapter described it, when television in Turkey meant only programming sanctioned by the state, the definition of what was Turkish was defined by the state. Only when private broadcasting opened up the media space was it possible for people who did not share the definition of "Turk" that TRT proclaimed to identify with images they saw on television. I have described how *Kanal 7* was able to promote its definition of the Islamic Turk. But other channels promoted other identities.

Up to this point I have not mentioned MED-TV, the Kurdish television station that is now closed, but served Kurdish viewers in Europe and the Middle East until April 1999. Constantly criticized by the Turkish government as being the voice of the PKK, the Kurdish revolutionary organization headed by Abdullah Ocalan, the Independent Television Commission in the U.K. finally withdrew their license. Though this book has not dealt with the Kurds or Kurdish identity among the migrants in Amsterdam, it is important to point out that Kurdish people with whom I talked did watch MED-TV up to the time of its closure and did identify with that channel to a much greater extent than they did with any Turkish channel. Many of the Kurds in Amsterdam are political refugees from Turkey. I did not want to get into the issue of the Kurdish conflict, the PKK, or Ocalan, so I tried not to select Kurds to be included in the interviews. In the end, several Kurdish people were interviewed, however. In one family where the mother was Kurdish and the father Turkish, the children had split loyalties. Though they opposed the PKK, they were concerned that Turkish media did not provide a space for them. The oldest girl in the family mentioned that the masthead of the largest Turkish daily carried a quote of Ataturk's under his picture and the Turkish flag that said, "Turkey is for Turks." She said that she presumed this did not include her, since she was half Kurdish, and she was offended by that statement.

MED-TV also targeted programming to the Alevi community (whether Turkish or Kurdish), so some people in this study who identified themselves as Alevis reported watching MED-TV. The Alevi form of Islam was described in chapter 3. Yavuz mentions that the Alevis who live in Berlin have their own local media, including a magazine, a radio station, and a television station that broadcasts four hours a week.[10] Nobody in this study expressed any awareness of these media. But all of these have as their purpose the promotion of Alevi identity. In Amsterdam, thirty-four Alevi organizations exist.[11] He also believes the media are responsible for the contestation and pluralization of Alevi identity in Turkey. He says there are now two separate identities for Alevis that have grown out of competing journals in Turkey. Yavuz concludes that for the Kurds and the Alevis,

> media, by offering many opportunities for politically conscious elites to diffuse their ideas, have brought ethno-linguistic and ethno-religious identities into public space and contributed to the fragmentation of authority by multiplying not just its voices but also their subjects and, most important, their contexts. Above all, it is the multiplication of media and of media outlets that contributes to this fragmentation.[12]

Though I accept that media have contributed to fragmenting identities, and that is true for the people who view any of the Turkish television channels alongside Dutch channels, the addition of media outlets has also allowed for more individuals to locate people like themselves in the media they consume.

Akşit, fifty-seven, a retired sanitation worker who now spends all his time in social service activities for the mosque, gets very upset by the image of the Turkish woman he sees on most Turkish channels. "They show covered women on those channels as if it were a sin. Here people accept the way we dress, but Turks in Turkey—the ones they show on those channels—look down on us. We watch *Kanal 7* because the people on that channel look and act more like we do," he said. Akşit said he gets so angry some days by the news out of Turkey that he can't even watch. Of course the political situation in Turkey is covered by *Kanal 7*, too. "The women who work in government offices ought to be able to go to their jobs covered," he says.

At least *Kanal 7* will reinforce his attitude about the situation in Turkey, and not oppose it. For that he is grateful. Before he was able to watch satellite television, Akşit and his family rented videos—the ones that reflected his values. Most of them were religious in subject matter. In this family, the important thing in selecting media was to be able to identify with the point of view of the content.

Though Filiz is not religious, she has the same concerns about identity. She thinks life is very hard for foreigners in the Netherlands, and particularly hard when you are trying to raise children in the culture that is both different from yours and not accepting of your ways.

> I look at the children. When a child is merely four years old here, he starts living the struggle. You watch the foreign children being treated differently. And you say, "these people are practicing discrimination." You take the child to Turkey and he isn't a Turk anymore. And here he has the other problems. It is very difficult to raise children here.

Filiz thinks that one way to counteract this problem is to use television as a connection for her children. By watching television, they don't forget their culture, she says. "They hold onto their identity." So the children raised with a solid sense of who they are have that identity reinforced in the programs they watch from Turkey. Filiz is critical of the quality of the programs and distressed by the political turmoil in the country presented on the news, but they continue to watch for the bond that it provides with the homeland.

Netwerk NTA—A New Generation's Identity

On June 5, 1999, a group of mostly young Turks gathered at the Balie Theater in Leidseplein in Amsterdam. The group of more than sixty said about themselves, "We are not a group who are waiting to return to Turkey. We are Dutch with Turkish roots. We are a group with two cultures." To adopt a phrase from a film by the same name, *Network*, they gathered because they were mad as hell and not going to take it anymore. The old timers, those people in the gathering who were over forty, had seen it happen before. The younger ones thought this might be a first-ever event.

The people came together on this day because they wanted to improve the image of the young professionals who lived in the Netherlands. As one of the organizers put it, "Their image of us is wrong and we have to change it. We don't fit their stereotypes." He said that the Turks who live here are not a group who have trouble learning in school, who can't achieve professional success. They are not part of a culture in which men have four wives, all of whom walk several paces behind them. And it is time to change that view of the people with Turkish roots who live in the Netherlands. Changing that stereotype should also lead to ending discrimination, he believes. Meryem feels the same way, providing an example in a separate conversation with me later.

> When you are in a public place, and people know you are Turkish, the conversation always moves to the issues of foreigners. If they want us to be integrated, why do they always focus on our being foreign or Turkish. The Dutch want us to turn into Dutch and assimilate into the Western culture. But they forget that we Turks have Western culture too, and it is older. But the Dutch people should also show an effort to learn about me and my culture. They ask my brother if he has four wives. They don't know that the Turkish Republic has been in existence for seventy-five years and polygamy has been illegal all that time. Stereotypes exist because of the lack of knowledge about the country.

The talk all day was of what strategy to adopt to obtain the most solidarity and power—to form a lobby or a foundation or something else. The group also discussed having a permanent physical location for their activity. The idea for the meeting came out of conversations among four friends. The big concern was whether the momentum for establishing such an organization could be maintained. The older people who attended were more skeptical, saying that such ideas had come up before and nobody was ever able to sustain the effort. Speakers had urged people to stay in touch with one another—in face-to-face meetings, by telephone, and by e-mail.

Familiar faces were everywhere in the room—from the media, from Turkish social services, and from other professional organizations. Sadık Yemni, the novelist, is one of the speakers. Though he too is concerned about whether there is enough energy to sustain the group, he applauds their effort. "It's nobody's fault that we've come this far without dealing with this issue. It's a matter of maturity and now we are able to establish such a group." Yemni ends with a Turkish proverb: "There is butter, flour, and sugar. Why don't they make *helva*?" In other words, the ingredients for establishing this group are all together. Finally they can make *helva*, or be able to work to accomplish their goal.

I don't know if this organization still exists. Given the myriad existing organizations of Turkish special and general interests, it likely appears on a list somewhere. But how much closer to reaching their goal of ending discrimination and changing their image is not known. The fact that such organizations spring up is indicative of the need of the second-generation, educated "Dutch with Turkish roots" to establish an identity for themselves in Dutch society apart from first-generation Turks and also from the Dutch.

Marriage and Identity

The selection of a marriage partner and the establishment of a family is a different kind of organization, but it has some things in common with the other associations described here. Choosing a marriage partner also involves issues of identity. Like other forms of association, marriage partners choose each other because of like interest. In most cases, Turkish migrants have selected Turks for marriage partners, either from the community in Holland or from Turkey. When they do this, the newly married couple strengthens the ties to the Turkish community and distances itself from the Dutch community, making it harder to bridge the gap than if a cross-cultural union had been formed. I am not suggesting that this should happen, only observing that Turks tend to marry within their own culture.

Three interviews shed some light on notions of identity and the establishment of a family. One was with the young women in the family that was very religious and where all the women in the family were covered. Demet, a nineteen-year-old who studies at vocational school and wants to work in tourism after her education is finished, thinks it wouldn't matter to her brother, who is not religious, if he married a Dutch girl or a Turkish girl. And that upsets her. For her it is different. Demet's religion is so important to her that it defines everything she does. She even reads books she borrows from the mosque (instead of the local library) in her spare time. Some are novels and others are about Islam. She said she would feel that she truly belonged in Amsterdam if she could only hear the call to prayer five times a day. When it comes to marriage partners, religious affiliation means more to her than ethnicity. "If he were Dutch and agreed to convert to Islam, then I could marry him. The most important thing to me is that he be Muslim," Demet said.

Elif is seventeen and not religious. Her mother is a teacher, and she has also grown up in Amsterdam. More than Demet, she has been exposed to the Dutch social and cultural life. And her mother is educated, while Demet's is illiterate.

But both young women express the same reservation about marrying a man who is Dutch.

> I don't think I could because their ways are so opposite to the way I think. No, I definitely couldn't think of marrying a Dutch man. But it could be. You never really know how it will turn out, but that's the way I feel now. Language—it is important. For example, I can say what I mean much better in Turkish than in Dutch. I much prefer Turkish. So when I think about speaking Dutch with my husband, I can't imagine it.

Nevin Özütok acted on the plans the young women have for marrying a Turkish man. Born in Adana, she was brought to Amsterdam by her parents while she was still in middle school. She said that because her parents had not adapted very well to Dutch culture or the lifestyle, she felt the same way about Dutch people—that they were not like her. So it was natural that she married a Turkish man. But after a few years, she realized that she was unhappy, and as more time passed, she became more unhappy. She said her parents noticed her unhappiness, too. Finally they separated, and after a time her parents changed their ideas about what was appropriate in the Turkish cultural environment.

> I changed my own views, too. I began to realize that life was not so black and white. We had been raised very separate from the Dutch. After I divorced, I lived by myself for awhile and began to think about things differently—after I lived life a little and was in the workforce. I didn't want to return to my family after I divorced. In that time I began to get to know the Dutch on a closer basis. And I realized that they were not a group to be afraid of. I also realized that they were not so different from us.

After a while, she met and married a Dutch man. She said that making such a move is particularly difficult for Turkish women, because it is the woman in the family who carries the culture from generation to generation. When they marry out of the culture, it is as if they had been unfaithful to it. Turkish men have it easier in this regard. They are more accepted when they marry Dutch women, she said.

Nevin's parents liked her husband from the beginning, but her mother worried about the language barrier. She felt that he would always be a foreigner to her. But she has accepted that, Nevin said.

Of all the people I talked to for this study, only Nevin, the artist Şenol, and the journalist Haluk Bakır had chosen Dutch people for their spouses. All of these people had higher levels of education and income than the majority of Turks in Amsterdam. Of course most of the first generation came to Holland with their Turkish spouses or brought them later. But it is significant that more people in the second generation have not married outside the culture of their parents. It speaks volumes about identity and a person's sense of belonging.

Dutch View of Migrant Identity

As the surveys have shown, Europeans admit to being racist—some even proud to hold racist opinions. In chapter 2, the results of a 1997 Eurobarometer study were discussed. It found that nearly half of the Dutch admit to being a little racist, more than a quarter said they are quite racist, and 5 percent said they are very racist. The study did not define the term "racism," but certainly religion played some role in the feelings of the respondents. Though most of the Turks are darker skinned than the Dutch, they are still Caucasians. So actual racial difference is more perceived than real here. Turkish difference in the Dutch context is composed of several characteristics that include color, dress, religion, and linguistic ability. A Dutch friend of mine overheard a comment by a person in a shop who had just had an unpleasant encounter on the street with a Turkish person. The woman burst into the shop saying, "This has turned into a goddammed camel country." The remark was obviously meant to be derogatory to the Turkish (and Moroccan) immigrants. It probably also referred to the complex of attributes considered when the remark was made. A "camel country" would be one filled with uneducated, backward people who practice Islam and who wear strange clothing and have not adopted the lifestyle of a modern European city.

People make racist statements like this one partially out of a sense that their own rights and privileges in a given society were threatened by the presence of "the other." In the same 1997 Eurobarometer study, more than half of the Europeans polled said there were too many children from minority groups in the schools, and as a result, education of their own children suffered. They were also concerned that minorities didn't pay as much into the social security system as they claimed (79 percent), that the religious practices of the minority threatened their way of life (29 percent), and that the presence of minorities increased unemployment (63 percent). At the same time, the Dutch respondents in the survey agreed that minorities in their country were the target of discrimination in the job market (74 percent). And 60 percent of the Dutch sample said that the country had reached its limits in accepting immigrants.[13]

To some extent, the Turks in this study felt their identities were formed as a reaction to the Dutch attitudes and practices. The people for whom this was of greatest concern are part of the second generation. The first generation never saw themselves as Dutch, and so did not seek acceptance on that basis. And as I have repeatedly said, they saw themselves as visitors to this country, not as permanent residents who wanted to be integrated or assimilated. That view of who they are has not changed. Of all the families interviewed, 46 percent said they felt closer to Turkey than the Netherlands, 33.3 percent said they felt caught in between the two cultures (or didn't feel close to either one), and only 20.5 percent said they felt closer to the Netherlands.

How close a migrant feels to Turkey can be seen through the number of trips made back. I asked each family how many trips they had made in the last five years. An average of 3.2 trips were made, and the average length of stay was four to five weeks. Only three families had not returned at all for economic reasons, while six families had traveled from six to twenty times in the last five years.

Another measure of closeness was the friends the participants reported. I asked whether their friends were exclusively Turkish, a blend of Dutch and Turkish, or all Dutch. Of those participants who responded to this question, 66.5 percent said they had only Turkish friends, 30.9 percent said they had a mixture of Dutch and Turkish friends, and 2.6 percent said they had no friends outside their family at all. This may be the most revealing result of the whole study. It means that many families who had been in the Netherlands for twenty to thirty years never made a real friend among the Dutch. Some of the participants said they used to know someone at work or in the neighborhood who was Dutch, but that person moved away or they no longer worked with that person. Not all of the people who reported having only Turkish friends were from the first generation either. Some young people said they were acquainted with Dutch young people at school or in the work place, but did not see them socially.

The second generation has had different experiences in Dutch society from their parents. Though many of them have a love-hate relationship with the Dutch, they neither wish to be Dutch nor to be Turkish. They want to be themselves—something different from either cultural definition. They are offended that they are seen as unacceptable to the Dutch. As several of the participants of this study said, they were born there, educated there, learned to communicate in Dutch, and now want to take their place alongside the Dutch as equals in the workplace and in social circles. Because that hasn't happened for many of them, they have retreated to their own culture to find solace among other Turks who have also been unfairly treated or not fully accepted. Yet, if they were fully accepted, it might be an acceptance based on how Dutch they were perceived to be—how much they had been assimilated into Dutch society. And to do that would mean leaving their Turkishness behind them. Stuart Hall said that there are "contradictory identities within us pulling in different directions so that our identifications are continuously being shifted about."[14]

Within the second generation, this sense of being pulled in several directions must be in constant play. Some of the young people who have been drawn back to Turkey for a time, thinking they would find acceptance and compatibility there, were surprised to find that there was as much difference between themselves and the Turks there as they found between themselves and the Dutch in Amsterdam.

The terms hybridization and creolization, as defined in chapter 1, have become widely accepted as defining the process that occurs in people who split their identities between cultures and then produce something new—an identity that is composed of both cultures, but not wholly belonging characteristic of either one. While I don't reject that as a possibility as described by Hall, Hannerz, Appadurai, and others, I am not sure that this process doesn't occur within a lot of people who never leave their culture of origin. In other words, it is not unique to migrants or to children of migrants. Growing up in a small college town in the Midwest, I never felt like I belonged in that community. As the years have passed and I have lived in several different places in the world, I have come to realize that parts of me belong in a lot of different places. Of course, a person is forced to confront the issue of conflicting cultures when he or she is born into one culture and has parents who were raised in a very different culture. That situation doesn't allow the individual the choice of ignoring the differences that appear in various life places—school, home, the playground, the mosque, the corner store, the soccer field. But it may also not allow total freedom in constructing an identity from the various elements of both primary cultures. Constraints are placed on migrant children growing up in the host culture. Language is one of those that has primary constraining power. Race is another. Religion is a third. And any children growing up in a culture where language, race, and religion of the family and host culture are different will not easily be admitted entrance to the other culture on the basis of those differences. So becoming assimilated or even integrated into the host culture may not be based on the choices made by the migrant.

Ayşe Çağlar also is concerned about using the concepts of hybridity and creolization to examine cultural identity, but for different reasons. She writes:

> Creolization and hybridization are thus conceived of as revolutionary antidotes to essentialist constructs of culture, identity and ethnicity. Yet these concepts are in danger of embracing the very reifications they seek to overcome. Above all, they fail to question some of the basic assumptions informing the critique of cultural holism. Here this danger looms especially large because hyphenation is anchored in ethnicity which could easily shift to an essential category, having continuity in time and space and thus undermining its relational character. Furthermore, this term limits the heterogeneity of German-Turks' cultural formations to two cultural wholes, namely to "Turkish" and "German" culture.[15]

In her critique of the hyphenated identity, she makes the point that when scholars focus on the hyphenation, they eliminate the possibility of other forms, new forms of identification that may be based on neither of their ethnic attachments. The young people who helped organize *Netwerk* were gathering partially in response to that problem. They wanted to define themselves as a group of individuals apart from the constraints of their family histories. They were seeking to forge new identities based on their experiences as Dutch citizens with Turkish roots.

Not only are hyphenated identities limiting on the one hand, but they may also be difficult to achieve on the other. It may be impossible for young people to break out of the culture of their parents in any significant way if members of the host society don't allow it. In this study people were criticized for living in culturally homogenous neighborhoods, for finding their friends and colleagues only from their home culture, for attending to media from Turkey and not from Holland, and for lack of participation in Dutch culture in general. Many of those in the study didn't have a lot of choice in the matter.

Stuart Hall also uses the term hybridity in his discussion of identity among diasporic peoples, but he does not define it in a limiting way.

> The diaspora experience as I intend it here is defined, not by essence or purity, but by the recognition of a necessary, heterogeneity and diversity; by a conception of "identity" which lives with and through, not despite difference; by *hybridity*. Diaspora identities are those which are constantly producing and reproducing themselves anew, through transformation and difference.[16]

People who live in a diaspora may be enriched by being forced to think about who they are in ways that most people may never have to. When children grow up in places where most everyone in their neighborhoods or schools has similar experiences and family heritage, they don't have to think about belonging. The Turkish migrants in this study have to think about that issue every time they step out of their front doors, every time they walk into the public school, every time they enter the workplace. That can't be easy.

Notes

1. Jean Tillie, Meindert Fennema, and Karen Kraal, "Creating Turkish Networks in Amsterdam: Personal or Organizational Strategies?" Draft version prepared for the workshop Associational Engagement and Democracy in Cities, Copenhagen, April 2000, 11.

2. Tillie, Fennema, and Kraal, "Creating Turkish Networks," 18-19.

3. Lale Yalçın-Heckmann, "The Perils of Ethnic Associational Life in Europe: Turkish Migrants in Germany and France," in *The Politics of Multiculturalism in the New Europe,* Tariq Modood and Pnina Werbner, eds. (London: Zed Books, 1997), 96.

4. Felice Dassetto and Gerd Nonneman, "Islam in Belgium and the Netherlands: Towards a Typology of 'Transplanted' Islam," in *Muslim Communities in the New Europe*, Gerd Nonneman, Tim Niblock, and Bogdan Szakowski, eds. (Reading, U.K.: Ithaca Press, 1996), 209.

5. Dassetto and Nonneman, 209.

6. Nilufer Göle, *The Forbidden Modern: Civilization and Veiling* (Ann Arbor, Mich.: U. of Michigan Press, 1996),

7. The Web site of the IGMG is http://www.igmg.de

8. Tillie, Fennema, and Kraal, "Creating Turkish Networks," 24.

9. M. Hakan Yavuz, "Media Identities for Alevis and Kurds in Turkey," in *New Media in the Muslim World: The Emerging Public Sphere*, Dale Eickelman and Jon Anderson, eds. (Bloomington, Ind.: Indiana University Press, 1999), 186.

10. Yavuz, "Media Identities," 188

11. Geke van der Wal and Mathijs Tax, *De vele gezichten van Turks Nederland: Een wie is wie* (Amsterdam: Uitgeverij Jan Mets, 1999), 24, 25.

12. Yavuz, "Media Identities," 195.

13. "Racism and Xenophobia in Europe," Eurobarometer Opinion Poll no. 47.1. First results presented at the Closing Conference of the European Year against Racism (18-19 December 1997).

14. Stuart Hall, "The Question of Cultural Identity," in *Modernity and its Futures*, Stuart Hall, David Held, and Tony McGrew, eds. (Cambridge: Polity Press in association with the Open University, 1992), 277.

15. Ayşe Çağlar, "Hyphenated Identities and the Limits of 'Culture,'" in *The Politics of Multiculturalism in the New Europe*, Tariq Modood and Pnina Werbner, eds. (London: Zed Books, 1997), 172.

16. Stuart Hall, "Cultural Identity and Diaspora," in *Identity: Community, Culture, Difference*, John Rutherford, ed. (London: Lawrence and Wishart, 1990), 235.

Chapter 7

Lessons Learned, Directions to Take

I began this research thinking that the television that was being beamed to Europe via satellite was probably having an incredible impact on the lives of the Turks who live in the several countries. I wondered how people who had spent the better part of their adult lives in western Europe away from their homes in Anatolia or the Black Sea coastal region could now turn back to the country of their birth and immerse themselves in the popular culture of that country. I have come to understand through the course of this research that those people who spend many hours watching Turkish television each day in fact may never have really left those homes on the Black Sea or the hills of Anatolia or in the south near the Mediterranean. Physically, yes, they closed up their houses, transported their families, and took employment in the Netherlands or elsewhere in Europe. But psychologically, most of the first-generation migrants never left. They just worked in Europe, while their hearts and minds were back in Turkey. And they returned home every chance they got. So when the opportunity to watch television from Turkey came along, they jumped at the chance. Their children were more confused about their cultural affiliation than they were. The second generation was Dutch in many ways, but the culture at home was Turkish. And the attraction to Turkey was strong. They spoke the language and had close relatives and friends who lived there. They returned annually for vacations. The presence of television from Turkey in their homes served to improve their proficiency with the language and provide a constant source of Turkish popular culture. Many of the men and women of the second generation now struggle with issues of identity.

Those who thought that the passage of time created the solution to the problem must remember that members of the second generation often return to Turkey to find a spouse and begin the process anew. Though the Dutch government has restricted immigration for family formation, it has not been able to prevent it entirely. On the other hand, the entry of new migrants from the home country offers some cultural advantages. In this book, I have mostly focused on the Turkish community in Amsterdam and their need to learn Dutch and fit into Dutch society. However, it seems that the Dutch also have an obligation to learn from the Turkish and other minority cultures within their midst. While they do shop in the Turkish stores and eat in Turkish restaurants, the Dutch are less likely to learn about other aspects of the migrants' culture. So as new generations of migrants keep arriving, there is additional opportunity to learn from them and their culture and be enriched by it. In Amsterdam an annual Roots Festival is held in Oosterpark. On a weekend in June, tents are erected there and music, food, and arts and crafts of the several cultures that now make up the city are represented. I attended this festival on two occasions, and I noticed that most of those attending were people who represented those cultures, not Dutch citizens. While the festival is intended to celebrate the diversity that is Amsterdam, it would be nice if more Dutch residents of the city used the occasion to learn more about the diverse cultures in their midst.

This research was initiated as a study of how the several generations of Turkish migrants used the opportunity to view television from Turkey and how they might have been affected by that use. But the time spent in Turkish homes opened up many more topics of relevance to the issue. Though television viewing was certainly not a trivial part of the lives of the migrants, it has probably been overblown as an issue to be concerned about in the integration of Turks in Dutch society. What follows is a summary of what was learned about the issue of communication and identity in the diaspora from both the Dutch and Turkish side of the issue.

Lessons for the Dutch

In earlier chapters, *allochtoon* was described as a term used to identify "nonindigenous" people. It was also pointed out that not all nonindigenous people in Holland are considered *allochtoon,* but only those who are somehow not as Caucasian as the Dutch. So the Turks, who are generally not blonde and blue-eyed, are in the category *allochtoon*, while German immigrants, for example, would not be. The continuous use of such a term in official language ends up preventing the very thing the Dutch say they are trying to accomplish: provide opportunities for minority groups to become equals with the Dutch and shed their disadvantageous position. In his thesis on the deconstruction of the term *allochtonen,* Glenn Isena also makes that point, as he cites some work by Fred Jongkind.

> I consider that too little attention is paid to [internal differentiation within migrant groups] in the Netherlands and would like to argue for an emphasis on policy supportive research that has scope for a more fundamental and theoretically orientated kind of approach. There would then be a greater chance that the ultimate aims of Dutch policy on minorities might be realized, instead of leading to the isolation of and alienation within ethnic communities which are caused by the implementation of current policy.[1]

When Dutch policy makers or media constantly refer to Turkish or other migrants as *allochtoon* it becomes impossible for them to shed the label. As several people in the second generation said, no matter what they do, they are always looked upon as the "other," not as full-fledged members of the Dutch culture. At some point Dutch policy will need to stop putting migrants in a special category and directing policy toward all of them as if they always needed special treatment and special services.

Herman Vuijsje believes that the Dutch made a big mistake in trying to avoid racist language and behavior because the result of that approach was to treat migrants with kid gloves and also avoid dealing with the very real problems the migrants were confronting.

> While the Netherlands was mobilizing for battle with the racism bacillus, social problems and deprivation continued to grow rampant. This is how the paradox of the Netherlands' good reputation in the area of racism, but the poor social prospects for *allochtoons*, came into being. The government promoted relatively peaceful racial relations in the Netherlands by "handing out" things. When, however, it came down to prescribing and requiring, the government dodged the issue.[2]

Consequently, according to Vuijsje, the Turkish and other migrants fell further behind. They had less education, competed less successfully for jobs, were more likely to be receiving welfare, and young migrants were more likely to participate in criminal behavior. It was not until the 1990s that changes began to occur. But Vuijsje says that by that time "it was too late for part of the second generation. They had had the bad luck to be at the crossroads of Dutch taboos: the ethnic taboo combined with the taboos on the invasion of privacy and government coercion."[3]

But he sees the problem as larger than just the migrants. He believes that the politically correct approach to many issues has caused more problems than it has solved. The intellectuals have prevented undesirable discussion of these issues, everything from ethnicity and immigration to the abuse of public assistance. "Thereby the progressive Netherlands has been caught empty-handed, now that the sea wall is turning the ship, public assistance is being cut down to the bone, asylum seekers are being sent back to murderous countries and personal data are being linked without much to-do,"[4] Vuijsje said. Perhaps some honest discussion about the amount of television from Turkey watched by the migrants might reveal why it was preferred to Dutch television. Since the Dutch consider what people do in the privacy of their homes their own business, they have done little research of this topic, however.

The second generation participants in this study would not mind bringing this discussion out into the open. They would just like to be treated fairly, but not be placed in a special category that sets them apart from *autochtoon,* or indigenous Dutch. In fact, it might be good if the two words were dropped altogether from the Dutch vocabulary. In the beginning of this book, I talked of the problem I had in deciding what to call the participants in this study. If they aren't migrants, *allochtoon*, minorities, or ethnic Turks, what are they? It seems to me that if they have Dutch citizenship, whether through birth or naturalization, then that is what they are. To label them as some sort of group apart has not helped them advance in Dutch society. While it is true that the first generation and many in the second generation still consider themselves Turks, once they have been accepted as full-fledged citizens of the Netherlands, they have become Dutch.

As I was conducting this research and investigating the history of guest-worker immigration and Dutch policy regarding that process, I was amazed to find little or no reference to the experience of the United States with race and with immigration. And this wasn't just characteristic of the Dutch. It marks the whole body of work—both academic and policy based—that treats issues of minorities in Europe. All along I have wondered why this is so. Why has America nothing to offer in the way of experience—whether positive or negative—that would help Europeans better deal with their own situations? It is not as if the experience of the United States is so old; it remains a country of immigration in the twenty-first century. If anything, in certain parts of the United States, immigration is on the rise. According to a 1999 survey of the U.S. Census Bureau, the proportion of foreign-born residents of New York City reached 40 percent, a level not equaled for a century. Though New York has not always dealt successfully with immigrants, it has been facing that issue for as long as it has been in existence. So problems of non-English-speaking adults and children, insufficient educational attainment, and job training have been issues in that city for a very long time. Certainly the United States does not have all the answers, but it might have tried out some solutions that didn't work here and perhaps shouldn't be tried elsewhere. For example, a recent examination of test scores of California students indicates that a move from bilingual education to English language immersion has resulted in improved reading and other skills in English.[5] Though the outcome of California's changed policy might not apply to Europe (or indeed to other states in the United States), it would seem that sharing expertise would be preferable to treating European migration as unique.

More research of the various migrant groups is needed. That research needs to be conducted on both a national and a local level. As this study reveals, there is a great amount of heterogeneity within a particular ethnic group. Once additional ethnic groupings are included, the diversity naturally becomes much greater. But the experiences of people also vary according to the place in which they live within the Netherlands. This study took place in various parts of a large city, but it is not known whether the experiences of people in Rotterdam differ from those of the people in Amsterdam. And when migrants settle in small- or medium-sized towns, their experiences may be much different still. When migrants live in more isolated settings, they may be confronted more directly with the local culture.

Of course, research is being conducted all of the time. The Institute for Migration and Ethnic Studies (IMES) at the University of Amsterdam is constantly producing publications. But little of that research is based on qualitative, in-depth household studies or on ethnographic method. Such an approach might be more valuable in discovering the nature of the cultural differences across and within groups. Arjun Appadurai would like this work to take a macroethnographic approach. As Appaduri put it,

> What a new style of ethnography can do is to capture the impact of deterritorialization on the imaginative resources of lived, local experiences. Put another way, the task of ethnography now becomes the unraveling of a conundrum: what is the nature of locality as a lived experience in a globalized, deterritorialized world?[6]

Appadurai would preserve the local observation of individuals' lived experiences but would add to it the ways people's lives are being imagined through the new media to which people can now get access.

The results of this study only go part way in accomplishing that goal. This study was not an ethnography, but rather a precursor to an ethnographic study. The next step would be to discover what individual entertainment programs and news do to help create these imagined lives. As long as researchers stand at an arm's length or more from the people they are seeking to understand, they will continue to place them into categories into which they might not exactly fit.

The Turks in this study may be receiving more information and entertainment via television from outside their communities of residence than most other people in the world, but their experience is not unique. I support Appadurai's argument that the mass media have presented us with a "rich, ever-changing store of possible lives, some of which enter the lived imaginations of ordinary people more successfully than others."[7] It is important that we understand the nature of that experience in greater depth. This study has begun that process for the Turkish people living in Amsterdam. Much more work needs to be done. But it will need to be done in the Netherlands through collaboration between Dutch and Turkish researchers. Each brings something to the table the other cannot.

I recommend all these things as an outsider to Dutch society. I began this study because of my interest and involvement with Turkish people living in the diaspora. I knew little about the Netherlands or the Dutch. That clearly put me at a disadvantage in this research. But it also helped me to want to explore the relationship between the values in Dutch society that led to certain policies. And I studied the areas of disconnection between Dutch culture and Turkish culture. I have come to admire the value placed on tolerance and individual privacy as well as the felt need to take care of the less fortunate. But I have also been able to see how these values have sometimes led to policies that do not benefit the migrants in the long run. For example, the concern for people's privacy may lead to overlooking certain illegal practices that don't benefit anyone. In particular, marriage between first cousins or keeping female children from school fit in this category of problems. More intrusive practices may be required to deal with these issues.

Lessons for the Media in the Netherlands

What the results of this study have told us above all is that the mass medium of television is used by people as a source of information and entertainment. And if the information and entertainment does not fit the cultural orientation and interests of the audience, viewers will select alternate sources of information and entertainment. The Turks who have chosen to watch Turkish television over Dutch television have done so for several reasons: they don't speak Dutch well enough to understand the programs; they don't see themselves or their circumstances in the programs that are designed for them; they want entertainment and they aren't finding enough of it in the programs directed to them. The Turkish media are also satisfying their needs. The music, comedy, and dramatic programs fit better with their interests and taste. Because the political situation in Turkey is often unstable, the news and public affairs programs present information that is exciting and attention holding. By contrast, Dutch politics are more predictable and stable. So people living there don't tune in to the news to see what happens next.

Many of the participants in this study say they don't see themselves on Dutch television. Though some effort has been made to include members of minority groups on a few television series, it is not common to have Turkish or other minority groups represented on a regular basis. On a given night, any member of a large minority group in the Netherlands ought to be able to find a channel and more than one program where that group is represented. The representation should also be balanced in its depiction. For Turks and Moroccans to only see themselves as perpetrators of crimes—or even victims of crimes—is not good. It will only work to drive the group away from local media and toward media from outside the country. When the minority group is represented in media content, it should happen frequently and across a wide variety of programs. It is only when that happens that the Dutch will be able to see a given group for what it is, a diverse population with all kinds of lifestyles and viewpoints. And only then will a given ethnic group be able to see itself. Ahmet Azdural, the man who directs the daily news program on Dutch radio, realized that. He knew that when he reported on the events in one part of the community that he made another part of the community angry. But he said that his job was not to make them all happy. His job was to reflect their diversity. His job was to present a picture of Turkish people living in Amsterdam such that everyone could tune in to find someone like themselves discussed or portrayed on a given day.

Migranten TV has a similar mission, but added to that is the goal of changing behavior or providing lessons to the audience about a variety of subjects. While some people listen regularly, others are bored by this approach and would rather watch an entertainment program on Turkish television. That is understandable. Audiences don't generally like to tune into programs that teach them lessons at the end of the day. But creating such programs to be more entertaining might lure the migrant audience back. The entertainment-education format might work as well here as it has for developing countries. Unfortunately, we don't have a lot of hard data about attitude or behavior change from the use of the soap opera format to teach, but the research of a variety of such programs by Singhal and Rogers is encouraging. In the conclusion to their book, they note: "If implemented in a systematic manner, with theory-based message design, formative research, and other necessary elements, the entertainment-education strategy can be a powerful influence in changing audience knowledge, attitudes, and behavior regarding an educational issue."[8] The British soap opera *Eastenders* might serve as a good guide for dealing with issues of social change. Though the producers of the series claim to be reflecting life rather than teaching lessons about how to live life, the program has dealt with issues of homophobia, family reactions to breast cancer, racism, adolescent sex, anorexia, euthanasia, and other social issues that clearly present ways to approach real-life situations. And because the characters and stories are so engaging, the series has attracted a large segment of British viewers for the past fifteen years. *Good Times, Bad Times* also attempts to address social issues (though many of the issues are Australian because of the program's origins) and has included a Turkish character on at least one occasion. The series is a production of commercial television, however, and its producers may not be interested in joining forces with *Migranten TV* to build in more educational content. Perhaps a new soap opera is called for, one that addresses a range of issues involving migrants, one that would be subtitled in Turkish and Arabic for the two primary immigrant groups, and one that would be interesting enough for audiences to want to watch on a regular basis.

Lessons for the Turkish Community

The Dutch are not alone in needing to examine the problems of the ethnic groups in the country. Each minority group, including the Turks, has made missteps and has failed to follow up on addressing the issues that confront them. In order for the relations between the Dutch and the various minority groups to improve, a new approach must be taken.

In my interviews with the Turks, I noted that although everyone was polite about the expression of their feelings toward the Dutch, few of them had made much real effort to get to know Dutch people or understand the culture. In the case of the Turks who had strong religious beliefs, they focused on the differences between themselves and the Dutch in their values. They claimed that the Dutch chose not to have children, that they did not have strong religious affiliations, and that many of them were immoral by Islamic standards. Those differences provided an excuse for not interacting with the Dutch. Such attitudes only serve to isolate and increase misunderstandings. Instead, Turkish people need to continue to make efforts to get to know Dutch people in a variety of settings—both in organizations and at work in more formal settings, and informally in their homes. Increased social interaction should at least lead to greater understanding of the context for certain cultural practices. And making more attempts to make social contact should not be too difficult for Turks. Being hospitable is a major characteristic of Turkish culture. But being rebuffed, or not having an invitation returned, has led many Turkish people to stop extending the invitations. Some renewed effort needs to take place on this front.

Of course social interaction becomes more difficult when the Turks have limited language skills in Dutch. Many Turks think that education finishes when a person leaves school. So those first-generation migrants who are in their forties, fifties, and sixties think that it is too late for them to learn to speak Dutch. They have grown comfortable in this environment with their Turkish neighbors and Turkish mosques and Turkish shops. They have little or no incentive to learn Dutch when their children or grandchildren can do the translation at the doctor's office, the tax office, or the department store. There may be a long waiting list to enroll in Dutch classes provided by the government, but a range of volunteer groups also provides classes in basic Dutch, and might welcome the older men and women who are motivated to learn. Speaking the language of the country where you live is the first step to understanding the culture and the political policies of that nation. All Turks need to make that effort. I'm not suggesting that total acculturation needs to take place. Turks have a rich cultural tradition, and they should be able to preserve their culture in the diaspora to the extent they wish. But that doesn't preclude learning something about the culture where they live from day to day.

All through this study I have pointed to the diversity of the Turkish population, a diversity that has been largely ignored by the Dutch. Here, I'd like to suggest that Turks put aside some of their differences and work together to solve their common problems. It is also a characteristic of Turkish culture that people allow their differences to get in the way of compromise. This has been the problem for Turkish politics for many years. Political parties with few ideological differences between them fail to work together to form solid governments. Instead, flimsy coalitions have frequently fallen apart because groups fight amongst themselves rather than focus together on the enormous social and economic problems the country faces. In this mini-Turkish environment in Amsterdam, the same thing occurs. It is utterly amazing that 156 mostly distinct organizations should have been created for a population of about 30,000 in Amsterdam. Many of those organizations exist because people focus on minor differences and decide it is better to create their own group than work together with an existing group. The result is that unemployment, illiteracy, drug use among youths, etc., worsen in their severity. Ahmet Azdural sees this problem up close. The community is so intolerant of other viewpoints that it complains to the radio station if it even appears to provide a platform to an unpopular view.

Azdural and the other media producers creating news and information programs for the Turks in the Netherlands are working hard to provide the information environment needed for the migrants to thrive. Though they might not always do this in the most exciting and interesting way possible, and certainly can't compete with the likes of a Turkish variety or comedy show, they are providing an important service. And the Turkish audience should try harder to respond to that effort. The audience needs much of the information provided by NPS or *Migranten* Television. A new way of thinking about educational media needs to be fostered in the community. That is partially the job of the media, but individual residents must do their part as well.

Future for Media and Identity in the Diaspora

This study of the Turkish migrants' use of media from Turkey and the Netherlands and how it relates to their identity may provide a framework for other studies. Marie Gillespie's work on the Punjabi community in Southall London encouraged me to conduct this study. Though my approach was different, this work does build on her findings. Like Gillespie, I believe that the understanding of the way media are involved in remaking ethnicity or cultural change requires the use of ethnographic approaches. Gillespie focused mostly on the use of British media by Asian youths living in England, while I dealt with the use of the domestic media to a much lesser extent. At the same time, both of us observed the difficulties of identity formation and change, and the role of media in that process. Gillespie explores the concept of cultural translation, both literally and metaphorically, as the youths "must acquire skills in negotiating from context to context between different cultures and various positions within each."[9] The adults in my study also needed to conduct cultural translation, but they seemed more rooted in the culture from Turkey than the culture in the Netherlands. While the youths and young, second-generation adults moved more freely between cultures, some of them also were closer to Turkish culture than Dutch. Others were constantly involved in cultural translation. But this study did not focus on the viewing of many specific programs. Rather, it examined a broader picture. The next step in this process would be to examine more closely the media use of individuals in a more in-depth fashion, using the ethnographic method.

Few other studies like this have ever been conducted—for obvious reasons. They are incredibly time consuming and need to be narrowly focused in order to make any detailed conclusions. Ideally, it would be important to understand the role of the media in identity for any cultural group in any location. But the difficulty of carrying out that research makes such a project impossible. As this study has shown, we cannot focus only on the media use of particular groups, but must understand the political and social context for viewing. That context will change depending on the group in question and the national, regional, and local setting of the study. As more research is conducted on additional groups, it will be easier to unravel the complex situation for migrants living in various parts of the globe. It is important to do this work as people continue to flee their countries of origin in search of better lives in new locations.

The viewing of television from far-off places is increasingly popular and possible around the world. In the United States, Spanish-language television has been available via cable and satellite for a long time. More recently, television from India, Turkey, the Arab Middle East, and some other countries has been sold in packages. Subscribers pay a monthly fee for service and a one-time fee for the satellite dish. So the situation that exists for Turks in Europe is now available to other ethnic groups in many parts of the globe. Based on this study, I would foresee that viewing television from one's birth country would not create a situation that would take people out of the media environment of the country where they live as it has in parts of Europe. As most people who emigrate from their home countries eventually learn the language of the adopted country well enough to conduct work, watch television, and read the newspaper, they would not have the problems that the first-generation Turks in this study had in understanding the local language. In the case of an Indian subscribing to Indian channels in the United States, the television content would likely enrich her life and provide a diversion, not cut her off from U.S. media. But that is only speculation. Empirical research would be needed to investigate the possible effects. As subscribing to media from a different nation becomes more popular, it suggests a new set of studies about the intersection of the global with the local. Up to this point, scholars have been most interested in the impact of Western media on citizens of developing countries. Political economists have been concerned that whole cultures might be wiped out as a result of the dominance of television and film from the United States. But the same technologies that carry messages from the west to the east and south can now send media content the other direction. That poses new research questions.

Media scholar Michael Schudson has summed up the perception of the power of mass media in a way that is applicable to this study.

> The mass media have often been seen as a powerful force for integration, both positively—assimilating different peoples to a common civil culture—and negatively—stripping different peoples of their folk culture and embracing them in an overbearing "hegemonic" culture produced by elites at the society's center.[10]

The Turkish participants in this study have demonstrated that neither of these things has happened to them, even though they may be consuming large amounts of television. By being able to select programs according to language, genre, and political and religious viewpoints, the Turkish people in Amsterdam reinforce the concept of the active audience. While they cannot dictate to producers the exact type of programming they wish to receive, they still have many choices to make among the wide variety of international and domestic offerings. Whether we like the choices they make or not is irrelevant here. What is important is how those choices help individuals define themselves and whether the selected media help them successfully navigate their environment. In the end, people will attend to messages that interest them, not what we force upon them.

And the more choices that are out there for the audience, the more compelling the content must be to attract that audience.

It will never be completely comfortable for the migrants who have made the Netherlands their home while they keep strong ties to Turkey. And that is so for most everyone who only partially adopts a new location to live. If the migrants decide to maintain their cultural base while living in a different culture, they will always be torn. Gaye, thirty-four, mother of two teenagers who doesn't work outside her home, best describes this problem as she explains how it is for her and her family. She says it is hard to live here as a Turk.

> Perhaps it is because I came here when I was so young. I was sixteen. I had a hard time. Perhaps now it is because I live so far away from my family. If the choice were up to me, I'd go back. And if my children get educated and we have enough money, I'll go back. My kids—particularly my son, used to wonder if it would be better to live in Turkey. Of course they only see how it is on vacation in the summer and they think it would be that way all the time. But now they see the students fighting on television and they don't talk about returning. And it couldn't happen anyway. Their education is going down a certain path and they couldn't just pick up and change it now.
>
> I'm comfortable here, but we don't put ourselves in situations where we would feel discriminated against—work, home, school—that's it. But we'd have a much more social life in Turkey. If we decided to go to a concert, it wouldn't cost very much there—but here it is too expensive for us.
>
> On the other hand, some things are easier here that become an ordeal in Turkey. For example, you go to the bank, take a number, get in line, and wait your turn. Then you do your business and leave. In Turkey you might need *torpil* [connections]. You will have to mention who your friend is, etc. It's different. Nobody will wait in line, for example. The cultural development is not great, yet. When my mother came to visit, she was impressed by the clean and orderly hospitals. The nurses treated her with respect. There is an arrogance in Turkey—a vanity. Turks look down on others who aren't in their class, who don't have money or connections, for example. I don't see these things here.
>
> If only I could be friends with some married woman who might live in the same building. I really have wanted to do that. I've lived in two different buildings here but haven't found anybody to make friends with. Then I could have spoken better Dutch—practiced it more often.
>
> I'd like to return to Turkey, but it is a dream. I couldn't leave my kids and their needs here and go back. If they all wanted to, then that would be OK, but since it is just me, it can't happen.

Gaye's feelings represent the problem of constantly comparing there with here and never being totally happy with either place. Gaye also watches a lot of Turkish television, though her children do not. And her Dutch language skills are weak. For her and many others, communication is still at the core of the problem, and language is the foundation.

Mass media can help in improving those language skills and communicating the cultural values, but it is only one way. While media should not be dismissed as insignificant in this effort, their importance should also not be blown out of proportion. Media do more to reinforce held values and opinions in this study. They might also function to change opinions over time in the way that cultivation theory holds. This approach claims that it is the cumulative exposure to certain types of television programming that has an effect on people—not any one program or set of programs—so that, over time, a child who watches violence on television on a daily basis, eventually has a certain reaction to that violence. Cultivation might also work to produce a good effect. If programs were designed to promote appreciation of the multicultural environment in the Netherlands, over time behavior might actually change.

More opportunities for interaction in interpersonal and small group settings need to be created where language skills can be improved and individuals can learn to appreciate one another's culture. Such occasions might also help the Dutch to explain their cultural framing of the issues that need to be addressed. As an outsider it is hard to understand the role of tolerance and respect for privacy and need to take care of the less fortunate in the determination of policies directed toward minorities. Teaching Dutch history to adult migrants, not just schoolchildren, might go a long way in communicating the rationale for the actions of government and other policy-making institutions.

Whatever is done, the process will be slow. Many people think it will take three generations for the situation to change. But if they mean it will take that long to make Dutch people out of Turks, then in my view this is not an appropriate position to take. The Turks and all the other ethnic minorities who make up the Netherlands in 2001 have something to offer to the Dutch, too. And encouraging cultural contributions from the migrants is as important as teaching them how Dutch culture works.

The concept of cultural orientation has also been explored in this work. Previous research had shown that socioeconomic and educational levels, amount of travel outside of a person's native country, strength of religious conviction, and foreign-language proficiency were related to the types of media people consume. This study advanced our understanding of the relationship between cultural orientation and media use. But the strongest factor in determining whether individuals would watch Dutch or Turkish media exclusively or a mix of the two was their language proficiency in Dutch. The more literate they were in Dutch, the more likely they were to read Dutch newspapers and watch Dutch television. Even those participants who reported watching a lot of Dutch television before the satellite television appeared, tended to watch game shows and musical variety programs when their Dutch was poor.

For those who were bilingual, consuming much television from Turkey often meant they felt closer to Turkish culture than Dutch culture. Because this study was not a survey of a random sample of Turkish people residing in the Netherlands, I cannot be at all sure whether the consumption of Turkish television was driving the feeling of closeness to Turkey or the reverse was true. I only know it would be more difficult to feed the interest in the Turkish culture without access to satellite television. Probably fewer than ten of the study's participants fit into this category. And I'm not sure that those bilingual or multilingual participants who retain a strong attachment to Turkey will always feel that way. Several of the participants in this study had acted on that attachment and actually returned to live in Turkey only to find that they felt a stronger sense of belonging to the Netherlands. They only imagined that they would be more comfortable in the homeland of their parents than they had been in Amsterdam. Perhaps driven by a rejection by Dutch people and being the target of subtle or obvious discrimination at school, in the neighborhood, or at work, they sought a home where their friends and colleagues were more "like them."

Much more empirical work must be conducted surrounding the concept of cultural orientation and mass media's role in its construction. As media become increasingly portable through the Internet and satellite connections, people will be able to have direct connections to nearly every cultural product available anywhere in the world. We will need to keep asking how that possibility affects our cultural orientation. As has always been the case, rather than closing the door with finality on a set of research questions, this study opens many more doors for investigation.

Notes

1. Glenn Constantino Isena, "Deconstructing 'allochtonen'; Socio-institutional Powers on the Lives of Children" (master's thesis, Free University of Amsterdam, 2000); http://home.student.uva.nl/glen.isena (28 May 2000).

2. Herman Vuijsje, *The Politically Correct Netherlands since the Sixties*, trans. and annot. Mark T. Hooker (Westport, Conn.: Greenwood, 2000), 29.

3. Vuijsje, *The Politically Correct Netherlands*, 26.

4. Vuijsje, *The Politically Correct Netherlands*, 170-171.

5. Jacques Steinberg, "Increase in Test Scores Counters Dire Forecasts for Bilingual Ban," *New York Times*, 20 August 2000, section 1, 1.

6. Arjun Appadurai, *Modernity at Large.* (Minneapolis: University of Minnesota Press, 1996), 33.

7. Appadurai, *Modernity at Large*, 32.

8. Arvind Singhal and Everett M. Rogers, *Entertainment-Education: A Communication Strategy for Social Change* (Mahwah, N. J.: Lawrence Erlbaum, 1999), 221.

9. Marie Gillespie, *Television, Ethnicity, and Cultural Change* (London: Routledge, 1995), 207.

10. Michael Schudson, "Culture and the Integration of National Societies," in *The Sociology of Culture*, Diana Crane, ed. (Cambridge, Mass.: Blackwell, 1994), 40.

Bibliography

Abadan-Unat, Nermin. "Summing Up." In *Migration and Development,* edited by Nermin Abadan-Unat. Ankara: Ajans Turk Press, 1975.

Abadan-Unat, Nermin, and Artun Unsal. "Migration through the Eyes of Political Parties, Trade Unions, Employer Associations, and Bureaucracy." In *Migration and Development*, edited by Nermin Abadan-Unat et al. Ankara: Ajans Turk Press, 1975.

Aksoy, Asu, and Kevin Robins. "Peripheral Vision: Cultural Industries and Cultural Identities in Turkey." *Environment and Planning* 29, no. 11 (1997): 1937-1952.

Anderson, Benedict. *Imagined Communities: Reflections on the Origins and Spread of Nationalism.* London: Verso, 1983.

Appadurai, Arjun. "Disjuncture and Difference in the Global Cultural Economy." In *Global Culture: Nationalism, Globalization, and Modernity,* edited by Mike Featherstone. Newbury Park, Calif.: Sage, 1990.

———. *Modernity at Large.* Minneapolis: University of Minnesota Press, 1996.

Aslaneli, Hakan. "The Ratings War Corrupts Turkey's Entertainment World." *Turkish Probe* 317 (7 February 1999); http://38.242.79.170/past_probe/02_07_99/dom2.htm#d20 (1 May 2000).

Baumann, Gerd. *Contesting Culture.* Cambridge: Cambridge University Press, 1996.

———. *The Multicultural Riddle.* New York: Routledge, 1999.

Balci, Kemal. "Anatomy of the Media Bosses." *Turkish Probe* 303 (1 November 1998); http://38.242.79.170/past_probe/11_01_98/contents.htm

Bhabha, Homi. *The Location of Culture.* London: Routledge, 1994.

Bourdon, Jerome. "Foreigners on Prime Time or Is Television Xenophobic?" In *European Television: Immigrants and Ethnic Minorities,* edited by Claire Frachon and Marion Vargaftig. London: John Libbey, 1995.

Brants, Kees, and Denis McQuail. "The Netherlands." In *The Media in Western Europe*, edited by Bernt Stubbe Ostergaard. London: Sage, 1997.

Broeder, Peter, and Guus Extra. "Language." In *Immigrant Policy for a Multicultural Society,* edited by Hans Vermeulen. Brussels: Migration Hans Vermeulen Policy Group, May 1997.

Browne, Donald R. *Electronic Media and Industrialized Nations.* Ames: Iowa State University Press, 1999.

Çağlar, Ayşe. "Hyphenated Identities and the Limits of Culture." In *The Politics of Multiculturalism in the New Europe*, edited by Tariq Modood and Pnina Werbner. London: Zed Books, 1997.

Castells, Manuel. *The Power of Identity*. Malden, Mass.: Blackwell, 1997.

Castells, Martin. "Muslims in the Netherlands." In *Muslim Minorities in the West,* edited by Syed Abedin and Ziauddin Sardar. London: Grey Seal, 1995.

Center for Turkish Studies. *Migration Movements from Turkey to the European Community*. Brussels: Commission of the European Communities, January 1993.

Chaliand, Gerard, and Jean-Pierre Rageau. *The Penguin Atlas of Diasporas*. New York: Penguin, 1995.

Dasetto, Felice, and Gerd Nonneman. "Islam in Belgium and the Netherlands: Towards a Typology of 'Transplanted' Islam." In *Muslim Communities in the New Europe,* edited by Gerd Nonneman, Tim Niblock, and Bogdan Szakowski. Berkshire, U.K.: Ithaca, 1996.

DeBruin, Joost. "'We Just Couldn't Behave Like That': Dutch Soap Opera, Adolescence and Ethnicity." Paper presented to the Crossroads in Cultural Studies Conference. Birmingham, U.K., June 2000.

de Jong, Mark-Jan. "The Immigration of Immigrants: A Challenge for the Netherlands." In *Democracy, Civil Society, and Pluralism,* edited by C. G. A. Bryant and E. Mokrzycki. Warsaw: IfiS, 1995.

Doomernik, Jeroen, Rinus Penninx, and Hans van Amersfoort. *A Migration Policy for the Future: Possibilities and Limitations*. Brussels: Migration Policy Group, 1997.

Drozdiak, William. "Citizenship Debate Divides Germans: Dual Nationality Is Proposed for Offspring of Immigrants." *Washington Post*, 5 November 1997, 28(A).

Eurobarometer Survey no. 48, EC Eurobarometer, 1998.

Fennema, Meindert, and Jean Tillie. "Political Participation and Political Trust in a Multicultural Democracy." Unpublished paper. Amsterdam: Institute for Migration and Ethnic Studies and Department of Political Science, University of Amsterdam, July 1999.

Frachon, Claire, and Marion Vargaftig. "The Netherlands." In *European Television: Immigrants and Ethnic Minorities*, edited by Claire Frachon and Marion Vargaftig. London: John Libbey, 1995.

"From Turks to Kids." *Haagsche Courant*, 13 July 2000, B10.

Gans, Herbert. *Deciding What's News: A Study of CBS Evening News, NBC Nightly News, Newsweek, and Time*. New York: Random House, 1980.

Gillespie, Marie. *Television, Ethnicity, and Cultural Change*. London: Routledge, 1995.

Güler, Emrah. "Tarkan: From the Stage to the Barracks," *Turkish Daily News*. (16 January 2000), Feature section; http://www.turkishdailynews.com (15 June 2000).

Hall, Stuart. "Cultural Identity and Diaspora." In *Identity: Community, Culture, Difference,* edited by John Rutherford. London: Lawrence & Wishart, 1990.

_____. "Old and New Identities: Old and New Ethnicities." In *Culture, Globalization, and the World System,* edited by Anthony D. King. Minneapolis: University of Minnesota Press, 1997.

———. "The Question of Cultural Identity." In *Modernity and its Futures,* edited by Stuart Hall, David Held, and Tony McGrew. Cambridge: Polity Press in association with the Open University, 1992.

Hall, Stuart, Tony Held, and David McGrew, eds. *Modernity and Its Futures.* Cambridge, U.K.: Polity Press in Association with The Open University, 1992.

Hannerz, Ulf. *Transnational Connections: Culture, People, Places.* New York: Routledge, 1996.

Het Amsterdamse Bureau voor Onderzoek en Statistiek. *Amsterdam in Cijfers: Jaarboek 1998*. Amsterdam: O+S, 1998.

Hiemstra, John L. *Worldviews on the Air: The Struggle to Create a Pluralist Broadcasting System in the Netherlands*. Lanham, Md.: University Press of America, 1997.

Hooker, Mark T. *The History of Holland.* Westport, Conn.: Greenwood, 1999.

Isena, Glenn Constantino. "Deconstructing 'allochtonen': Socio-institutional Powers on the Lives of Children." Master's thesis, Free University of Amsterdam, 2000; http://home.student.uva.nl/glen.isena (28 May 2000).

"Islamic Evangelists." *Economist* (8 July 2000), 52.

Karakasoğlu, Yasemin, and Gerd Nonneman. "Muslims in Germany, with Special Reference to the Turkish-Islamic Community." In *Muslim Communities in the New Europe,* edited by Gerd Nonneman, Tim Niblock, and Bogdan Szajkowski. Reading, U.K.: Ithaca, 1996.

Kloosterman, Robert. "Migration in the Netherlands and the Emerging Post-Industrial Social Divide in Urban Areas." In *Immigrants, Integration, and Cities: Exploring the Links,* edited by OECD. Paris: OECD, 1998.

Kruyt, Arrien, and Jan Niessen. "Integration." In *Immigrant Policy for a Multicultural Society*, edited by Hans Vermeulen. Brussels: Migration Policy Group, May 1997.

Kuzum, Mustafa. Personal interview. Ankara, Turkey (1 May 1997).

Lucassen, Jan, and Rinus Penninx. *Newcomers: Immigrants and their Decendents in the Netherlands, 1550-1993.* Amsterdam: Het Spinhuis, 1995.

McQuail, Denis. *McQuail's Mass Communication Theory.* 4th ed. London: Sage, 2000.

Mendelsohn, Matthew, and Richard Nadeau. "The Magnification and Minimization of Social Cleavages by the Broadcast and Narrowcast Media." *International Journal of Public Opinion Research* 8, no. 4 (1996), 374-389.

Ogan, Christine. "The Audience for Foreign Film in the United States." *Journal of Communication* 40, no. 4 (autumn 1990): 58-77.

———. "Communications Policy Options in an Era of Rapid Technological Change." *Telecommunications Policy* 16, no. 7 (September-October 1992): 565-575.

———. "Developing Policy for Eliminating International Video Piracy." *Journal of Broadcasting and Electronic Media* 32, no. 2 (spring 1998): 163-182.

———. "Media Imperialism and the Video Cassette Recorder: The Case of Turkey." *Journal of Communication* 38, no. 2 (spring 1988): 93-106.

Öncü, Ayşe. "Packaging Islam: Cultural Politics on the Landscape of Turkish Commercial Television." *Public Culture* 8, no. 1 (1995): 51-71.

Onulduran, Ersin, and Herman van Renselaar. "International Relations, Legal and Political Dimensions." In *Migration and Development*, edited by Nermin Abadan-Unat et al. Ankara, Turkey: Ajans Turk Press, 1975.

Panayi, Panikos. *Outsiders: A History of European Minorities.* London: Hambledon, 1999.

Penninx, Rinus, and Herman van Renselaar. "Evolution of Turkish Migration before and during the Current European Recession." In *Migration and Development,* edited by Nermin Abadan-Unat et al. Ankara, Turkey: Ajans Turk Press, 1975

Penninx, Rinus, Jeannette Schoorl, and Carlo van Praag. *The Impact of International Migration on Receiving Countries: The Case of the Netherlands*. The Hague: Netherlands Interdisciplinary Demographic Institute, 1994.

Pope, Nicole, and Hugh Pope. *Turkey Unveiled: A History of Modern Turkey*. Woodstock, N.Y.: Overlook, 1998.

"Racism and Xenophobia in Europe." *Eurobarometer Opinion Poll 47.1.* First results presented at the closing conference of the European Year against Racism. Luxembourg, 18-19 December 1997.

Rath, Jan. "The Netherlands: A Dutch Treat for Antisocial Families and Immigrant Ethnic Minorities." In *The European Union and Migrant Labour*, edited by Mike Cole and Gareth Dale. Oxford: Berg Publishers, 1999.

Rath, Jan, and Robert Kloosterman. "Outsiders' Business: A Critical Review of Research on Immigrant Entrepreneurship." *International Migration Review* 34, no. 3 (fall 2000): 657-681.

Rath, Jan, Rinus Penninx, Kees Groenendijk, and Astrid Meyer. "The Politics of Recognizing Religious Diversity in Europe: Social Reactions to the Institutionalization of Islam in the Netherlands, Belgium, and Great Britain." *Netherlands' Journal of Social Sciences* 35, no. 1 (1999): 53-68.

Safran, William. "Diasporas in Modern Societies: Myths of Homeland and Return." *Diaspora* 1, no. 1 (spring 1991): 83-99.

Sahraoui, Myriam. "Putting More Colour into the Dutch Media." *Media Development* 45, no. 3 (1998): 22.

Schiller, Herbert. *Mass Communication and the American Empire.* Boulder, Colo.: Westview, 1992.

Schothorst, Yolanda, Dick Verzijden, and Ingmar Doeven. *Mediagebruik Etnische Publieksgroepen 1998*. Amsterdam: Veldkamp Marktonderzoek bv, June 1999.

Schudson, Michael. "Culture and the Integration." In *The Sociology of Culture*, edited by Diana Crane. Cambridge, Mass.: Blackwell, 1994.

Shadid, W. A. R., and P. S. van Koningsveld. *Religious Freedom and the Position of Islam in Western Europe*. Kampen, The Netherlands: Kok Pharos, 1995.

Singhal, Arvind, and Everett M. Rogers. *Entertainment-Education: A Communication Strategy for Social Change*. Mahwah, N.J.: Lawrence Erlbaum, 1999.

Stalker, Peter. *Workers without Frontiers*. Boulder, Colo.: Lynne Rienner, 2000.

Steinberg, Jacques. "Increase in Test Scores Counters Dire Forecasts for Bilingual Ban." *New York Times*, 20 August 2000, section 1, 1.

Sunier, Thijl, and Astrid Meyer. "Religion." In *Immigrant Policy for a Multicultural Society*, edited by Hans Vermeulen. Brussels: Migration Policy Group, May 1997.

Tan, Dursun, and Hans-Peter Waldhoff. "Turkish Everyday Culture in Germany and Its Prospects." In *Turkish Culture in German Society Today*, edited by David Horrocks and Eva Kolinsky. Providence, R.I.: Berghahn, 1996.

Ter Wal, Jessika, Amy Verdun, and Karin Westerbeek. "The Netherlands: Full or at the Limit of Tolerance." In *New Xenophobia in Europe*, edited by Bernd Baumgartl and Adrian Favell. London: Kluwer Law International, 1995.

Tillie, Jean, Meindert Fennema, and Karen Kraal. "Creating Turkish Networks in Amsterdam: Personal or Organizational Strategies?" Draft version prepared for the workshop, Associational Engagement and Democracy in Cities, Copenhagen, April 2000.

Tomlinson, John. *Cultural Imperialism: A Critical Introduction*. Baltimore: Johns Hopkins University Press, 1991.

Tungate, Mark. "Battle of the Big Four." *Media International* (September 1998): 40.

"TV Watchers Vote News as Favorite Program." *Turkish Daily News*. Domestic news. Ankara, Turkey, 24 September 1997; http://www.turkishdailynews.com (25 September 1997).

Valdez-Rodriguez, Alisa. "Pop Beat: Turkish Singer's Latin Success Sealed with a Kiss or Two." *Los Angeles Times*, 22 July 2000, F1.

van den Bedem, Ruud. "Towards a System of Plural Nationality in the Netherlands." In *From Aliens to Citizens: Redefining the Status of Immigrants in Europe*, edited by Rainer Baubock. Aldershot, U.K.: Avebury, 1994.

van der Horst, Han. *The Low Sky: Understanding the Dutch*. The Hague: Scriptum Books, 1996.

van der Wal, Geke, and Mathijs Tax. *De vele gezichten van Turks Nederland: een wie is wie*. Amsterdam: Uitgeverij Jan Mets, 1999.

Veldkamp Marktondeerzoek bv. *Invloed Schotelantennes op Kijkgedrag Turken en Marokkanen.* Amsterdam: Veldkamp, 1996.

_____. *Mediagebruik Etnische Publieksgroepen 1998.* Amsterdam: Veldkamp, June 1999.

Vuijsje, Herman. *The Politically Correct Netherlands since the Sixties.* Translated and annotated by Mark T. Hooker. Westport, Conn.: Greenwood, 2000.

Wicker, Hans-Rudolf. "From Complex Culture to Cultural Complexity." In *Debating Cultural Hybridity*, edited by Pnina Werbner and Tariq Modood. London: Zed Books, 1997.

Yalçın-Heckmann, Lale. "The Perils of Ethnic Associational Life in Europe: Turkish Migrants in Germany and France." In *The Politics of Multiculturalism in the New Europe,* edited by Tariq Modood and Pnina Werbner. London: Zed Books, 1997.

Yavuz, M. Hakan. "Media Identities for Alevis and Kurds in Turkey." In *New Media in the Muslim World: The Emerging Public Sphere*, edited by Dale Eickelman and Jon Anderson. Bloomington: Indiana University Press, 1999.

_____. "Towards an Islamic Liberalism?: The Nurcu Movement and Fethullah Gülen." *Middle East Journal* 53, no. 4 (autumn 1999): 606-620.

Index

About the Author

Christine Ogan is professor of journalism and associate dean for graduate studies and research in the School of Informatics at Indiana University. She has conducted research and published numerous articles and book chapters on the uses of new communication technologies and accompanying policy in Turkey and western Europe. She specializes in issues related to Turkish media.